In Pursuit
of a Dream
Deferred

PETER LANG
New York • Washington, D.C./Baltimore • Bern
Frankfurt am Main • Berlin • Brussels • Vienna • Oxford

In Pursuit of a Dream Deferred

Linking Housing and Education Policy

EDITED BY

john a. powell, Gavin Kearney, & Vina Kay

PETER LANG
New York • Washington, D.C./Baltimore • Bern
Frankfurt am Main • Berlin • Brussels • Vienna • Oxford

Library of Congress Cataloging-in-Publication Data

In pursuit of a dream deferred: linking housing and education policy / edited by
john a. powell, Gavin Kearney, and Vina Kay.
p. cm.
Includes bibliographical references.
1. Discrimination in education—United States. 2. School integration—United
States. 3. Education and state—United States. 4. Discrimination in
housing—United States. 5. Housing policy—United States. I. powell, john a.
(john anthony). II. Kearney, Gavin. III. Kay, Vina. IV. Series.
LC212.2 .I52   379.2'6'0973—dc21   2001029038
ISBN 0-8204-3943-6

Die Deutsche Bibliothek-CIP-Einheitsaufnahme

In pursuit of a dream deferred: linking housing and education policy
/ edited by john a. powell, Gavin Kearney, and Vina Kay.
–New York; Washington, D.C./Baltimore; Bern; Frankfurt am Main;
Berlin; Brussels; Vienna; Oxford: Lang.
ISBN 0-8204-3943-6

Cover design by Lisa Dillon

The paper in this book meets the guidelines for permanence and durability
of the Committee on Production Guidelines for Book Longevity
of the Council of Library Resources.

Printed in the United States of America

In loving memory of my mother Florcie Mae Powell
—j.a.p.

Acknowledgments

The editors would like to thank the following members of the Institute on Race & Poverty for their hard work and insight in helping to produce this anthology: Rachel Callanan, Tinisha Davis, Susan Hartigan, Jennifer Holt, Lisa Jabaily, and Colleen Walbran.

Contents

Introduction

Gavin Kearney

What happens to a dream deferred?
Does it dry up
like a raisin in the sun?
—Langston Hughes "Harlem", *Selected
Poems of Langston Hughes*

The Institute on Race and Poverty at the University of Minnesota Law School brought together some of the nation's leading scholars and advocates around issues of race, housing, and education to discuss the persistent and interrelated segregation of America's residential markets and educational systems to commemorate the fortieth anniversary of the *Brown v. Board of Education* decision. A collection of articles emanating from that forum was published in the *University of Minnesota Law Review* the following year.[1] The title of the forum, shared by this anthology, invokes the plaintive language of Langston Hughes in the context of the dream of educational integration articulated in the 1954 Supreme Court decision *Brown v. Board of Education*.[2] Forum participants critically evaluated our failure to adequately account for the interconnection of housing and education in carrying out the *Brown* mandate and explored possible avenues for achieving a renewed and emboldened commitment to an integrated society.

The central issues of this forum remain important today. As we begin the twenty-first century it is clear that the "problem of the color line" of which W. E. B. DuBois spoke has outlived the twentieth century.[3] This color line, which segregates African Americans from full participation in American society, remains strong, albeit more subtle and insidious. Moreover, the problem of twenty-first century America may be that of color *lines*. Although blacks may bear the brunt of racist exclusion in our society, rapidly changing demographics and political backlash, as evidenced by recent political attacks against immigrants, suggest that future society may be increasingly ordered along multiple lines of race and ethnicity. Realizing the dream of *Brown* is as important as ever. If we are ever to attain our democratic ideal of equality of opportunity, then we must recognize the central role that segregation plays in maintaining inequality and denying communities of color key resources and opportunities. We must resolve ourselves to the achievement of a fully integrated society in which all members are empowered to fully participate in and construct those institutions and structures that define our world and ourselves.

Recent Jurisprudential Developments

Much of the discussion at the forum critically focused on Supreme Court jurisprudence in the area of educational segregation. As several of the authors discuss, since the time of *Brown* a series of key Court decisions have frustrated the goal of educational integration by narrowly construing the harms of segregation and restricting the breadth of remedies that may be employed to address them. A key component of this jurisprudence is the refusal to account for the role that residential segregation plays in creating educational segregation. Courts have increasingly relied on this jurisprudence to relieve school districts of desegregation orders, even where racial demographics reveal continued segregation. Tellingly, the Charlotte-Mecklenburg School District was ordered to end race-based student busing in 1999, thirty years after it became the first to do so.[4] This order came over the objections of parents and administrators and despite general consensus that the district's desegregation plan was working. Unfortunately, this episode is more the rule than the exception, and this trend is closing the door on desegregation even as schools remain segregated and racial achievement gaps persist.

Although there have been no new Supreme Court opinions dealing directly with educational segregation since the forum proceedings were published in 1996, there has been at least one noteworthy judicial development. In 1995 the Court heard the case of *Aderand v. Pena*, in which a white subcontractor brought an equal protection challenge against a federal program designed to ensure that minority business enterprises received federal highway contracts.[5] In declaring the program unconstitutional, the Court overruled its own earlier decision in *Metro Broadcasting* and held that all racial classifications employed by governmental actors would be evaluated with the same strict level of scrutiny regardless of whether their purpose was benign or remedial.[6]

Unclear in the *Aderand* decision was whether this ruling applied to the context of education where prior case law had recognized the unique goal of achieving diversity as a legitimate justification for employing race-specific criteria.[7] Despite this ambiguity, a number of subsequent lower court decisions have held that *Aderand* does apply to educational policies. In 1996 the Fifth Circuit Court of Appeals invalidated an admissions policy employed by the University of Texas Law School to increase its enrollment of African American and Latino students. Citing the *Aderand* decision, the court stated that "there is now absolutely no doubt that courts are to employ strict scrutiny when evaluating all racial classifications, including those characterized by their proponents as 'benign' or 'remedial.'"[8] Other courts have also employed Aderand's decontextualized analysis of race (or as some have stated, its conflation of race and racism) to invalidate antiracist remedies on behalf of white plaintiffs.[9]

This lack of clarity on race as a factor in admission has impacted grammar and high schools as well. For example, in March of 2000, the Supreme Court denied review of a Fourth Circuit Court of Appeals decision to invalidate a school district policy that considered race as a factor in evaluating requests to transfer schools.[10] The Fourth Circuit similarly invalidated a weighted lottery plan that ensured minority attendance at a kindergarten magnet school in a case up for consideration by the Supreme Court.[11]

Recent Policy Responses to Racial Inequality in Education

Contemporary policy discussions around racial disparities in education echo the judiciary's move away from integration and toward formal "color blindness." Although educational quality is a major policy issue at the local and national levels, much of the debate around educational reform focuses on intra-school and district-level measures, such as smaller class sizes, neighborhood schools, and stronger curricula. While reform at these levels is clearly necessary, particularly in our nation's most troubled school districts, the omission of integration as part of these reform efforts overlooks decades of research and experience that point to the negative effects of racial and economic segregation on student achievement.[12]

Many advocates of educational reform have also begun to push for greater accountability from administrators, teachers, and students. For example, a number of states have adopted "high stakes testing" policies that prevent students from receiving their diplomas if they do not score above a certain level on standardized tests. This movement is troubling in that it ignores the effects of systemic issues such as segregation on student performance and holds students accountable for conditions beyond their control. It implies that student failures are largely responsible for our educational crisis and ignores the effect of our extensive and continued history of segregative practices in housing and education.[13] Not surprisingly, students of color and students from racially segregated and poor school districts are performing consistently worse than their peers on these high stakes tests. One result of this will be an increase in the number of people of color who must confront the job market with no diploma in hand.

In those instances where race is acknowledged as legitimate grounds for policy making, it is most often in the context of pursuing diversity and not in the context of addressing racism. A prominent example of this comes from "One America in the Twenty-First Century: The President's Initiative on Race," launched by President Clinton with much fanfare in 1997. After studying and dialoguing around issues of race, the initiative released a report entitled "Pathways to One America in the Twenty-First Century: Promising Practices for Racial Reconciliation" in January of 1999. Of the numerous education practices highlighted for their promise, the vast majority dealt with enhancing our appreciation for diversity and not one addressed systemic educational problems or the need for racial integration.[14]

Current Demographic Trends in Education and Housing

While courts and policy makers move away from *Brown*'s integrative ideal, we are seeing increasing racial and economic segregation in our neighborhoods and significant resegregation racially and economically in our schools. Moreover, racial and economic segregation overlap heavily in both contexts: areas of economic segregation are almost always areas of racial segregation, and vice versa. Although this intersection of race and poverty has tremendous consequences for people of color, current jurisprudence and policy making largely ignore it.

Census data reveal that racial segregation has persisted in the great majority of our metropolitan areas over the last several decades, particularly for African Americans.[15] During this same time period, economic segregation has increased tremendously as indicated by the dramatic rise in concentrated poverty.[16] Between 1970 and 1990, the number of people living in concentrated poverty census tracts nearly doubled. As of 1990, nearly eight million Americans live in these areas. Over half of all concentrated poverty residents are African American and another quarter are Hispanic.[17]

A recent report by Gary Orfield and John T. Yun documents the rise of racial and economic segregation in our schools. According to Orfield and Yun, the last few years have seen the South achieve its highest levels of racial segregation in schools since early in the desegregation process. The rest of the country's schools are also witnessing an increase in racial segregation over the last few years. Given economic demographics, these trends mean that more students of color are attending schools in which large proportions of their classmates are poor. Orfield and Yun report that the average black or Latino student attends a school with twice as many poor classmates as the average white student.[18] As noted earlier, it is this overlap of racial and economic segregation and the effect of economic segregation on student achievement that make the issue of integration far more than an issue of racial comity. Segregation is a direct cause of racism and racial inequality, and integration is an issue of equality of opportunity and democratic participation.

The mandate of *Brown* is as imperative today as when it was originally issued. While current decision-making and policy discussions would suggest either that *Brown* is no longer relevant or that its ideal has been attained, reality strongly suggests otherwise. It is clear that if we are to serve the educational needs of children of color, we must rekindle the drive for integration. The chapters that follow provide an initial step in that direction.

Overview of the Chapters

In chapter 1, "Beyond *Brown v. Board of Education*: Housing and Education in the Year 2000," Kenneth B. Clark expresses his naivete at the time of the *Brown* decision in thinking that it would provide the necessary push to move us to an integrated society. He discusses the manner in which subsequent events revealed the subtle, complex, and persistent nature of American racism. Clark concludes with the charge for new energy and leadership in our commitment to racial equality and integration.

john a. powell, in his chapter entitled "Living and Learning: Linking Housing and Education," moves beyond racial rhetoric to examine just what is at stake in discussions of educational integration. He articulates the crucial link between housing and education and critiques the Supreme

Court's failure to acknowledge this and other important realities in its racial jurisprudence. powell suggests what a more responsible jurisprudence might look like and points to some exemplary policies.

Meredith Lee Bryant describes the weak and at times contradictory nature of Supreme Court jurisprudence in the area of educational segregation in chapter 3, "Combating School Resegregation Through Housing: A Need for a Reconceptualization of American Democracy and the Rights It Protects." Bryant situates current jurisprudence around race within a weak conception of democracy and argues for a more substantive, positivist commitment to our democratic ideals, a commitment that explicitly acknowledges the goal of achieving racial equality. She concludes by suggesting a path for moving to this stronger vision through a reconceptualization of the rights to property, contract, and free association.

Nancy A. Denton lends an empirical eye to policy discussion of residential and educational segregation. In "The Persistence of Segregation: Links Between Residential Segregation and School Segregation," she discusses the current state of knowledge of residential and educational segregation in America and debunks prevailing "myths" of their causes. Denton explores the specific dynamics of segregation at the neighborhood and metropolitan levels and concludes with a discussion of multiethnic neighborhoods, key players in an integrative agenda for the future.

In "Metropolitan School Desegregation: Impacts on Metropolitan Society," Gary Orfield draws upon our forty year history of desegregation efforts and current demographic trends to inform his assertion that the desegregation of schools is both feasible and an expression of our democratic norms. Orfield demonstrates that substantial integrative measures can not only be successful in the long run, but also may lead to a broader form of democracy in school policy.

In chapter 6, "The Current State of School Desegregation Law: Why Isn't Anybody Laughing?" Drew S. Days evaluates Supreme Court jurisprudence in light of the variety of governmental actions that contribute to school segregation. He argues that segregated schools result from several actions of constitutional significance and questions the failure of desegregation law to acknowledge this.

Charles R. Lawrence focuses on the Court's construction of segregation in the landmark decision *Milliken v. Bradley* in his chapter, "Segregation Misunderstood: The *Milliken* Decision Revisited."[19] Lawrence articulates key characteristics of the institution of segregation, including the fact that it is systemic, self-perpetuating, and stigmatizing. He then goes on to describe how Supreme Court decision making, leading up to and including *Milliken*, misunderstands segregation and in so doing precludes an adequate remedy to it.

In chapter 8, "Discrimination: A Pervasive Concept," Michael H. Sussman writes from the perspective of a civil rights litigator who was involved in one of the few cases to acknowledge and account for the link between residential and educational segregation, *United States v. Yonkers*.[20] Sussman discusses several important characteristics of racism and of segregation that ought to inform litigation in the area. In the final section of his chapter, he articulates how a litigator might adopt a more informed approach in the context of school districts seeking a declaration of unitary status.

In chapter 9, "The Boundaries of Race: Political Geography in Legal Analysis," Richard Thompson Ford expands upon the role of segregation in disempowering communities of color. He also discusses the manner in which seemingly neutral practices interact with a racialized geographic landscape to create and maintain racial hierarchy. Ford concludes with an attempt to mediate the tensions between working within local communities of color and addressing segregation through a broader focus.

The final chapter, "Equality and Educational Excellence: Legal Challenges in the 1990s," is a transcript of the remarks of Theodore M. Shaw, deputy director of the NAACP Legal Defense and Education Fund, from the original forum. Shaw draws from his extensive experience as a civil rights litigator to critique the current status of desegregation law and the nature of public discourse surrounding it. He concludes with the charge that, while no integration remedy has been perfect, we must remain committed to the struggle for racial equality because the struggle has meaning in itself.

Notes

1. 80 *U. of Minn. L. Rev.* 743–910 (1996).

2. 347 U.S. 483 (1954).

3. W. E. B. DuBois, *The Souls of Black Folk*, 1. New York: Bantam Books (1903).

4. *Capacchione v. Charlotte-Mecklenburg Schools*, 1999 WL 709975 (W.D.N.C., September 9, 1999).

5. 515 U.S. 200 (1995).

6. 515 U.S. 200, 227 (overruling *Metro Broadcasting, Inc. v. FCC*, 497 U.S. 547 (1990).

7. 438 U.S. 265 (1978).

8. *Hopwood v. Texas*, 78 F.3d 932, 940 (1996).

9. See e.g., *Tuttle v. Arlington County School Board*, 195 F.3d 698 (4ᵗʰ Cir. 1999)(relying upon *Aderand* to invalidate an integrative magnet school policy).

10. *Eisenberg ex. rel. Eisenberg v. Montgomery County Public Schools*, 197 F.3d 123 (4ᵗʰ Cir., 1999, cert. denied by *Montgomery County Schools v. Eisenberg*, 1999 WL 1272568 [2000]).

11. *Tuttle v. Arlington County School Board*, 195 F.3d 698 (4ᵗʰ Cir., 1999).

12. See e.g., James Coleman, *Equality of Educational Opportunity.* Washington, D.C.: National Center for Educational Statistics (DHEW), 1966. ("The inequalities imposed on children by their home, neighborhood, and peer environment are carried along to become the inequalities with which they confront student life."); Robert Crain and Debora Sullivan, "The Role of School Segregation and Educational Discrimination in the Multigenerational Transmission of Educational Disadvantage," *Columbia University Report* (1996); M. Dawkins, "Black Students' Occupational Expectations: A National Study of the Impact of School Desegregation." 18 *Urban Education* 98 (1983); Vivian Ikpa, "The Effects of Changes in School Characteristics Resulting from the Elimination of Mandated Busing for Integration upon the Academic Achievement of African-American Students," *Education Research Quarterly* (1993).

13. In this respect it is analogous to the welfare "reform" movement which has ignored structural causes of poverty and dependency in favor of a behavioral model that absolves the majority of our society of responsibility for the plight of the poor in general and poor people of color in particular.

14. The President's Initiative on Race, "Pathways to One America in the 21ˢᵗ Century: Promising Practices for Racial Reconciliation" (January 1999). It is an unfortunate sign of the times that President Clinton deserves some credit for merely

recognizing the obvious: race is significant in contemporary society. The manner in which the initiative has construed issues of race may, however, be counterproductive. In fact, one is hard pressed to find the word "racism" or recognition of the disparate benefits and harms of racial hierarchy in the initiative's publications. Focusing solely on the initiative's publications, one would be left with the impression that better interracial relations is the only barrier to a racially just America.

15. See Douglas Massey and Nancy Denton, *American Apartheid: Segregation and the Making of the Underclass*, Cambridge: Harvard University Press, 1993; Roderick J. Harrison and Daniel Weinberg, *Racial and Ethnic Segregation in 1990*, Washington D.C.: U.S. Bureau of the Census, 1992.

16. Concentrated poverty refers to areas in which 40 percent or more of residents live below the federally defined poverty level.

17. Paul A. Jargowsky, *Poverty and Place: Ghettos, Barrios, and the American City*, New York: Russell Sage Foundation, 1997.

18. Gary Orfield and John T. Yun, "Resegregation in America's Schools," The Civil Rights Project, Harvard University (June 1999).

19. *Milliken v. Bradley* 418 U.S. 717 (1974)

20. 624 F. Supp. 1276 (S.D.N.Y. 1985), aff'd 837 F.2d 1181 (2d Cir. 1987), cert. denied 486 U.S. 1055 (1988).

Chapter 1

Beyond *Brown v. Board of Education*: Housing and Education in the Year 2000

Kenneth B. Clark

The Supreme Court's 1954 decision in *Brown v. Board of Education* spawned a collective hope and dream for an end to racial segregation in American public schools.[1] I joined in the optimism. I spoke and wrote buoyantly, confident in our future.[2] At the time, I believed there would be positive changes within a decade or more. I thought that I, and the small group of like-minded persons with whom I worked, would successfully raise these issues, combat all signs of segregation, and remain persistent in opposing racism in our local schools. Although I knew of the de facto pattern of segregation that existed at that time in the New York City public school system, I thought the problem of segregation essentially was a southern problem. I now confess this was naïve. I recall being oblivious of the extent to which the board of education and school officials, including the commissioner of education, had developed curious subtle and covert social maneuvers for maintaining segregated schools in New York City. As a social psychologist, I can say now that wishful thinking colored my ideas and beliefs. I did not realize the tenaciousness of racism in American culture.

At the time, the North rationalized its racism by contending that racially segregated schools were a manifestation of a larger pattern of our racial culture. Segregation in housing patterns and racially segregated communities created segregated schools. I thought taking important steps in modifying the racial housing pattern would address the segregated housing problem. This, in turn, would resolve the reorganization of our public school system seriously and successfully. I did not understand, however, that the maintenance of segregated housing excused persistent patterns of school segregation in that segregated housing itself represented a form of deeply embedded racism that resisted all attempts at desegregation. Ironically, this phenomenon appeared particularly entrenched in the North. I was perplexed. Thus, while in writings and speeches I highlighted the gains in our society, such as the civil rights gains, affirmative action, and the increasing numbers of elected black political officials, I underestimated the significance of racism's staunch hold on the American people.

Recent developments have made me reflect on the early stages following the Court's *Brown* decision. I now see more clearly the curious way that our early optimism prevented us from anticipating how racial progress would result in a form of backlash. The current resistance to affirmative action, for example, reflects the depth of American racism. We now are confronted with various manifestations of the belief that affirmative action essentially represents a rejection of or penalty against white males. This argument, however, conceals the fact that affirmative action was designed to remedy the past rejection, prejudice, and exclusion of minorities, particularly blacks. It is disheartening to see that these attempts to remedy social injustices now are being used to maintain those prior injustices.

As another example, segregated schools and segregated housing still pervade the American landscape, but they are not being discussed as manifestations of racism. Similarly, desegregation and integration are not being discussed as attempts to resolve former and persistent forms of injustice. Instead, these issues are discussed as issues of poverty and choice rather than as lasting symbols of our history of racism.

Significantly, many liberals and many Supreme Court decisions now follow this pattern of racial exclusion. In fact, institutions of higher learning explain racial isolation in terms of beneficial conditions for blacks in general, despite the earlier beliefs that segregation not only damaged black children, but also interfered with the human growth and development of white children. I am particularly fascinated by the fact that some blacks approve of segregated living quarters and segregated communities. The rise of the black separatist movement in the 1960s manifested blacks' identification with the reasoning of their oppressor. Black separatists internalized the reasoning of the proponents of racial separation.

It is clear to me, however, that the failure to desegregate our schools at all levels, including elementary, high school, and college, despite our awareness of the harm that segregation inflicted on all of our children, has demoralized our society. It has weakened our social fabric. Yet we are being told not only that segregated schools and segregated housing in ghettos are desirable, but that blacks should feel grateful.

I often wonder how Thurgood Marshall and Robert Carter would present their case today before the present Supreme Court. How would they cope with present patterns of resegregation that so pervade our society? As one of the social scientists who worked with Marshall and Carter during the *Brown* cases, I would argue that segregation, not only in Clarendon County, South Carolina, but also in New York City, in the Twin Cities, and in America at large, is as damaging now as it was then. The dream so long deferred should be reexamined, but not because the premise of the *Brown* decision has changed. The Supreme Court in *Brown* said, "We conclude that in the field of public education the doctrine of separate but equal has no place."[3]

In the forty years since those statements, we have seen copious examples of the harm inflicted upon our society by the racism onto which we have held. It is time that educators, who have been dormant for so long, assume their role as leaders in this campaign for justice. Educators can become crucial participants in helping society protect our children and protect itself from the persistent damage of racism and segregation. Our schools, our neighborhoods, and, in fact, our society as a whole must be mobilized. We cannot apologize about freeing ourselves from the damage that is being done to our children and to the very fabric of our society. Our society desperately needs rejuvenation and a renaissance of positive and constructive policies by which we can all become constructive partners.

Notes

1. 347 U.S. 483 (1954)

2. See, e.g., *Dark Ghetto: Dilemmas of Social Power* (1989) (recounting life in urban ghettos in the 1960s); Introduction to Symposium, "Desegregation in the Public Schools," 2 *Soc. Probs.* 197, 197–98 (1955) (discussing the social scientist's role in facilitating the process of desegregation); "The Desegregation Cases: Criticism of the Social Scientist's Role," 5 *Vill. L. Rev.* 224 (1959) (examining the arguments of some of the leading critics on the social scientist's role in school desegregation cases); "Current Trends in Desegregation," *Am. Child*, Nov. 1954, at 1, 4 (discussing how communities affected by the *Brown v. Board of Education* decision were dealing with desegregation of schools); "More Effective Techniques," in "What Next? Five Negro Leaders Reply," *New York Times*, Sept. 29, 1963 (magazine), at 27, 91 (urging blacks to go beyond public civil rights marches and demonstrations and to join together in actively exerting pressure on the government, businesses, labor organizations, financial and other like institutions, ultimately to eliminate any and all forms of racial injustice); "The Negro Is Tired of Waiting," *U.S. News & World Rep.*, June 10, 1963, at 38 (responding in an interview to questions regarding the growing militancy of Negroes in the North).

3. 347 U.S. 483, 495 (1954).

Chapter 2

Living and Learning:
Linking Housing and Education

john a. powell

As state and federal courts struggle with the issue of racial segregation in America's public schools, confusion and contention persist over who bears ultimate responsibility for the harm of segregation, and even what constitutes harm in the context of segregation. Justice Thurgood Marshall, in his dissent from the Supreme Court's 1974 *Milliken v. Bradley* decision, broadly construed the harm produced by racially segregated educational systems.[1] He stated, "Our Nation, I fear, will be ill served by the Court's refusal to remedy separate and unequal education, for unless our children begin to learn together, there is little hope that our people will ever learn to *live* together."[2] Twenty-one years later, Justice Clarence Thomas took a much narrower view of segregation in his concurrence in the *Missouri v. Jenkins* decision.[3] Thomas stated, "It never ceases to amaze me that the courts are so willing to assume that anything that is predominantly black must be inferior."[4] Years of inadequate and uncommitted attempts at integrating our schools through busing and other limited means separated these divergent opinions; today we find ambivalence regarding integration, even from those sincerely committed to racial justice. Although our concept of how to achieve integration should have certainly been affected by our abortive experiences, it is perplexing that our view of the harm of a segregated society has been so completely lost over time.

Debate over the causes of, and responsibility for, educational segregation has mirrored and contributed to this confusion about the assumptions and goals of integration, particularly within the court system. Writing for the majority in *Milliken*, Chief Justice Warren Burger narrowly defined the state's responsibility for segregation in education, concluding that an educational desegregation remedy is warranted only in conjunction with a finding of de jure segregation. Burger limited the scope of respon-sibility, moreover, by holding that a remedy may only be implemented within the bounds of the school district where said de jure segregation exists.

In contrast, Justice William O. Douglas, in his dissent, asserted that "there is so far as the school cases go no constitutional difference be-tween *de facto* and *de jure* segregation."[5] To Justice Douglas, the majority's focus on individual district responsibility, effectively separating city from suburb, was an arbitrary distortion of reality. Douglas described the myriad ways that segregation of the Detroit public school system (at issue in *Milliken*) implicated state action as evidence of the fact that segregation in a particular school district is part of a larger theater of segregative forces. Specifically, Douglas described suburban school board actions, state-enforced restrictive covenants in housing, and state school depart-ment siting of schools.

The Court's five-four split in *Milliken* left a rift over how to affix re-sponsibility, and thus how to determine the scope of remedies, in school desegregation cases. In fact, a consensus on the issue of who is respon-sible for segregation has eluded the Court since its unanimous decision in *Brown v. Board of Education*.[6] When the Court ruled in 1995 in *Mis-souri v. Jenkins* that an interdistrict plan was not an appropriate means of desegregating the Kansas City public school system, it severely limited the remedies available for children trapped in segregated educational sys-tems, and it signaled its unwillingness to address substance, rather than follow form, in its efforts to help poor, minority children. *Jenkins* fol-lowed the trend of a more conservative majority, emergent in the *Milliken* decision, to reject state responsibility for segregative conditions in schools and communities. This trend places blame for the deterioration and seg-regation of city schools on "normal pattern[s] of human migration."[7] Writing for the majority in *Jenkins*, Chief Justice Rehnquist denied the existence of a causal link between de jure segregation and white flight, attributing the phenomenon to demographic changes outside the scope of govern-ment control (and hence outside a court's remedial reach).[8] While the members of the Court and the parties agreed that the Kansas City schools and neighborhoods were segregated, the majority of the Court refused to examine seriously the causes of the city's severe segregation. The major-ity opinion never discussed the history of housing discrimination, lending bias, public housing construction, federal home mortgage loan programs, or other governmental causes of racial segregation.

Unfortunately, this disturbing trend is not peculiar to the judiciary; it is a mood that has come over much of the nation as we contemplate past attempts at school integration. Whereas over forty years ago, the *Brown* Court recognized and condemned the unique harm experienced by black students forced to attend racially segregated schools, today many Americans are ambivalent about or indifferent to the fact that most urban schools remain segregated. And while the explicitly segregationist policies of the *Brown* era seldom exist today, a more subtle network of social and institutional barriers works to maintain segregation in our schools and communities.

The *Brown* Court's observation that separate is inherently unequal continues to ring true.[9] Yet somehow we have failed to challenge seriously the educational and housing segregation that persists in this country. This failure is not due simply to a lack of commitment to integration or the creation of opportunities for people of color. Rather, this failure in part is attributable to the movements we have seen over the last fifteen years, movements that embrace racial segregation as a necessary and worthy policy goal and construe integration as a racist objective.[10] Worse yet, this type of thinking has brought with it an attempt to minimize and fictionalize the negative effects of segregation on society in general and schoolchildren in particular.[11]

Why are we giving up on integration? In all likelihood, these policy surrenders are partially a response to the hopelessness and frustration experienced when we consider the persistence of segregation. Integration is a difficult concept to embrace when one considers that it cannot claim many examples. Another cause, especially for those who would otherwise support the idea of integration, is the conflation of the terms "integration" and "assimilation." The implications of assimilation have appropriately been criticized by a number of scholars.[12] Integration and assimilation, unfortunately, have become synonymous concepts in the minds of many. Because of this confusion, some individuals have gone so far as to suggest that *Brown* was wrong and that separation of the races may be the only means of creating adequate educational opportunities for poor, minority children.[13]

But reality is not so easily altered by such rhetoric. An exploration of the educational conditions that children face within segregated schools and neighborhoods demonstrates that such a system does not serve the needs of students and the larger society.[14] Instead, segregation perpetuates a legacy of both racial hierarchy and dominance.[15] If we are to achieve a racial democracy, we must renew and deepen our commitment to achieving true integration, not only in our schools, but also in the communities where we live and work.[16] It is not enough to recognize the value of living in an integrated society in theory. We must transform our theory into practice.[17] Our failure to act perpetuates the injury of apartheid in education, housing, and, indeed, in our very psyche. If we are to heal a fractured society continuously at war with itself, we must make it possible for everyone to participate equally in our communities. We must challenge the racial hierarchy implicit in segregation and remove the barriers to discovering our common humanity.

Segregation persists on multiple levels. We must therefore develop multiple strategies for breaking down segregation in our society. These approaches must be organized around the principles of participation and democracy. Focusing on the desegregation of schools alone cannot produce lasting results and ultimately does not integrate society or increase and enhance participation in our democracy. This is the path we followed with busing. The answer lies substantially in linking education and housing policies. Linking policies designed to integrate schools with housing provides a path to building integrated communities. Such a remedy requires both a theoretical and practical commitment to abolishing racial exclusion and hierarchy and to promoting participation and democracy.

Part 1 of this chapter defines what it means, in both a policy and a legal sense, to link housing and education and shows why this connection is crucial for creating a permanently integrated society. Part 2 critiques some of the approaches courts have taken to examining segregation and suggests a more comprehensive and searching legal analysis. Part 3 examines the need to continue pursuing integration. Finally, part 4 considers the positive quantitative and qualitative effects of integration, including the overarching goal of building a true democracy. I conclude by calling for an inclusive effort to racially transform our society. Anything short of this damages not only our children but also our entire society. The ultimate goal is daunting, but necessary. We must make our society one in which we all participate as equal citizens, sharing both our problems and solutions in the pursuit of a deeper manifestation of our democratic vision.[18]

Housing and Education: The Existing Relationship Between Living and Learning

What It Means to Link Housing and Education from a Policy Perspective

Twenty-five years ago, the Supreme Court recognized that the quality of schools has a profound impact on housing choices.[19] More recently, the Court not only has ignored this reality, but has been hostile to it. Instead of recognizing the relationship between housing and schooling, the Court has created myriad legal fictions under the rubrics of state action and causation.[20]

Housing and education have played central roles in the segregation of our society. Given the relationship between where we live and where our children go to school, the quality of local education is one of the most important factors behind a parent's choice of neighborhood. More often than not, the public schools considered best are in middle-class and upper-middle-class neighborhoods. This link between housing and schools maintains residential and educational segregation. For example, the return to neighborhood schools, for which many policy makers are now calling, may maintain or increase the racial and economic segregation of communities.

Policy makers have failed to explicitly acknowledge and address this relationship, however. A generous reading of this failure is that policy makers, isolated within their areas of expertise, are not sufficiently aware of the relationship between housing and education. Instead of recognizing this connection, policy makers often operate within the confines of housing policy or education policy, oblivious to the consequences of one for the other. This failure to connect the two policy objectives has resulted in inadequate or short-lived solutions to problems in either area.

The efforts of federal courts to treat housing and school segregation as independent are counterfactual. State courts and policy makers, however, are not bound by the federal approach to segregated schools and housing. Policy makers have it within their power to address the interrelationship of housing and education. Confronting these issues holistically is a more effective approach to addressing housing, education, and other community concerns. In addition, by more fully understanding the connection between housing and education, and the implications for other policy concerns and society at large, policy makers can better tackle some of the most troubling challenges facing the nation, not the least of which is an increasing polarization along racial and economic lines.

Part of the difficulty in adequately understanding segregation in our society is that our language and our national consciousness about segregation have been shaped by the federal courts. Even non-lawyers use legalistic language when they think about and discuss these issues. Despite the power of federal jurisprudential language, there remains a deep knowledge that we are separated by race and class. This knowledge constantly threatens to destabilize the official narrative on these issues. Our choice of schools, neighborhoods, and cities is very sensitive to racial and socioeconomic makeup. The language of federal courts, then, is in dissonance with this lived reality. Whereas the language of the federal judiciary suggests there is no real harm in segregation and that much of our segregation is a natural consequence of legitimate social choice, the anxiety and even violence around issues of segregation strongly suggest otherwise.

The legal narrative of the federal courts suggests that the primary, perhaps sole, harm that results from racial segregation is stigma. This exclusive assertion of racial stigma comes from the law's narrow understanding of segregation. Legal segregation, which is frequently viewed as synonymous with all segregation, is caused by intentional state endorsement of the segregation of disfavored minorities. Socioeconomic segregation does not play a part in this narrative. In fact, socioeconomic segregation is considered a form of benign or "natural" segregation that the government will not remedy. If intent is missing, there is a strong reluctance to recognize harm and an even stronger reluctance to move toward a remedy.

To overcome the limitations of this discourse, we must recognize that the harm of segregation occurs across racial and socioeconomic lines. When poor whites, like poor blacks, are segregated and isolated from the middle class, their life opportunities are diminished.[21] The intense segregation in urban areas, however, is almost always a function of both race and socioeconomic status. Race and class work together to create a particularly virulent form of segregation that cannot be explained by either race or socioeconomic status alone. The injuries caused by segregation are multiple. Isolated, poor communities are not merely isolated from people of a different race and class. They are isolated from those opportunity structures, including education, health care, and employment, that Americans rely on for health, stability, and advancement.[22] The social and economic harms of segregation become clear when we consider both the immediate and cumulative effects of prolonged isolation and concentration of communities by race and class. Furthermore, these harms manifest regardless of explicit intent or legal actionability. An adequate understanding of these compels action by policy makers. Agreement on the causes of segregation should not be a predicate to action when the harms are so great.

The causes of segregation, like the harms that result, are multiple. Policy makers and state courts are not limited by causation in their ability to respond to segregation. Under most state constitutions, for example, education is a fundamental right, and this enables state courts to compel the state to act regardless of evidence of intent.[23] But as a matter of policy it is important to understand causation in order to fashion an effective remedy. For example, by recognizing that there is an important relationship between a particular school and the area that surrounds it, remedies may be more apparent than if the focus is solely on the school itself.

When patterns of segregation mirror municipal boundaries, the interrelationship of housing and schools becomes even stronger.[24] In such cases, exclusionary housing practices on the part of local government directly determine the catchment area of local schools, particularly in areas where municipal boundaries and school district boundaries are contiguous. Metropolitan-wide school integration strategies have been more successful at promoting and maintaining a greater level of integration than city-wide approaches because they remove the ability of local municipalities to control attendance at their schools. Successful metropolitan school plans also have increased housing integration by removing a significant incentive for segregative housing practices. The successes of even these plans, however, are difficult to sustain over the long term without actively addressing the fundamental issues that arise from the connection between housing and education.

Despite the attention school desegregation has received in the federal courts, we have never come close to eradicating the effects of centuries of legal racial separation.[25] An effective strategy requires addressing housing and school issues with a comprehensive and coordinated plan. Our failure to link housing and education is an implicit acceptance of segregation as a policy matter.

Creating a Legal Analysis That Links Housing and Education

State and federal jurisprudence for housing and school desegregation differ in several respects. Whereas the most widely known developments in school desegregation have been in federal courts, states have recently developed a number of important innovations, especially in the area of education. Although education is not a fundamental right under federal law,[26] a number of state courts recently have found that education is a fundamental right under their state constitutions,[27] and nearly all states ensure adequate schooling under their constitutions.[28] These constitutional mandates create an affirmative duty on the part of individual states to address issues of education and obviate the need for showings of intent or causation. States should be, and have been, held liable for segregative and inadequate conditions in housing and schools, even where these harms cannot be linked directly to state action.[29]

The racial and economic segregation of schools often stems from the policies and actions of multiple actors, including housing and planning authorities and education officials.[30] Likewise, housing segregation often results from the measures implemented by school officials in addition to those enacted by land-use authorities. Because of the way federal courts fracture the responsibility for segregation among government agencies, litigators often fail or cannot join all the necessary parties.[31] Failure to include nonschool officials and agencies in the school litigation process or school officials in the housing litigation process means that school and housing integration cannot be fully addressed, even where the courts find liability. By including all culpable actors and thus addressing the link between housing and education, however, lawyers can make more complete relief possible for aggrieved parties.

Because it is difficult to join or even identify all the possible governmental parties that have contributed to housing and school segregation, suing the state itself, rather than attempting to identify individual, lower-level government actors and entities, is the more effective legal approach.[32] Because local governmental authority emanates from state delegations of power, the state is often ultimately responsible for the agencies that implement both housing and school policies. Put another way, whereas the state may delegate its powers, it may not delegate its duty to ensure that those powers are exercised constitutionally. Because the state has an affirmative obligation to remedy these injuries, a remedy that addresses both housing and education is more plausible.

In addition to guarantees of an adequate education, state constitutions also require that police powers, such as the power to zone, be exercised for the general welfare of all state citizens. This has allowed plaintiffs to argue that the state's general welfare clause does not allow the passive acceptance of housing practices that cause injury through segregation. If a state has been found liable for housing segregation, plaintiffs can draw the link between housing and school segregation in court. For example, plaintiffs can demonstrate that implementing a neighborhood schools program in a community with segregated housing will knowingly or intentionally segregate schools and is thus legally impermissible under state and federal law.[33]

Proving state responsibility for segregated housing can be more difficult than proving state responsibility in the area of education because the state does not have the same degree of control in housing as it does in education. The federal government, banks, and other actors in the private market play large roles in establishing housing policy. Nevertheless, the state has nearly exclusive authority in the area of zoning. As a result of this power, in the *Mt. Laurel* court decisions the New Jersey Supreme Court compelled the state to remedy segregative housing conditions based on the state's responsibility for zoning policies. [34]

In only a few cases have federal courts recognized that school segregation can create and reinforce housing segregation and vice versa. Moreover, federal courts that acknowledge housing segregation may cause school segregation usually have denied liability, asserting that the causes of housing segregation are unknown,[35] that housing patterns result from the natural forces of the market rather than state action,[36] or that boards of education are responsible for schools but not for housing.[37] Rarely have federal courts moved beyond their simplistic analysis of causation to explore the many interrelated actions and policies that contribute to segregative conditions.[38]

Where states are bound by general welfare and adequacy mandates, plaintiffs may be able to avoid intent and causation difficulties faced in federal court, as was the case in the *Mt. Laurel* decisions. When the state grants an entitlement in school or housing, there are two ways it legally can be compelled to act. One is by demonstrating that the state was responsible for creating segregated schools or communities. The other is by showing how the state could take reasonable action to remedy these harms, even if it did not cause them. Illustrating the link between housing and education is always crucial, both in demonstrating responsibility and in constructing a remedy.

The Failure of Current Legal Analysis to Take Integration Seriously

Formal approaches to school segregation cases have narrowed the broad language of the Court in *Brown v. Board of Education*. In fact, federal courts have developed legal doctrines that *shelter* state officials from liability for continued segregation. In particular, the doctrines of intent and unitary status mask the reality of the continued involvement of state government and policies in segregation. The direct consequences of these policies, even though diluted across a number of state actors, contradict *Brown*'s principle that governments may not segregate black students from the rest of the community.

The formal approach of much current federal analysis elevates legal form above substantive analysis and in doing so fails to recognize the link between housing and education. Ignoring this link between housing and education policies blinds courts to the pervasive segregation of our society and the role of government policies in maintaining this segregation. A careful examination of current federal jurisprudence exposes the limitations of the federal analysis of segregation and informs efforts on the state level to develop effective approaches to these issues.

The Intent Standard: Turning the Tables on the Victims of Segregated Education

One of the most significant and debilitating components of federal school desegregation jurisprudence is the intent standard.[39] This standard requires plaintiffs harmed by segregated schools to prove that school officials intentionally created and maintained racial segregation.[40] In practical terms, this protects segregation in our society by reducing segregation and racial discrimination to individual torts, that is, discrete explicit actions that directly cause a specific harm.[41] By imposing this analysis, the court fails to recognize and redress the complex dynamics of segregation and the equally complex, often hidden, motives of segregative actors. It presumes that racism is the product of deliberate, conscious thought processes and turns a blind eye to segregative contexts in which a less overt process is at work. Under such an approach, only the most extreme and explicit forms of discriminatory practices are actionable. This focus fails to appreciate the very real, but sometimes obscured, dynamics that comprise state action. Current formalist legal analysis fails to recognize state action as the culmination and combination of the policies and actions of schools, housing authorities, and other city, state, and federal officials taken together. Moreover, the current focus fails to see *inaction,* or the failure of the state to remedy segregation and counteract segregative forces, as state action.

Consistent with this rigid, overly simplistic tort model is the Supreme Court's elevation of the autonomy of local school districts above the interests of students victimized by segregation. The decision in *Milliken v. Bradley* made clear that local control over education was to be taken literally, that independent local school districts would not be held responsible for the problems of neighboring school districts, much less the condition of schools across the state. In emphasizing local autonomy, the *Milliken* Court absolved numerous government actors of their responsibility to integrate schools and curtailed desegregation efforts. Unfortunately, emphasizing local autonomy in education decisions also means that under federal law neither state governments nor the courts are left responsible for making integrated education a reality. It also means that

white families who have succeeded in creating segregated suburban enclaves have also succeeded in shielding themselves from any liability for
doing so.

This emphasis upon motives shifts the heart of the inquiry away from
the harms of segregation and allows such harm to persist where intent is
unproven. At the time of the *Brown* decision, segregated education, at
least in the South, was clearly the result of the intentional segregation of
black children by state officials.[42] The harm was explicit and was manifested in schools that were vastly unequal in terms of structure, resources,
and quality. Although the same kind of blatant and invidious discrimination seldom exists today, and never existed to the same extent in the
North as in the South, our schools remain segregated by race and socioeconomic status and continue to be vastly unequal in terms of quality.
Thus, the legacy of federal jurisprudence since *Brown* is that we have
succeeded in eradicating the *means* of segregation employed in the mid-
twentieth century without succeeding in eradicating the *harms* of segregation. Form has triumphed over function.

Justice Douglas recognized this failure in his concurring opinion in
Keyes v. School District No. 1.[43] In response to the Court's conclusion
that intentional segregation in one area is relevant to determining the
school board's intent in other school decisions, Douglas urged the Court
to go further and not differentiate between de facto and de jure segregation. State action is implicated in both cases, he argued, and he pointed to
judicial enforcement of restrictive covenants and uneven dispersion of
public housing as examples of policies that create segregation in neighborhoods, thus creating segregation and inequality in schools.[44] The Court
has not adopted Justice Douglas's views, however, and has used the heightened requirements of intentional segregation to avoid recognizing the harm
of our current segregated school system.

Nothing in the Constitution requires the Court to place the burden of
proving intent on those suffering from segregated schools. Placing the
burden of showing intentional segregation on those harmed by segregated education creates a presumption that only intentionally segregated
education is harmful. It also implicitly assumes that racial segregation is
an exception to the norm, a product of aberrant decision-making. Such
an assumption, given our country's long history of racism, is clearly erroneous. It ignores the experiences of children of color who attend poor,
segregated schools and live in poor, segregated areas. This presumption
makes it difficult for such children to tell their stories and to right the
wrong of segregation.[45] This limiting legal approach absolves government

officials of accountability for their policies and concomitantly silences those whom segregation harms most by making the federal courts largely inaccessible on the issue of educating poor, minority children.

Unitary Status: Cutting Off the Possibility for True Integration

The legal concept of "unitary status" is another barrier to integration. Unitary status, as opposed to dual status, describes the state of school districts that the court has deemed desegregated as a matter of law. A finding of unitary status does not mean that actual equality or integration in education exists, however, only that a *local* school district is not officially condoning segregation and that it is doing everything in its power to eliminate actual segregation within its district boundaries.[46] A unitary, or desegregated, school district is rarely an integrated school district for several reasons. Local school districts have little influence over housing, which plays a major role in the segregation of schools. A school board is also only one of several instruments of the state and has limitations on its influence in the educational arena. This again speaks to the need for a broader definition of state action and responsibility. Unitary status reflects an unrealistic insistence on defining community at such a small level that policy makers' hands are tied when attempting to formulate a remedy for segregation.

In granting unitary status, courts only require narrow and limited remedies. Such courts pay no attention to how neighboring school districts, housing officials, other policymakers, or the state as a whole are implicated. Thus, school districts that are nearly 100 percent poor and of color will still be considered desegregated if none of the individual schools within this district deviate substantially from district-wide averages. This will be the ruling even though, as is often the case, neighboring school districts have student populations that are nearly all white and middle to upper class. A grant of unitary status cuts short the inquiry into the reality of continued segregation and possible broader remedies. Thus school districts have an easy threshold for obtaining an end to court-ordered desegregation even if they have not achieved desegregation.[47] School districts argue that there is nothing they can do to alter the district's population; as individual actors they are largely correct.

In *Freeman v. Pitts*, the Supreme Court held that courts may relinquish control over desegregation once districts have obtained unitary status.[48] Eager to encourage local autonomy in public education, the *Freeman* Court refused to consider de facto segregation or the cumulative effects of state action on housing and education.[49] Unfortunately, using unitary status as the standard not only creates an over-simplified legal analysis, it also represents a dramatic departure from the goals of integration. Even where desegregation efforts have been successful, resulting in higher test scores and greater neighborhood integration,[50] early ends to enforced plans under the theory of unitary status have resulted in rapid resegregation.[51]

The Need to Link Housing and Education: A Crucial Step Toward Achieving Integration and Equality

Linking housing and education in legal doctrine and policy making creates the possibility for a transformation of our communities, one that will not only change how we perceive the value of integration, but also improve the economic and social conditions of many people. For this transformation to take place, we must move away from conceptions of assimilation and avoid formalistic notions of desegregation. If we examine the limitations of current understandings of integration and the possibility for a more comprehensive approach, we see that integration remains a worthy and necessary goal.

The Conflation of Integration and Assimilation

Integration policies often have resulted in a push for assimilation of minority populations into the majority culture rather than an attempt to achieve a *shared* understanding among different groups within a community. The belief that assimilation is necessary for minority groups to live successfully in American society stems from the historical experiences of European ethnic groups immigrating to this country.[52] From these experiences, the idea of a common American culture emerged, designed to embrace the experiences of white European immigrants, who brought with them different languages, religions, and customs. At the same time, there was room within this larger vision for these immigrants to identify and distinguish themselves from each other according to ethnic group.[53]

The widely accepted idea of integrating the many European ethnic groups into American society is premised upon the notion that, despite minor cultural differences, there is a more fundamental shared white racial identity. This ethnic identity paradigm, however, has not smoothly fit the experiences of different racial groups. Despite having different ethnic backgrounds, Americans are assumed to be of the white race.[54] Applying this idea of ethnic integration to the experiences of different racial groups requires African Americans, Asian Americans, Latinos, and Native Americans to assimilate into a white, European American culture rather than become part of an integrated society.[55]

School integration policies have accepted the assimilation model, too often focusing on "fixing" black children in an attempt to improve their assimilation into white culture. Because of the assumption that only blacks gain from integration, black children have been bused to white schools, while white children are rarely bused to black schools. The misconception is that students of color must become like white, middle-class students in order for their educational experiences to improve. This paradigm is destructive to people of color, and particularly to blacks.

It has been suggested that there is something wrong or deficient with black children, something that is alleviated by placing them in the company of white children.[56] The assumption has been that racial problems will be resolved when all blacks are assimilated into whiteness.[57] In one sense, this assumption results from the view that urban schools provide a less-than-satisfactory education because the students are black, while suburban schools, because the students are white, provide greater opportunities. This assumption ignores the reality of socioeconomic status in urban and suburban society and the role that racialized space plays in maintaining this reality. The problem of racism in a racialized societal structure is conflated with race itself. The goal becomes removing the blackness from black students. To accomplish this, black students must assimilate into white, middle-class culture.[58]

The assimilation model, then, is one of racial supremacy. It assumes that only the dominant race or culture is valuable and healthy. Acceptance into the community requires acceptance of the experiences of the dominant race as one's own. Despite this country's long history as a multicultural and multiracial society, relationships between different racial and ethnic groups continually suffer from such assertions of dominance and power.

Assimilation ignores the problems of both racial hierarchy and class. It assumes that blacks are poor because of their failures, not as a result of how benefits and opportunities have been distributed by the dominant society. It assumes that black schools are substandard because they are black, not because they lack economic and community resources. The contradiction, of course, is that blacks are expected to behave like whites in a society in which their very blackness defines them as inferior.

The language of assimilation is slippery. Although policy makers and judges may not intend to exclude groups of people in creating desegregation policies, their positions as members of the dominant community become intertwined in their legal reasoning.[59] The result may be a failure to see the harm of assimilation. Policies such as one-way busing subtly create a perception of one community as more valuable than another. Children who are bused out of their communities as well as those in suburban schools experience the harm of assimilation. The students bused from urban areas come to see their communities and experiences as inferior.[60] Suburban students, meanwhile, develop a narrow view of the world, preventing an understanding of experiences other than their own.[61]

Rather than recognize that African American is both an ethnic and a racial identity with a distinct history and experience, the ideal of a color-blind society treats blackness as irrelevant, at best. As black intellectuals begin to expose the racism of assimilation, however, many are rejecting integration and arguing instead for segregation. This, too, is a flawed conclusion. Integration is not the problem. Whereas segregation and assimilation support the status quo, integration, when properly conceived, is inclusive and transformative.

A true integration model challenges racial hierarchy and the need to be colorless or white. Such a model entails a redistribution of resources and opportunities, as well as a shift in ideology. Additionally, a real problem with the idea of assimilation is the assumption that whites have not been affected by growing up in a racialized society. Although whites may be injured differently by assimilation, they are harmed nonetheless. An inclusive approach cannot simply fit individuals into existing norms and structures; it must transform those structures to accommodate all individuals and groups. Put another way, a true model of integration recognizes that whites do not occupy a neutral position and does not seek to place people of color in this same position.

Linking Housing and School Creates More Stable, Integrated Communities

Despite recent criticism of, and confusion over, the benefits of integration, it still receives widespread support.[62] Moving toward lasting integration, however, requires efforts beyond sporadic, narrowly defined education goals. The lack of a long-term, practice-oriented commitment to the ideal of integration has resulted in a series of abortive attempts to achieve integrated schools. As John Dewey taught, education comprises far more than formal schooling.[63] Although integration may improve test scores and graduation rates for low-income minority students, an equally important and related benefit is the more complete democracy that Dewey envisioned. Through education, we strive to create good citizens and active participants in our communities; integration policies should reflect and further this higher goal.

Policy makers and courts are guilty of shortsightedness for failing to look beyond the immediate consequences of actions necessary to achieve integration.[64] A frequently expressed fear is that integration will weaken communities and create "white flight." For example, mandatory busing is perceived to weaken communities, rather than being an effective step toward achieving integration, and this perception drives many school districts to return to neighborhood schools.[65] What policy makers fail to notice is that hints of the potential for lasting integration have surfaced in communities implementing aggressive plans, even where the plans were short-lived.[66] Our imperative today is to take the ideological commitment and the potential for long-term change seriously and to focus on creating and implementing lasting integration plans.

Recharging the public's commitment to the goal of integration requires an approach that recognizes the importance of integration at all levels. We must build our own communities while simultaneously supporting a much larger community. The world beyond our own neighborhood or town is extremely diverse, and a more expansive view of this world, and of our relationships to each other, forces us to understand our shared needs and differences. With this new understanding, we must realize that we cannot build a democratic nation by preserving some communities and abandoning others.[67]

Breaking down barriers to adequate and affordable housing in all communities must be a central goal in a broad integration policy. There are both blatant and subtle barriers to acquiring housing in middle-class suburban neighborhoods for many minority families. In addition to the lack of affordable housing, discrimination in the real estate and lending markets prevents minority families from moving to these communities, even when their economic status would allow such a move.[68]

Accomplishing integration in the areas of housing and education signals a commitment to full societal integration and also recognizes the multiple barriers to integration. Integrating schools ought to be one part of a broad policy of integration albeit a central one due to the far-reaching effects of integrated education.[69] This can be seen in the case of Jefferson County, Kentucky, where stereotypes and prejudices began to break down at the very beginning of a county-wide desegregation and mandatory busing plan:

> [I]t is essential to remember that the exaggerated emotionalism which accompanied implementation of the transportation aspect of desegregation rapidly began

to die away after classes began. By the end of the first year of desegregation, the tension and upset which spilled into the hallways and classrooms from the initial turbulence on the streets had largely given way to relaxed acceptance. Inside the schools, if not in all parts of the community, old misconceptions and misapprehensions receded into the past.[70]

This episode points out that creating more integrated communities is possible and desirable when people of different racial and economic groups begin to recognize that, despite their differences, they share many goals and concerns.

Negative perceptions of urban schools contribute to the unwillingness of white families to move to urban neighborhoods. Part of the reason urban schools have a negative reputation is, of course, that they are segregated by race and class. The concentration of poverty in urban schools is indeed a problem and affects the resources available in those schools. Overwhelmingly poor communities have access to few resources despite their greater needs.[71] When communities achieve broad and lasting integration, neighborhood schools become integrated schools. Moreover, when housing and school policies work together, fears of integration dissipate and integrated communities can maintain stable, diverse populations.[72]

The potential of such an expansive approach makes clear that busing students to schools outside their neighborhoods is, at best, a weak tool for achieving integration. However, until policy makers address the issue of housing segregation, busing students remains both an appropriate and a necessary way to achieve integration. Although perhaps not comforting to those who oppose the immediate consequences of busing, including distance between home and school and long bus rides, busing is an important step toward broad, long-term integration.[73] Combining mandatory and voluntary incentive-based approaches to desegregation addresses the importance of achieving some form of integration immediately.

Desegregation or Integration? Striving for a More Inclusive Community

Distinguishing desegregation from integration is one necessary step in moving beyond assimilation. Desegregation has traditionally referred to the removal of legally redressable barriers to integration, or the simple placement of students of different racial and ethnic backgrounds in physical proximity to one another. Both interpretations, however, are too narrow and have limited utility. Segregation is not just the exclusion or separation of people, but also the limitation of opportunities and economic resources. It creates and maintains a culture of racial hierarchy and subordination. Integration, as a solution to segregation, has a broader meaning; it refers to community-wide efforts to create a more inclusive society in which individuals and groups have opportunities to participate equally.

Integration, then, transforms racial hierarchy. Rather than creating a benefactor-beneficiary distinction along lines of race and class, true integration makes benefits possible for all groups. Poor minorities, in particular, have increased access to social, cultural, economic, and educational resources in integrated communities. At the same time, as Dewey acknowledges, integration brings us closer to our shared democratic ideal:

> A democracy is more than a form of government; it is primarily a mode of associated living, of conjointed communicated experience. The extension in space of the number of individuals who participate in an interest so that each has to refer his own action to that of others, and to consider the action of others to give point and direction to his own, is equivalent to the breaking down of those barriers of class, race, and national territory which kept men from perceiving the full import of their activity.[74]

The desegregation policies this country has adopted have not and cannot produce integration. Given this, desegregation policies can be seen as an accommodation of continued segregation and discrimination. The history of desegregation policies focuses on desegregation as a right of African American children who have been denied the quality of education received by white students. Integration goes further, recognizing desegregation as a benefit to the entire community rather than as the right of a few. *Brown v. Board of Education* recognized the harm experienced by segregated schoolchildren. Our responses to that harm must change, however, as time clarifies the severity of the damage to our children caused by segregated communities. Efforts at desegregating schools have simultaneously demonstrated the possible benefits of integration and proved that desegregation alone is not enough. What began as a discussion of individual rights has moved into a deeper analysis of how to better our communities for all.

Elizabeth Schneider's articulation of the dialectic of rights and politics illustrates that rights are useful and necessary to achieve some version of equality, but that the language of rights can also be limiting.[75] Black schoolchildren intentionally placed in segregated, unequipped schools needed courts to recognize their right to something better. Focusing only on individual rights, however, leads to legal fictions such as the concept of unitary status. Rather than examining the reality of inequality in housing and education, for example, rights-based analysis focuses narrowly on such issues as equalized funding or classroom size. Although these single issues are important in striving to achieve adequate education for all children, they do not capture the larger, more pervasive problems of segregation and isolation of schools and communities by race and class.

A narrow rights-based analysis cannot adequately remedy what truly troubles our communities. Integrationist policies are a response to the rights expressed through desegregation and these social realities. Integration, rather than simply representing a remedy for existing harms, affirmatively moves our communities toward a goal that is good in itself.

Opposition to Integrationist Policies: The Diversion of Resources Argument

The most common response to the failure of poor, segregated schools is that resources should be expended to make such schools more educationally effective. This solution, common among critics of integrationist policies, focuses on using tangible, quantitative improvements in education to bring about social and economic change in poor, largely minority communities.[76] Some claim that resources spent on school integration could be better channeled toward improving conditions in urban schools and neighborhoods.[77]

Some scholars, such as David Armor, suggest that minority groups choose to remain segregated from white communities and that to disregard this choice is paternalistic and racist.[78] Others suggest that as communities become more viable, they will naturally integrate. These critics also argue that the push for integration ignores the real needs of poor, urban neighborhoods. They view integration as a middle-class aspiration that will only benefit those with the economic resources to participate fully in an integrated society.[79] Many of the proponents of this position argue that blacks and other minorities would more likely choose to live in their respective communities if adequate resources were available to these communities.

Arguments in support of self-imposed segregation have a number of flaws. The reality is that the segregation of poor minorities is not self-generated; rather, it is imposed by the dominant society. One of the major tenets of racism in the United States has been the right to exclude the disfavored race. The economic, social, and cultural impacts of this belief are both profound and destructive for poor, minority communities and for society as a whole. Despite the fact that officially enforced segregation is now often attributed to the "natural choice" of excluded groups, segregation is neither natural nor a choice.[80] While it is true that the middle class is likely to see the benefits of a more integrated society first, this does not suggest that poor people of color will not benefit as well.

Most middle-class blacks who have the choice do not choose to live in poor, segregated communities or send their children to predominantly black schools. Thus, in thinking about preferences, we should remember that some apparent "choices" are not voluntary at all, but result from societal restrictions of choice.[81] Moreover, choices are easily distorted and manipulated by a lack of accurate information.

In the 1920s and 1930s, many blacks chose to live in the black community because of the constant threat of violence by whites. Despite the continuation of this threat, the majority of blacks today favor living in an integrated community. Achieving that goal requires breaking down widespread, subtle, and institutionally entrenched discrimination in all parts of society. Building up urban communities through economic development, improved education, and quality housing contributes to dismantling racism in significant ways.[82]

Affirmative integration policies also contribute to this project. Integration helps to achieve improvements in urban communities by attracting resources and renewed political commitment to cities. When poor and middle-class minorities and whites live in the same urban communities, they develop a shared concern for the problems tearing away at the nation's cities. Increasing resources in urban communities is crucial in addressing issues of urban decay, as critics of integrationist policies argue. Integration, however, remains necessary for effective and long-lasting change.

The Effect of Integration: Meeting and Moving Beyond Our Expectations

The benefits of fully integrating our schools and neighborhoods extend beyond an adherence to our constitutional equal protection ideals. Studies persuasively illustrate the devastating effects of segregated schools and communities and indicate just as powerfully the benefits of integration to all members of society.

Quantitative Consequences of Integration Efforts
There are immediate and easily identifiable benefits to an integrated education. When communities integrate their schools, even if the communities themselves do not become integrated, the overwhelming result is

improvement in academic achievement. The improvements are especially pronounced for minority students bused to integrated schools.[83] In cities across the country, the achievement gap between black students and white students has narrowed considerably with the implementation of school integration plans. For example, between 1980 and 1989, the achievement gap between African American and white students in Dallas narrowed from 35 percentage points to 16 percentage points following the implementation of an integration plan. Similar gap reductions occurred in language ability and reading. The achievement gap between African American and white students in Louisville elementary schools narrowed by as much as 7 percentage points after the implementation of an integration plan in 1975. Although white students experienced higher academic performance overall, African American students experienced a greater rate of improvement.[84] The results of improved learning extend well beyond the high school classroom, with students of color educated in integrated schools more likely to obtain full-time employment or to attend college.[85] The costs of school integration to white students, in academic terms, are nonexistent. Indeed, white students in integrated schools experience stable or improved academic achievement.[86]

The beneficial effects of social integration run deep and continue to influence the lives of students from integrated schools long after their formal education. Students taught in an integrated environment are better able to adapt to our rapidly changing world once they leave school. These students are also more likely to choose to live in an integrated community as adults.[87]

The trend in many communities to abandon integration efforts, in favor of a narrow focus on improving achievement, has ironically resulted in lower academic achievement among both white and minority students. For example, black students' academic achievement has declined since the return to a segregated neighborhood school system in Norfolk, Virginia, and the achievement gap between black and white students has increased. When Norfolk ceased mandated busing, African American elementary school students' achievement scores dropped from a mean of 52.57 to 47.15. Furthermore, white students' mean test scores decreased by 2.92 points.[88] These declines occur even when school districts commit significantly greater funding and other resources to segregated neighborhood schools.[89] The resegregation of schools has a devastating effect on poor, minority students, creating an environment of diminished community resources and lower expectations.[90]

The Effect of Integration on Our Communities:
Building a Participatory Democracy

The social value of integration is consistent with the founding ideals of this country. A central goal of integration policies involves the opportunity for everyone to participate actively in our democracy. Active participation requires resources and tools, such as housing, income, and education, that provide stability and allow for expression. Another necessary element of participation is the connection of individuals to the community as valued members of the polity. Segregation excludes community members, even when formal rights to participate exist.

Integration makes it possible for those historically excluded from participating in society to be a part of a larger community while transforming that community. Deliberate and formal schooling is only part of the educative experience. Association provides another avenue for learning. As Dewey noted, through association we learn to consider the effect of our actions upon others.[91] We no longer can act in isolation once we know each other.

Dewey also saw education, in his broad understanding of the term, as a means of continuous renewal.[92] Through education, we constantly work to equip our children with the tools to live. The formal learning environment provided in schools is one place where children of different backgrounds and experiences come together.[93] The school setting provides both academic and social tools for participating in society. The less formal environment of our neighborhoods and social circles provides equally important tools for everyday life. Integration of both schools and housing demonstrates for all of us how the practice of living and learning together can inform our understanding of the world. A truly participatory democracy results from an informed and active citizenry. Integration promotes this vision of participation by educating citizens in a broad sense, both formally and informally.

Conclusion

America cannot afford to maintain two societies, white and minority, separated by race, class, and space. Nor can it afford to waste the potential of any of our children simply because they live in the forgotten parts of our urban centers. None of us can afford to turn our backs on the imperative of *Brown v. Board of Education*. We must understand *Brown* to require the integration of two societies into one, not by assimilating one into the other, but by breaking down the barriers that prevent the two from enriching one another. Linking housing and education has proven the most effective way to ensure the integration of both. Attorneys, judges, and policy makers should adopt this strategy as the next step in implementing the *Brown* imperative and breaking the cycle of hopelessness caused by the intersections of isolation, racism, and poverty.

Notes

1. 418 U.S. 717 (1974).

2. Ibid., 783 (Marshall, J., dissenting).

3. 515 U.S. 70 (1995).

4. Ibid., 114 (Thomas, J., dissenting).

5. *Milliken*, 418 U.S. at 761 (Douglas, J., dissenting).

6. 347 U.S. 483 (1954).

7. *Pasadena City Board of Education v. Spangler*, 427 U.S. 424, 436 (1976).

8. *Jenkins*, 515 U.S. at 94–95. The Court explicitly absolved itself and other state actors of responsibility for continued segregation: "Just as demographic changes independent of *de jure* segregation will affect the racial composition of student assignments, so too will numerous external factors beyond the control of the [Kansas City, Missouri, School District] and the State affect minority student achievement. So long as these external factors are not the result of segregation, they do not figure in the remedial calculus. Insistence upon academic goals unrelated to the effects of legal segregation unwarrantably postpones the day when the [school district] will be able to operate on its own." Id. at 102 (citations omitted).

9. While some experts have questioned the validity of the stigma theory relied upon in *Brown*, most still acknowledge that segregated schools do not provide an equal education. Those who favor segregated schools often argue that with enough resources these schools can provide an education equal to that of majority white schools. This claim ignores the fact that schools segregated by race also are segregated by class. The focus then shifts to class and to the assertion that states cannot address class because class is not a constitutional issue. The inextricable link between race and class undermines these claims. Recent approaches to the problem of segregation, including educational adequacy suits under state constitutional provisions, raise the issue of the link between class and race.

10. Some argue that, because desegregation has not produced the predicted leaps forward in black educational achievement, there is "no reason to think that black students cannot learn as well when surrounded by members of their own race as when they are in an integrated environment. . . . [B]lack schools can function as the center and symbol of black communities, and provide examples of independent black leadership, success, and achievement." *Missouri v. Jenkins*, 515 U.S. 70, 121–22 (1995) (Thomas, J., concurring); see generally David Armor, *Forced Justice: School Desegregation and the Law* (1995) (discussing the recent trend toward "resegregation" within the school choice movement).

11. For a discussion of some of the negative effects of segregation, see George C. Galster, "A Cumulative Causation Model of the Underclass: Implications for Urban Economic Development Policy", in *The Metropolis in Black and White: Place, Power and Polarization*, 190, 194–200 (George C. Galster & Edward W. Hill, eds., 1992).

12. See *infra* text accompanying notes 55–64 for a discussion of assimilation.

13. "The ideal of integration can only be achieved by respecting this unique [African American] culture through the maintenance and operation of *separate* institutions." Alex M. Johnson Jr., "Bid Whist, Tonk, and *United States v. Fordice*: Why Integration Fails African Americans Again," 81 *Cal. L. Rev.* 1401, 1403 (1993).

14. See Jonathan Kozol, *Savage Inequalities: Children in America's Schools*, 112–24 (1991).

15. See David Theo Goldberg, *Racist Culture: Philosophy and the Politics of Meaning*, 187–90 (1993).

16. See generally, Douglas Massey and Nancy Denton, *American Apartheid: Segregation and the Making of the Underclass* (discussing the negative impact of segregation on the African American community); Howard Winant, *Racial Condition: Politics, Theory, Comparisons* (1994) (comparing the liberation of racial identity in the United States and Brazil).

17. Even the Supreme Court has recognized this. For example, the Court has declared that the deprivation of an integrated living environment is a cognizable harm extending standing to both white and minority plaintiffs. See *Trafficante v. Metropolitan Life Insurance Co.*, 409 U.S. 205, 212 (1972).

18. See Kenneth L. Karst, *Belonging to America: Equal Citizenship and the Constitution*, 28–42 (1989) (discussing equality and inclusion as foundational theories of the American civic culture).

19. *Swann v. Charlotte-Mecklenburg Board of Education*, 402 U.S. 1, 20–21 (1971).

20. For a more detailed discussion of the legal analysis of state action, causation, and linking education and housing, see *infra* notes 26–41 and accompanying text. See also Alan Freeman and Elizabeth Mensch, "The Public-Private Distinction in American Law and Life," 36 *Buff. L. Rev.* 237, 238–42 (1987) (analyzing liberal legalism based on the premise that the public-private distinction is an artificial construct).

21. See Robert B. Reich, *The Work of Nations*, 203–04 (1991) (discussing how segregation along economic lines is harmful to lower-middle-class whites).

22. See George C. Galster and Edward W. Hill, "Place, Power, and Polarization," in *The Metropolis in Black and White*, *supra* note 11, at 1, 1–7 (discussing how segregation operates as a web-like system with cumulative effects).

23. This is the basis of an adequacy suit. The liability arises when the state creates an entitlement to an adequate education but then allows conditions to develop that undermine this entitlement.

24. This was the very situation that the Court refused to acknowledge in *Milliken v. Bradley*, 418 U.S. 717 (1974). The *Milliken* Court held a multi-district, area-wide remedy inappropriate in the absence of violations by each included district. Id. at 744–45.

25. See Florence Wagman Roisman, "Intentional Racial Discrimination and Segregation by the Federal Government as a Principal Cause of Concentrated Poverty: A Response to Schill and Wachter," 143 *U. Pa. L. Rev.* 1351, 1351–52 (1995) (arguing that federally sanctioned racial discrimination and segregation continue to pervade society, especially in the area of federal housing programs).

26. *San Antonio Independent School District v. Rodriguez*, 411 U.S. 1, 33–39 (1973) (refusing to equate "fundamental" with the term "fundamentally important").

27. See, e.g., *Alabama Coalition for Equity, Inc. v. Hunt*, Nos. CIV.A.CV-90-883-R, CV-91-0117-R, 1993 WL 204083, at notes 56–57 (Ala. Cir. Ct. Apr. 1, 1993) (noting that education plays an essential role in advancing societal interests); *McDuffy v. Secretary of Executive Office of Education*, 615 N.E.2d 516 (Mass. 1993) (interpreting Massachusetts Constitution, pt. II, ch. 5). Contra: *Idaho School for Equal Educational Opportunity v. Evans*, 850 P.2d 724, 732–33 (Idaho 1993) (holding that the Idaho Constitution does not establish education as a fundamental right).

28. See, e.g., Massachusetts Constitution, pt. II, ch. 5, § 2 (establishing a duty to provide education); New Hampshire Constitution, pt. 2, art. 83 (imposing a duty on the state to provide adequate education); New Jersey Constitution, art. 8, § 4, para. 1 (providing for "free public schools"); North Dakota Constitution, art. VII, §§ 1–2 (establishing state schools); Tennessee Constitution, art. XI, § 12 (providing for free public schools).

29. See *United States v. Yonkers*, 837 F.2d 1181, 1226 (2d Cir. 1987), cert. denied, 486 U.S. 1055 (1988) (holding both the school board and the city liable for school segregation); *Liddell v. Board of Education*, 667 F.2d 643, 653–55 (8th Cir.), cert. denied, 454 U.S. 1081 (1981) (affirming a court-ordered desegregation plan that required the state of Missouri to pay one-half of its cost); *United States v. Board of School Commissioners*, 637 F.2d 1101, 1107 (7th Cir.), cert. denied, 449 U.S. 838 (1980) (finding discriminatory intent in state legislation); *Evans v. Buchanan*, 582 F.2d 750, 766 (3rd Cir. 1978) (holding states, rather than the federal government, responsible for operating a nondiscriminatory school system); *Newburg Area Council v. Board of Education*, 489 F.2d 925, 932 (6th Cir. 1973) (imposing a duty on the school board to eliminate all vestiges of state-enforced discrimination).

30. See *Yonkers*, 837 F.2d at 1219-20 (affirming a district court finding that the city's policy of constructing low-income housing only in minority areas led to

increased segregation); *Liddell*, 667 F.2d at 652–53 (noting that the board of education is ultimately responsible for desegregation); *Newburg Area Council*, 489 F.2d at 931 (holding that neutral geographic zoning assignments cannot be upheld if they fail to eliminate segregation within a district under a court-imposed mandate to do so).

31. See *Milliken*, 418 U.S. 717, 728–30 & nn.8–9 (1974) (noting the effects of a failure to join 85 independent school districts as defendants); see also *Missouri v. Jenkins*, 515 U.S. 70 (1995).

32. See Michael H. Sussman, "Discrimination: A Unitary Concept," 80 *MNLR* 875 (1996).

33. This is the case in Minneapolis, where a settlement in the *Hollman v. Cisneros* lawsuit has resulted in admission of the intentional segregation of public housing residents. The city's mayor and school board have considered a move to neighborhood schools. Doug Grow, *The Mayor Stands Strong, Even if the Time Has Come to Clash with an Old Mentor*, Star Tribune (Minneapolis), July 2, 1995, at 3B.

34. *Southern Burlington County NAACP v. Township of Mount Laurel* [*Mount Laurel I*], 336 A.2d 713 (N. J. 1975); *Southern Burlington County NAACP v. Township of Mount Laurel* [*Mount Laurel II*], 456 A.2d 390. The court relied upon the general welfare clause of the New Jersey Constitution. *Mount Laurel I*, 336 A.2d at 725–27 & n.11 (citing New Jersey Constitution, art. I, para. 1).

35. See *Milliken v. Bradley*, 418 U.S. 717, 745 (1974) (denying a metropolitan area remedy for interdistrict segregation in Detroit-area schools because the respondents did not show that the racially discriminatory acts of one or more school districts caused the segregation).

36. See *Freeman v. Pitts*, 503 U.S. 567, 494–95 (1992) (discussing the notion that residential segregation patterns are not a result of state action but rather of private choice); *Board of Education v. Dowell*, 498 U.S. 237, 242–44 (1991) (discussing the district court finding that residential segregation resulted from private choices and economics rather than from school segregation).

37. *Missouri v. Jenkins*, 515 U.S. 70, 102 (1995) (noting that demographic changes that are independent of de jure segregation, along with many other factors, will affect the racial composition of students at schools and that these demographic changes do not "figure in the remedial calculus").

38. *U. S. v. Yonkers*, 837 F.2d 1181, 1236-38 (2d Cir. 1987).

39. See, e.g., *Washington v. Davis*, 426 U.S. 229, 239-42 (1976) (discussing the necessity of proving intent to succeed in an action for racial discrimination under the Fourteenth Amendment); *Keyes v. School District No. 1*, 413 U.S. 189, 208–09 (1973) (holding that intent to segregate is necessary to establish that school authorities have segregated schools or school systems); *Swann v. Charlotte-Mecklenburg Board of Education*, 402 U.S. 1, 32 (1971) (holding that a

district court need not intervene if there is no evidence that school authorities or other state agents intentionally have segregated schools).

40. See *Freeman v. Pitts*, 503 U.S. 467, 494 (1992) (requiring a remedy for racial imbalance in a school only if a de jure policy of segregation caused the imbalance); *Board of Education v. Dowell*, 498 U.S. 237, 250 (1991) (holding that a desegregation decree should be dissolved if a school board no longer intentionally discriminates and has acted in good faith to eliminate the "vestiges of *de jure* segregation . . . as far as practical"); *Milliken v. Bradley*, 418 U.S. 717, 745 (1974) (holding that, to obtain an interdistrict remedy, a plaintiff must show that racially discriminatory acts of the state or local school districts were a substantial cause of the interdistrict segregation).

41. See Kimberle W. Crenshaw, "Race, Reform, and Retrenchment: Transformation and Legitimation in Antidiscrimination Law," 101 *Harv. L. Rev.* 1331, 1384 (1988) (arguing that "the belief that racial exclusion is illegitimate only where the 'White Only' signs are explicit—coupled with strong assumptions about equal opportunity"—makes it difficult to address underlying racism because society is satisfied with "neutral norms and formal inclusion"); Alan Freeman, "Legitimizing Racial Discrimination through Antidiscrimination Law: A Critical Review of Supreme Court Doctrine," 62 *Minn. L. Rev.* 1049, 1054–55 (1978) (arguing that, if only intentional discrimination violates the antidiscrimination principle, a person can escape responsibility for conduct which may have been discriminatory merely by "showing that the action was taken for a good reason, or for no reason at all"); Neil Gotanda, "A Critique of 'Our Constitution is Color-Blind,'" 44 *Stan. L. Rev.* 1, 44–45 (1991) (criticizing the Supreme Court's use of "formal-race unconnectedness" as a standard that covers up racism and allows it to continue); see generally Charles R. Lawrence III, "The Id, the Ego, and Equal Protection: Reckoning with Unconscious Racism," 39 *Stan. L. Rev.* 317 (1987) (positing that the intent requirement protects racism because discrimination often is unintentional).

42. The Court implied that only intentional segregation is harmful. See *Brown v. Board of Education*, 347 U.S. 483, 493–94 (1954) (addressing the issue of segregation "solely on the basis of race"). Although the injury caused by intentional segregation may be greater, there is little doubt that de facto segregation also is harmful.

43. 413 U.S. 189, 216-17 (1973) (Douglas, J., concurring) (stating that there is no constitutional difference between de jure and de facto segregation and that both are the result of state action).

44. "When a State forces, aids, or abets, or helps create a racial 'neighborhood,' it is a travesty of justice to treat that neighborhood as sacrosanct in the sense that its creation is free from the taint of state action." *Keyes v. School District No. 1*, 413 U.S. 216. Justice Douglas expressed the same views in his dissent to the Supreme Court's decision in *Spencer v. Kugler*, 404 U.S. 1027 (1972). In *Spencer*, the Court allowed the state of New Jersey to maintain school district boundaries that had a segregative effect. Id. at 1028 (Douglas, J., dissenting). Douglas

saw redistricting as the solution, drawing an analogy to voting redistricting to achieve diverse voting districts. Id. He added that housing segregation was a result of state action and led, undeniably, to segregated schools. Id. at 1029 n.1.

45. See Alan Freeman, "Antidiscrimination Law: The View from 1989," 64 *Tul. L. Rev.* 1407, 1409–23 (1990), for a discussion of the victim perspective versus the perpetrator perspective. The victim perspective, according to Freeman, focuses on the injury while the perpetrator perspective focuses on fault. Id. at 1411–13. Freeman notes that the courts have adopted the perpetrator perspective. Id. at 1413. Given the injury and our history, what presumption should apply? One approach is for courts to place the burden on the state to show that it has not caused segregation. This is the approach in employment law and Title VIII cases. See *United States v. Black Jack*, 508 F.2d 1179, 1185 (8th Cir. 1974) (holding that once a plaintiff establishes a *prima facie* case under Title VIII by showing discriminatory effect, the burden shifts to the government to show that its allegedly discriminatory actions were necessary to promote a compelling governmental interest).

46. See *Missouri v. Jenkins*, 515 U.S. 70, 90 (1995) (noting that "[t]he proper response to an intradistrict violation is an intradistrict remedy . . . that serves to eliminate the racial identity of the schools within the affected school district by eliminating, as far as practicable, the vestiges of *de jure* segregation in all facets of their operations.").

47. For instance, in Norfolk, Virginia, a federal court found that the city's school district had achieved unitary status only three years after federal courts ordered desegregation. Christina Meldrum and Susan E. Eaton, *Resegregation in Norfolk, Virginia: Does Restoring Neighborhood Schools Work?* 3 (1994). The school district used this finding to disregard Norfolk's history of segregation. Id.

48. 503 U.S. 467 (1992).

49. The Court found no de jure segregation and attributed racial imbalances to demographic forces, for which the school district and other state actors had no responsibility. *Freeman v. Pitts*, 503 U.S. 494–95. "Where resegregation is a product not of state action but of private choices, it does not have constitutional implications." Id. at 495.

50. Jefferson County, Kentucky, provides a good example of this result. See generally Kentucky Commission on Human Rights, *School and Housing Desegregation Are Working Together in Louisville and Jefferson County* (1983) (discussing the narrowed education gap between blacks and whites when black families move to suburban communities as part of housing and education desegregation programs) [hereinafter Kentucky Commission Study].

51. Kentucky Commission Study, "School and Housing," 1–3 (noting that Louisville, which had implemented a voluntary desegregation plan in 1956, had a segregated school system again by 1972).

52. See generally Michael Omi and Howard Winant, *Racial Formation in the United States from the 1960s to the 1990s* (2d ed., 1994) (discussing the conceptions of race in American society).

53. Ibid., 14–23.

54. The simplicity of this view is unfortunate in that the search for a definition of our American community is more complicated. According to Kenneth Karst, "The question, Who belongs? turns out to be a question about the meanings of America. To speak of self-definition, of the sense of community, and of the community-defining functions of law is not to identify different parts of a machine but to view a complex social process from several different angles." Karst, *supra* note 18, at 13.

55. Ibid.

56. See Omi and Winant, *supra* note 52, at 17 (referring to the work of Gunnar Myrdal, in particular his 1944 study, *An American Dilemma*).

57. See generally Arthur M. Schlesinger Jr., *The Disuniting of America* (1992) (noting that integration often emphasizes the need to assimilate into white culture).

58. Criticizing the focus of some educators on teaching about separate cultural heritages, Schlesinger asks, "But would it not be more appropriate for students to be 'continually' encouraged to understand the American culture in which they are growing up and to prepare for an active role in shaping that culture? Should public education strengthen and perpetuate separate ethnic and racial subcultures? Or should it not seek to make our young boys and girls contributors to a common American culture?" Schlesinger, *supra* note 57, at 90. Schlesinger fails to address the possibility that the "common American culture" is not made up of multiple perspectives and experiences, but rather consists of the dominant perspectives in society, those of middle-class, white individuals who never experience the stigma of being "different" or outside the majority. If this is true, then education already perpetuates a separate culture, one that is "ethnic and racial" to everyone who is not a part of this cultural experience.

59. Karst sees the failure of policy makers and judges to recognize the different experiences of members of a multicultural society not as callousness or lack of sympathy on the part of these individuals, but as part of a "deep-seated problem that begins in the acquisition of cultural identity and gender identity, a problem that is especially acute in a multicultural society." Karst, *supra* note 18, at 11. A person from a white, middle-class, Protestant background acquires a "community of meaning." Id. For this person, "poor people and black people and non-Protestants are apt to be seen as Others, whose differences define boundaries between communities—boundaries policed by ignorance and fear. Such a boundary is not inevitably a barrier preventing a legislator or a judge from imagining the experience of people on the other side, but surely the boundary complicates that process." Id.

60. See, e.g., Kozol, *supra* note 14, at 152–53 (1991) (noting students' perceptions of conditions in integrated schools as superior to their perceptions of conditions in nonintegrated schools).

61. By contrast, white students who attend integrated schools are more likely to be socially integrated as well. Jomills Henry Braddock II and James M. McPartland, "The Social and Academic Consequences of School Desegregation," *Equity and Choice*, Feb. 1988, at 5, 63–64. Dewey remarked that an isolated community "makes for rigidity and formal institutionalizing of life, for static and selfish ideals within the group." John Dewey, *Democracy and Education* 99 (1916).

62. Massey and Denton, *supra* note 16, at 91–92.

63. See Dewey, *supra* note 61, at 1–22.

64. Achieving *any* further integration, in fact, may require a broader approach. Using data from the Department of Justice's Office of Civil Rights, Steven Rivkin found that isolated school districts had integrated to the best of their ability by 1988. Steven G. Rivkin, "Residential Segregation and School Integration," 67 *Soc. of Educ.* 279, 285 (1994). Changes in urban populations have resulted in the majority of poor, minority families living in urban centers, and white, middle-income families moving to suburban school districts. Id. As a result, district-focused attempts at racial and class integration cannot be completely successful. Rivkin concludes that "[o]nly the movement of students across district boundaries, either through interdistrict integration programs or changes in housing patterns, can significantly reduce the racial isolation of Black students in any of the four [Midwest, Northeast, South, and West] regions." Id.

65. See Gary Orfield, Foreword to Meldrum and Eaton, *supra* note 47, at i.

66. Jefferson County, Kentucky's, county-wide desegregation plan resulted in some black families moving to predominantly white suburbs even after only four years. *Kentucky Commission Study*, *supra* note 50, at 1. Between 1975–1976 and 1981–1982, the use of buses for desegregation purposes decreased and the average time students spent riding buses decreased. These cuts resulted from the numbers of black families moving out of the cities to the suburbs. Civil rights groups promoting fair housing and provisions in the desegregation order prompted these moves. The key desegregation order provisions provided for exemptions from busing for integrated neighborhoods. In 1975, many schools had no black students; by 1980 almost every school had students from black families living in the neighborhood. Id. at 16.

    The Jefferson County desegregation plan ended after four years when, in 1980, a federal district court declared Jefferson County Public Schools desegregated, moving the case to inactive status. See Kentucky Commission on Human Rights, *New Elementary and Middle School Assignment Plans Creating Dual School System, 1985–86*, 50 (1986). In that year, student assignment was the most desegregated it had ever been. Id. That success was undone by school board decisions to exempt a white suburban school from busing and to reduce desegregation busing of black elementary students without concurrently increasing busing of white students. The result was a quick increase in resegregation. Id. at 50–51.

67. It is this conceptual inability to look beyond constructed political boundaries that has led to disconcerted, ineffective efforts at urban revitalization and the

consequent reinforcement of the isolation and disempowerment of central city residents.

68.   See, e.g., Reynolds Farley, "Neighborhood Preferences and Aspirations among Blacks and Whites," in *Housing Markets and Residential Mobility*, 161, 183–85 (G. Thomas Kingsley and Margery Austin Turner, eds., 1993); Martha R. Mahoney, "Segregation, Whiteness, and Transformation," 143 *U. Penn. L. Rev.* 1659, 1669–75 (1995); Margery Austin Turner, "Limits on Neighborhood Choice: Evidence of Racial and Ethnic Steering in Urban Housing Markets," in *Clear and Convincing Evidence: Measurement of Discrimination in America*, 117, 125–40 (Michael Fix and Raymond Struyk, eds., 1993). The lack of mobility is especially true for blacks. Massey and Denton, *supra* note 16, at 85.

69.   Racial segregation plays a significant role in widening the education gap between white and minority students. The Harvard Project on School Desegregation found that after Norfolk, Virginia, abandoned a school desegregation plan and returned to neighborhood schools, the achievement gap between races and between black students attending segregated and integrated schools grew. In 1991, black third-graders in integrated schools scored on average 16 percentage points below their white counterparts. But black third-graders in segregated schools scored even worse than the black third-graders in integrated schools, an average of 21 points lower than white third-graders. Meldrum and Eaton, *supra* note 47, at 48. Some of the consequences of integrated and segregated schools may take a generation or more to develop. For example, research indicates that children who attend integrated schools are more likely to live in integrated communities as adults. Gary Orfield, "Segregated Housing, Educational Inequality, and the Possibility of Urban Integration," in *Urban Institute Symposium on Residential Mobility and Minority Incomes*, 1, 28 (1988).

70.   Kentucky Commission Study, *supra* note 50, at 3; see also generally Donald L. DeMarco and George Galster, "Prointegrative Policy: Theory and Practice," 15 *J. Urban Aff.* 141 (1993).

71.   As the Kansas City school system demonstrates, simply pumping in more resources is not an adequate solution. See *Missouri v. Jenkins*, 515 U.S. 70, 99–102 (1995) (explaining that many factors beyond funding affect minority student achievement). "In-place" strategies are not sufficient precisely because they do not address effectively the lack of access to critical institutions and resources that increasingly are located outside of low-income neighborhoods. See, e.g., Helen F. Ladd, "Spatially Targeted Economic Development Strategies: Do They Work?" 1 *Cityscape: J. Pol'y Dev. & Res.* 193, 208 (1994) (discussing the inadequacy of place-based enterprise zones); see also generally Justin D. Cummins, "Recasting Fair Share: Toward Effective Housing Law and Principled Social Policy," 14 *Law & Inequality* 339 (June 1996) (arguing that every community in a region needs to provide its proportional share of low-income housing).

72.   One way to create stability is to exempt families living in integrated neighborhoods from mandatory busing to preserve the community-wide integration achieved in these neighborhoods. See Kentucky Commission Study, *supra* note 50, at 16 (discussing the Jefferson County desegregation plan).

73. See generally Meldrum and Eaton, *supra* note 47, at 9–10 (arguing that Norfolk's decision to end busing produced "racial isolation, and, consequently, concentrated poverty" in the city's schools).

74. DEWEY, *supra* note 60, at 101.

75. See generally Elizabeth M. Schneider, "The Dialectic of Rights and Politics," 61 *N.Y.U. L. Rev.* 589 (1986).

76. Derrick A. Bell Jr., "Serving Two Masters: Integration Ideals and Client Interests in School Desegregation Litigation," 85 *Yale L. J.* 470, 479 (March 1976).

77. John O. Calmore, "Spatial Equality and the Kerner Commission Report: A Back-to-the-Future Essay," 71 *N.C. L. Rev.* 1487, 1494–95, 1517 (1993).

78. David J. Armor, *Forced Justice: School Desegregation and the Law*, 198 (1995).

79. See Calmore, *supra* note 77, at 1498.

80. Only 12% of African Americans prefer to live in all-black neighborhoods, while 31% are unwilling to move into such a neighborhood, given a choice. Massey and Denton, *supra* note 16, at 89–90. Although a majority of blacks consider a 50-50 ratio ideal, 95% would willingly live in a neighborhood that is merely 15% black. Id. For discussions of choice in education, see generally Wendy R. Brown, "The Convergence of Neutrality and Choice: The Limits of the State's Affirmative Duty to Provide Equal Educational Opportunity," 60 *Tenn. L. Rev.* 63 (1992); Paul Gewirtz, "Choice in the Transition: School Desegregation and the Corrective Ideal," 86 *Colum. L. Rev.* 728 (1986).

81. See Amy Stuart Wells and Robert L. Crain, "Perpetuation Theory and the Long-Term Effects of School Desegregation," 64 *Rev. Educ. Res.* 531, 536–41 (1994) (noting that segregation tends to limit the fulfillment of black students' occupational aspirations).

82. Calmore, *supra* note 77, at 1492–96, 1501–07.

83. Students of color bused to desegregated suburban schools experienced reading improvement. These students also experienced improvements in mathematics scores that were far superior to those of minority students in segregated schools. Voluntary Interdistrict Coordinating Council for the Settlement Agreement, *Complete Eleventh Report to the United States District Court, Eastern District of Missouri*, 25 (1995).

84. See Kentucky Commission Study, *supra* note 50, at 6–8.

85. Seventy-five percent of minority suburban school attendees obtain full-time employment if they do not attend college while 41% of urban school attendees obtain full-time employment if they do not attend college. Fifty-four percent of suburban school attendees go on to college while 21% of city school attendees go on to college; 95% of suburban school attendees graduate from high school while 80% of urban school attendees graduate. James Rosenbaum et al., "Can the Kerner Commission's Housing Strategy Improve Employment, Education, and

Social Integration for Low-Income Blacks?" 71 *N.C. L. Rev.* 1519, 1533–35 (1993).

86. See Meldrum and Eaton, *supra* note 47, at 48.

87. Wells and Crain, *supra* note 81, at 551.

88. See Vivian W. Ikpa, "The Effects of Changes in School Characteristics Resulting from the Elimination of the Policy of Mandated Busing for Integration upon the Academic Achievement of African-American Students," 17 *Educ. Res. Q.* 19, 23–24 (1993).

89. See Meldrum and Eaton, *supra* note 47, at 5.

90. The higher the socioeconomic status of classmates, the higher a given student's achievement. See Carla J. Stevens and Micah Dial, "Comparison of Student Academic Performance at Multi-Ethnic Schools versus Single-Ethnic Schools," paper presented at the annual meeting of the American Educational Research Association, 4–5 (April 1993) (copy on file at the Institute on Race and Poverty, University of Minnesota Law School). The high correlation between race and poverty means that confining students of color to racially segregated schools also confines them to economically segregated schools.

91. Dewey, *supra* note 61, at 20.

92. Ibid., 3.

93. Ibid., 25–26 ("The intermingling in the school of youth of different races, differing religions, and unlike customs creates for all a new and broader environment.").

Chapter 3

Combating School Resegregation Through Housing: A Need for a Reconceptualization of American Democracy and the Rights It Protects

Meredith Lee Bryant

In June of 1995, the Supreme Court delivered another blow to the fulfillment of racial equality in America. In *Missouri v. Jenkins*, a case involving school desegregation in Kansas City, the Court denied minority children the right to attend integrated schools.[1] The rationale: the minority
children's addresses fell within, rather than without, the racially defined
city limits. The Court refused to address the residential segregation that
had effectively resegregated the Kansas City school district. According to
Justice Thomas's concurrence, "'it is beyond the authority and beyond
the practical ability of the federal courts to try to counteract' these social
changes."[2] The Court in effect said that it "*is powerless to eradicate
racial instincts*" in housing preferences.[3] Any such attempt would be
"inconsistent with the typical supposition . . . that 'white flight' may
result from desegregation, not *de jure* segregation"[4] and could "*only
result in accentuating the difficulties of the present situation.*"[5] The
irony of these views is that the quotations in roman type come from the
1995 *Jenkins* decision, while the italicized quotations come from the
infamous 1896 *Plessy v. Ferguson* "separate but equal" decision. The
tragedy of these views is that unlike *Plessy*'s judicial acceptance of "separate," the "separate" authorized by *Jenkins* does not require "equality."[6]
By refusing funding increases intended to enhance the "desegregative
attractiveness" of the less-desirable city schools, the Court was willing to
allow inner city schools to remain inferior.[7]

Jenkins highlights two major misconceptions, surrounding the housing-school connection, that have become accepted dogma for many opponents of school desegregation. The first is that school desegregation is the cause of white flight and city-suburb racial segregation. The second is that courts are powerless to remedy school resegregation because the residential segregation causing it is a result of natural private decisions protected by legal rights such as property, contract, and the right to free association. As demonstrated in part 1 of this chapter, these misconceptions are empirically and historically false. Furthermore, they are at odds with each other. The Court based its reasoning on two contradictory notions about the relationship between schools and housing. The Court's acceptance of the "typical supposition" that desegregation plans cause white flight is based on a theory that court actions in the school arena have had external effects in the housing arena. Conversely, its reliance on the assumption of natural preferences for segregated housing is based on a theory that court actions to desegregate housing are futile in terms of desegregating schools. The recent Court's simultaneous commitment to these contradictions can be attributed to its abandonment of the legal realism and judicial activism that has brought the Court and the country their only successes in the complex arena of urban racial segregation. To correct the drastic state of minority isolation in our nation's cities, the Court must return its attention to the realities of the law's operation over the past four decades and create a new construction of rights that will allow an appropriate response to these realities.[8]

To do this, the Court must look past school desegregation orders and address residential segregation head-on. No longer can this nation afford to ignore housing segregation. In the 1950s, civil rights activists made the realistic decision to choose schools as their battleground for racial equality. The activists should not be criticized for making this decision; schools were, as they still are, America's weakest institution. However, it is now time for civil rights supporters to wage the more important, and the more difficult, war. It is time to challenge ingrained and sacred notions associated with housing. It is time to reexamine the legal doctrines that have sheltered housing from the requirements of the Fourteenth Amendment's guarantee of equal protection and subject such doctrines to analysis in light of a new conceptual model of protected rights in American democracy. In part 2 of this chapter, a four-tiered model of American democracy is presented, one that supplies a historically inspired rationale for the adoption of a new construction of rights to racial equality. Under the ultimate formulation of this new construction of rights, racial equality is made an explicit goal. That is, racial equality is formulated as a goal to be furthered, rather than hampered, through traditional rights to property, contract, and free association.

Finally, in part 3, this chapter concludes by formulating an action plan for the future of school and housing desegregation. Based on the analyses and hypotheses explored in the rest of the chapter, it attempts to demonstrate the superiority of a positive rights-based model of democracy. It offers concrete solutions to the current problems of racial segregation by valuing rights to property, contract, and free association in terms of racial integration rather than in terms of racial isolation.

The History of State-Sponsored Housing Discrimination

The Historic Reality of Urban Housing Discrimination

Recent judicial justifications of residential segregation as "natural," and thus acceptable, have consistently been refuted by social scientists, historians, and commentators on race and federal housing policy.[9] Residential segregation can be attributed to government involvement at the local, state, and federal levels.[10] However, the legacy of official discriminatory actions has a much more extensive history. This section will attempt to give a broad overview of this history and demonstrate how today's racial segregation in inner cities is a direct result of official state discrimination. As the 1968 Kerner Commission report noted of the "racial ghetto," "[W]hite institutions created it, white institutions maintain it, and white society condones it."[11]

The present pattern of discrimination against blacks can be traced to the black exodus from the South that began during World War I. Pulled by labor shortages created during the war and pushed by the decline of the cotton industry, millions of rural southern blacks migrated to northern cities. A combination of public and private forces confined these blacks to inner city ghettos. Public housing projects were built near factories in order to accommodate the initial wave of new black workers. As increasing numbers of families were enticed by rumors of economic opportunity, they gravitated to the same public housing neighborhoods inhabited by their relatives and friends. Thus blacks were channeled into the same inner city neighborhoods, in part because of personal, private decisions.

However, this initial channeling does not explain why blacks remained in segregated inner city ghettos. Part of the explanation is that blacks experienced increasing levels of racial violence that kept them imprisoned behind "black-belts" and isolated in "darkytowns." Whites did not welcome the black influx into their cities. Working-class whites who, prior to World War I, lived relatively peacefully with their few black neighbors now resented the sudden surges of black workers in their neighborhoods and in their workplaces. Middle-class whites, infused by racist ideologies of black inferiority and black criminality, feared that black invasion into their previously all-white communities would decrease their property values and increase levels of crime.

These racist hostilities led to a wave of race riots in the large industrial cities. Blacks who were found in white neighborhoods were beaten and lynched as reminders of the impermeable color line that kept racial ghettos successfully fenced in. Even wealthier blacks attempting to cross the solidifying racial divide were subjected to mob intimidation. Racial violence against blacks went virtually unpunished by public officials; the white perpetrators of such riots were rarely arrested. Instead, the majority of arrests were of blacks. This police toleration of violence against blacks gave coerced residential segregation the imprimatur of the state.

State complicity in and encouragement of residential segregation were not limited to police acceptance of violence aimed at intimidating blacks from leaving the ghettos. Many cities actively engaged in policies designed to foster racial separation. Through the use of zoning and city planning powers, many cities enacted laws and regulations prescribing where blacks could live. The Supreme Court eventually outlawed racial zoning as a violation of the Fourteenth Amendment in the 1917 case of *Buchanan v. Warley*,[12] but many cities continued to enforce it. Even without the option of racial zoning, city planners were able to accomplish the same result through exclusionary zoning laws prohibiting low-income housing development. These laws effectively prevented poorer blacks from escaping inner city ghettos. Exclusionary zoning has been declared illegal in some states, but remains legal to this day in many others.

Once racial zoning was no longer available as a legal option, whites who feared black intrusion organized themselves into neighborhood cooperatives. Such cooperatives adopted restrictive covenants contractually forbidding property owners from selling to black buyers. Restrictive covenants were routinely upheld by the courts and received the Supreme Court's implicit blessing in the 1926 case, *Corrigan v. Buckley*.[13] In the opinion dismissing the case, Justice Sanford characterized the challenge to racially restrictive covenants as "so insubstantial as to be plainly without color of merit and frivolous."[14]

As a result of the combination of fear of violence, racial zoning, and restrictive covenants, black households throughout the 1920s and 1930s were confined within deteriorating inner city neighborhoods. These neighborhoods were significantly cut off from any growth, thus creating incredible demand for scarce and overused housing. Housing prices were kept at artificially high prices, while maintenance declined. Landlords took advantage of the shortage of housing, converting single-family homes into multi-unit dwellings. Black families were forced to double up in already overcrowded homes. Whites saw black willingness to live under such conditions as evidence of inferiority. These views fueled beliefs that allowing blacks to move into their own neighborhoods would result in similar blight and decay.

Discriminatory federal mortgage policies helped further fuel the racist fire. The Home Owner's Loan Corporation (HOLC), created by the Roosevelt administration to promote greater home ownership, refused mortgages to households living within redlined inner cities and integrated outlying areas. The HOLC devised a rating system to evaluate the risks of making loans in urban neighborhoods; redlined areas were determined to be the riskiest and loans were virtually never given in such areas. The HOLC routinely redlined any neighborhood with even small black populations. In addition, neighborhoods with the potential to attract black families were denied funding. With state actors overtly discriminating against such households, whites fled from neighborhoods as soon as they perceived possible black in-migration. Thus, the vicious cycle that kept blacks in isolated ghettos was directly fueled by the public actions of the HOLC.

Furthermore, the HOLC's discriminatory lending practices had an even greater impact, given its status as a role model for other public and private lending institutions. By imitating the redlining practices of the HOLC, these other institutions ensured that black families had virtually no options for receiving credit to purchase homes. Most significantly, the HOLC's redlining practices influenced the underwriting policies of the Federal Housing Administration (FHA) and the Veteran's Administration (VA). Created in 1934 as a program to insure and guarantee private-lender, long-term home mortgages, the FHA has had "a more pervasive and powerful impact on the American people over the past half-century" than any other government agency.[15] Much of this impact can be attributed to discriminatory redlining practices. Backed by U.S. Treasury bonds, FHA guarantees gave banks little reason not to offer low-interest loans for home purchase and improvement. However, without FHA or VA backing, applications for mortgages in unstable black neighborhoods became even more unattractive to banks and other lending institutions.

The FHA only granted loans to families in "stable" and "desirable" neighborhoods. Black or integrated neighborhoods met neither of these requirements. According to the FHA Underwriting Manual, "inharmonious racial or nationality groups" were cause for serious concern.[16] "If a neighborhood [was] to retain stability, it [was] necessary that properties . . . continue[d] to be occupied by the same social or racial classes."[17] Suburban neighborhoods were thus encouraged to enact racially restrictive covenants; those that did were able to enhance their chances for receiving FHA mortgages. Even after the Supreme Court, in *Shelley v. Kraemer*,[18] ruled that judicial enforcement of such covenants was unconstitutional, the FHA continued to advocate the use of racially restrictive covenants for almost two years.

Thus, due to an elaborate system of government-sponsored segregation, nearly all FHA subsidized loans went to white families, as black neighborhoods fell further into decline. Fueled by the government's refusal to contribute mortgage capital to badly under-capitalized inner city ghettos, minority communities became the victims of wholesale public and private disinvestment. This unfortunate turn of events coincided with the second great migration of southern blacks to the North after World War II. As federal programs subsidized white flight to the suburbs, the arrival of millions of blacks to the inner city encouraged an even more impermeable color line around the ghettos. The devastating downward spiral of disinvestment created by the unavailability of FHA loans was intensified by the increasing numbers of black migrants in the mid-1940s. Without options for housing outside the ghettos, blacks had no choice but to move into neighborhoods plagued by disrepair and deterioration. The increased use of these neglected units only hastened urban blight. Soon, without any infusion of capital, these overused houses and apartments became uninhabitable, causing widespread vacancies and abandonment.

Eventually, the government was forced to respond to the urban disaster it had helped to create. In the 1950s, white elites who had economic and other ties to the universities, hospitals, libraries, foundations, and businesses located in the cities demanded that the federal government offer relief to stop the deterioration. Urban renewal programs were the chosen solution. These programs offered local housing authorities federal funds to purchase and condemn slum properties for redevelopment. Given the long history of discrimination, it was not surprising that most of the neighborhoods targeted for "slum clearance" were inhabited by blacks and other minorities. Suburbs with small minority neighborhoods lobbied for federal funds to level those neighborhoods and keep blacks out of their towns and schools. As a result, many black families were displaced.

Though local authorities were, technically, obligated to guarantee suitable and affordable replacement housing for displaced families, local housing officials solved the problem as quickly and cheaply as possible by building inadequate public housing projects. These projects were located in the inner city because suburban politicians waged bitter battles to block construction of projects in their neighborhoods. For example, local politicians in Chicago were able to get state legislation enacted that gave the city council the right to reject sites proposed by the Chicago Housing Authority. This veto right was then delegated to individual neighborhoods; white areas were, in effect, able to prevent the siting of public housing projects in their neighborhoods. As a result, only one of thirty-three projects was located in a neighborhood with a black population of less than 84 percent. Thus, government urban renewal programs and public housing only exacerbated the drastic situation of segregation by "shifting the problems of blight, crime, and instability from areas adjacent to elite white neighborhoods to locations deeper inside the black ghetto."[19]

In 1968, Congress finally responded to obvious patterns of housing discrimination by passing the Fair Housing Act.[20] Many courts have recently used the passage of the act as a justification for their determinations that housing discrimination can no longer be attributed to government agencies. However, the act's impact on eliminating segregation has been minimal. Although, in theory, the act required all federal housing programs to foster fair housing, segregation actually increased throughout the 1970s and 1980s. The failure of the Fair Housing Act has been attributed, in part, to its inherent weakness. The U.S. Department of Housing and Urban Development (HUD) was established to orchestrate the goals of the act. HUD was responsible for investigating allegations of housing discrimination and for engaging informal efforts at conciliation. However, HUD was given virtually no enforcement powers; the agency could refer violators to the Justice Department, but could not prosecute violators in order to force compliance with the law. Unfortunately, the Justice Department chose to pursue only a small percentage of the cases HUD referred to them. The lack of effective enforcement was further exacerbated by the fact that, although thousands of complaints were filed annually, HUD referred only about 10 percent of the cases they received to the Justice Department.

The only realistic means of achieving relief involved filing a private suit under Title VII of the Fair Housing Act. Private citizens were granted the right to initiate civil actions in federal court irrespective of HUD's investigative and referral determinations. However, this required the victims to understand that they had been subjected to discrimination prohibited by the act. In addition, the victims had to find legal counsel willing to take on the case. Although fair housing organizations worked diligently to assist victims of housing discrimination, the act's short 180-day statute of limitations and the difficult burden of gathering sufficient evidence of discrimination for each individual plaintiff rendered the private right-of-action provision a largely ineffective tool for attacking systematic housing segregation. Thus, the ultimate effect of the Fair Housing Act was to allow individual and institutional discrimination to continue, even as federal government officials were given more information about the growing extent of residential segregation and discriminatory housing patterns. Understanding this history, courts can no longer assume that housing discrimination ended upon passage of fair housing legislation.

After the relative failures of urban renewal, public housing, and the Fair Housing Act, "privatization" became the buzzword for federal and local housing policies. In the market-based incentive programs of the early 1970s, segregation was once again reinforced by government actions. Section 235, for example, was a program designed to promote home ownership among low-income households. However, by pouring money into the few integrated neighborhoods of the city, Section 235 made it easier for whites to escape to the nearby white suburbs. In offering poor white families the opportunity to purchase small homes at the same cost as public housing, Section 235 subsidized white flight.

Additionally, Section 235 led to a process called "blockbusting." Realtors would sell a few homes in previously all-white neighborhoods to black families able to purchase homes as a result of Section 235. The realtors would then spread rumors that the neighborhood would soon become entirely black. These rumors would spur a wave of panic selling, and whites would flee further into the suburbs. Alternatively, black buyers were convinced to use their subsidies to purchase old homes within segregated inner city neighborhoods already in a state of decline. These homes often had severe structural flaws that real estate agents bribed FHA appraisers to overlook. Because such homes were in such bad disrepair, many of the new black owners eventually resorted to abandonment. Not uncommonly, entire neighborhoods were destroyed. The result was severe: by 1979, of the ninety-thousand-plus homes subsidized by Section 235, 18 percent had been assigned to HUD or foreclosed.

The Section 8 program was equally unresponsive to existing segregation and the problems it posed for market-based housing incentives. The objective of Section 8 involved offering rent subsidy certificates to qualifying lower-income tenants. Housing developers honoring such certificates were given federal funds to help construct apartment developments. However, in spite of the fact that "affirmative marketing" requirements were supposed to ensure minority audiences were made aware of the program, in reality, the requirements have been ignored. Because this program was never brought to the attention of inner city blacks, Section 8 suburban developments primarily benefited white families. Meanwhile, eligible minority applicants were confined to developments in the segregated cities.

As recognized by the Civil Rights Commission, "[t]he Federal Government . . . has . . . been most influential in creating and maintaining urban residential segregation."[21] The effects of historical discrimination in housing have yet to be corrected. Both HUD and President Clinton have acknowledged the federal government's failure to affirmatively promote fair housing. The government-sponsored placement of development sites and the assignment of tenants on a racial basis have had significant, long-lasting effects on creating and maintaining isolated, racially defined communities. Most important for the purpose of this chapter has been the unambiguous discriminatory effect on schools. Years of conscious placement of housing projects and subsidized developments in neighborhoods already segregated as a result of racial zoning, restrictive covenants, and redlining by federal mortgage agencies have virtually ensured segregated school systems. Many cities had schools specifically built to service tenants in segregated projects. Often school attendance lines were carefully drawn to ensure that black children from the projects were not sent to the same schools as white children from neighboring areas. Given that most federal housing programs have been subjected to repeated cuts, black neighborhoods are falling into even greater disrepair. Because their residents are often impoverished, there is insufficient money to fund inner city schools. Thus, black city schools remain drastically inferior to white schools located in outlying neighborhoods. Not only have federal and local housing policies led to segregated schools, but they have also created unequal schools.

Judicial Findings of Housing Discrimination

Courts consistently find evidence of state-sponsored housing discrimination. In Chicago, for example, a federal district court determined that the city council had vetoed housing sites on racial grounds for decades:

"[U]ncontradicted evidence [proves] . . . that the public housing system operated by CHA was racially segregated, with four overwhelmingly white projects located in white neighborhoods and with 99.5 percent of the remaining family units located in Negro neighborhoods."[22] The Supreme Court agreed that the discriminatory site selection and tenant assignment violated the Fourteenth Amendment. On appeal, the circuit court found not only that the Chicago Housing Authority (CHA) discriminated against blacks in administering the public housing program, but that HUD was guilty of aiding and abetting racial segregation in the Chicago area. The court ordered a metropolitan-wide remedy, requiring HUD and CHA to incorporate the suburbs into their desegregation plan.

In *United States v. Yonkers Board of Education*, the first combined legal attack on housing and school officials, it was found that 96.6 percent of public housing for poor people was located in the city of Yonkers' predominantly black southwest quadrant.[23] The court further found that "the extreme concentration of subsidized housing in [predominantly black] Southwest Yonkers today is the result of a pattern and practice of racial discrimination by City officials, pursued in response to constituent pressures to select or support only sites that would preserve existing patterns of racial segregation, and to reject or oppose sites that would threaten existing patterns of segregation."[24] The court also determined that these discriminatory housing policies resulted in government-linked racial segregation in city schools.

In *Young v. Pierce*, the court described HUD's involvement in creating and perpetuating segregated public housing in East Texas, specifically, and across the nation.[25] In Dallas, a federal district court found that the city was guilty of intentional segregation in housing siting and tenant placements.[26] Clear evidence of discrimination led the court to hold both HUD and the city of Dallas responsible for school segregation. More recently, a class action was filed in Baltimore, Maryland, challenging the intentional and continued segregation in the city's public housing program.[27] According to a federal report, public housing officials sited adjacent projects intentionally to "offer a splendid barrier against the encroachment of colored" people into a "good white residential neighborhood."[28]

Past Housing-School Combined Efforts

Both local and federal governments are aware of the history of housing discrimination and its impact on school desegregation. In the early 1980s, the Department of Justice, responding to criticism of its uncoordinated enforcement policies, made attempts to investigate the connected problems of residential and housing segregation. Such efforts in Chicago led to a negotiated consent decree that forced federal and local housing and school officials to work together to find solutions for the segregation problem.

Chicago provides evidence that such coordinated efforts are possible. The best example of such an effort, however, comes from Saint Louis. In 1980, a federal district court approved a school desegregation order that included several housing-related features.[29] First, integrated neighborhoods and those that became integrated were exempted from busing. Second, incentives were established to entice white neighborhoods to accept subsidized housing. Neighborhoods that created public housing sufficient to ensure that 20 percent of the public school enrollment was black were allowed to return to neighborhood schools. Finally, and most significantly, the court required the city government, the school board, the state government, HUD, and the Department of Justice to submit a coordinated housing plan to help implement the school desegregation plan and support integration in the entire metropolitan area. Though similar coordinated plans are rare, the existence of this possibility proves that housing and school agencies at the federal, state, and local level can learn to cooperate. Contrary to the assumptions of recent courts, the problems addressed by these various agencies are interconnected and can be attacked together. Courts may shy away from such coordinated plans in order to avoid confronting principles of federalism or because they believe such tasks are the proper province of the legislative or executive branches. Nonetheless, where coordinated efforts offer the most efficient and promising means to ensure effective desegregation, courts should utilize the full extent of their equitable powers to promote protection of the constitutional right to equal education.

Housing counseling is another solution that has proven effective for desegregating schools and neighborhoods. In connection with a court order recognizing the benefits of encouraging residential integration in Louisville, Kentucky, the Kentucky Human Rights Commission used housing measures to help school desegregation. Counselors worked to increase residential integration by taking black recipients of rental subsidies outside the ghetto through education about housing choices in primarily white areas. Families that made pro-integrative moves were automatically exempted from busing. As a result of these efforts, half of the subsidy recipients decided to move to white areas. The success in Louisville's integration was not attributable to unusually favorable attitudes about racial integration. Gary Orfield's studies of the Louisville program found that discriminatory attitudes were prominent in the neighborhoods that eventually accepted integration. Thus, Louisville's experience shows that integration-resistant attitudes are not immutable; they can be changed by affirmative actions.

Building on the lesson of Louisville, this chapter next presents an alternative rights model. This model challenges present legal doctrines of racial equality and provides a new conception of rights, one that would enable Americans to overcome the types of discriminatory attitudes responsible for resistance to integration in housing and education. An analysis of the progression of American democracy and the rights it has sought to protect legitimizes this new theory of rights for American democracy. Acceptance of this new theory would allow courts to acknowledge the failure of present legal doctrines in addressing the housing-school segregation connection. Furthermore, it would enable courts to recognize and remediate the effects state-sponsored housing discrimination has had on school integration.

The Four-Tiered Model of Racial Equality in American Democracy

Our American democracy is founded upon the doctrine of equality. Though the extent to which the Founding Fathers of our Constitution, and even the Founding Fathers of the civil rights amendments, were committed to racial equality is unclear, it is now clear that democracy as we perceive it today includes formal racial equality before the law. Current debate focuses on how that formal equality should be achieved. Some individuals advocate a strict application of the principle of color blindness: race should never be a factor in decisions affecting our society and government.[30] This chapter takes another view. Though supposedly committed to the ideal of racial equality revealed in the revolutionary case of *Brown v. Board of Education*, the Court's present equal protection clause jurisprudence does not enable America to fully attain it. In light of our country's history of slavery,[31] de jure segregation,[32] and explicit[33] and implicit racial discrimination,[34] a strict application of the color-blind, antidiscrimination principle espoused by the present Court's conservative wing stops short of formalizing a commitment to true racial equality.

Brown envisioned a democratic ideal wherein the right to racial equality is as important as all other protected rights, such as the rights to property, contract, and freedom of association. As articulated below, *Brown* created a four-tiered model of American democracy with each successive tier affirming a greater right of participation in the American polity.

Fulfillment of the journey through each tier, however, depends upon positive conceptualizations of rights that equate the right to racial equality with all other rights guaranteed under our Constitution. This part observes that outdated conceptions of protected rights have blocked American society's natural progression toward its destined democracy. Our society is still tied to legal doctrines that prevent equal protection of the laws, largely in the name of protection of private property, liberty of contract, and private decisions of association. The State Action Doctrine is the most obvious example of this tendency. Though the importance of the constitutional rights to private property, contract, and association cannot be ignored, the government must do more to ensure the protections of the Fourteenth Amendment before these other rights can be secured on a racially equal basis. Instead of bringing American society closer to the achievement of the goals of *Brown*, recent court decisions have started the nation on a backward swing toward *Plessy*. In order to stop this regression, it is necessary to reformulate the ways in which we understand the rights our democratic society guarantees. Such a reformulation is necessary in order to avoid the tragedy foreseen by Justice Marshall in *Regents of the University of California v. Bakke*.

> I fear we have come full circle. After the Civil War our Government started several "affirmative action" programs. This Court in the Civil Rights Cases and *Plessy v. Ferguson* destroyed the movement toward complete equality. For almost a century no action was taken, and this nonaction was with the tacit approval of the courts. Then we had *Brown v. Board of Education* and the Civil Rights Acts of Congress, followed by numerous affirmative action programs. Now, we have this Court again stepping in, this time to stop affirmative action programs of the type used by the University of California.[35]

The following rights-based model of democracy facilitates an understanding of the history and the future of racial equality in American society. It envisions different conceptions of American democracy and offers a new construction of rights based on substantive equality for all races.[36] The purpose of the model is to present a framework in which rights to equality in education and housing are afforded the same protections as the rights to private property, contract, and association. In order to move American society toward the democracy it is destined to achieve, we must place these equality rights on an equal footing with other traditional rights.

The Four-Tiered Framework
The fulfillment of true racial equality in our country can be symbolized as a climb through four tiers of American democracy, as first envisioned in

Brown. At the first tier, racial equality plays no part in society's, or the Court's, conception of democracy. No rights are given to racial minorities. At the second tier, racial equality within our democracy is conceived as the right to be free from government discrimination on the basis of race. These are negative rights of racial equality. At the third tier, racial equality within our democracy is conceived as the right to reparation for present inequalities that exist as a result of past invidious discrimination. These are positive rights in the negative sense (positive rights to counteract negative losses). At the fourth and highest tier, racial equality within our democracy is conceived as the right to have one's racial identity legitimized and celebrated within a legal framework where all races are treated with total equality. These are positive rights in the positive sense (positive rights to move forward toward an assertion of race as a positive factor in a legally equal society).

Our nation has firmly accepted second-tier democracy and has made tentative advances toward achieving third-tier democracy.[37] Fourth-tier democracy has been suggested in various forms by different Supreme Court justices[38] and commentators,[39] but has yet to be fully developed in a form truly committed to the type of racial equality proposed by this chapter. A democracy of true racial equality must consist of two crucial elements: (1) total equality of opportunity before the law, with specific and narrow allowances for celebration of racial diversity and racial pride; and (2) social equality allowing and even encouraging individuals to choose freely which racial connections, if any, they want to make. This conception of democracy, ironically, should sound familiar to those who use notions of private property rights, liberty of contract, and the freedom of association to justify both residential and school segregation. However, in order to allow these more traditional rights to exist in a truly equal democracy, we must redefine property, contract, and free association rights in terms of racial equality. We must look at property, contract, and free association rights independent of the legal conceptions legitimated through decades of state-sponsored actions in contravention of equality in housing and education.

The present Supreme Court has been unwilling to address the connection between housing and school segregation, precisely because of its blind adherence to a negative conception of rights embodied in second-tier democracy. Rights to racial equality in education and housing cannot coexist with rights to private property, contract, and free association when these more traditional rights are defined primarily by the right to exclude. Thus, our country has seen a wide-scale occurrence of resegregation.

The Supreme Court has allowed this resegregation by portraying housing segregation as a problem beyond the capabilities of the courts to either solve or address. Such an assertive refusal to address the problem can only be justified where private property, contract, and association rights are defined as negative rights that include, most importantly, the right to exclude others. With these traditional rights so defined, the Court's argument for permitting such exclusionary rights to reign supreme over rights to racial equality is hard to rebut. By allowing the negative right to exclude others to trump positive rights to racial equality, the Court is able to ignore the political and social reality of decades of state-sponsored discrimination in housing. Ironically, such state-sponsored discrimination constitutes a clear violation of negative-rights equal protection. This is precisely why a negative-rights democracy can never succeed. When rights are defined only in the negative, the temptation to allow one form of negative rights to trump another is irresistible, almost natural.

Negative rights are "unknowable," that is, their precise boundaries are unknown. Thus, negative rights to property, contract, and association become proxies for unknowable, unknown instances of racism while negative rights to be free from government discrimination become themselves unknowable and unknown because the connections to state action seem too tenuous when private rights to exclude others are involved. The inability to precisely define any negative right encourages the Court to preference those rights more easily identifiable. When the right to be free from racial discrimination is pitted against the rights to private property, contract, and association, the latter rights are always more easily identified. Racism in our country, especially state-sponsored racism, is (1) much more subtle and invisible than property and contract rights, which by their very nature must be explicitly documented and recorded; and (2) much less central to the sacred notions of local government than the right to free association. Thus, under a negative-rights democratic conception, racial equality will never become a reality in America.

The negative rights enabling people to isolate themselves in communities without concentrations of minorities are, of course, absolute and cannot be constitutionally challenged. Nor, necessarily, should they be. One of the greatest privileges of being an American is the freedom to live wherever one chooses. However, it must always be remembered that this freedom is, for many, untenable. Even today, legal exclusionary practices such as minimum lot sizes and zoning bans on certain types of lower-income housing prevent low-income minorities from moving out of predominantly black inner cities.[40] This chapter's major criticism of the Court's resegregation decisions is not that the Court misinterprets the present doctrinal balance between private property rights, contract rights, rights to free association, and rights to racial equality. Its criticism aims at how the Supreme Court characterizes, or rather refuses to characterize, this balance. As will be seen, to the present Court, negative property rights, and thus the move away from integrated communities, are seen as normal. Equally normal, implies the Court, are minorities' lack of rights to attend desegregated schools. Thus, even second-tier democracy suffers a setback when property owners are allowed to move to the suburbs without assuming any responsibility for the racially identifiable and often unequal schools they leave behind. Without metropolitan-wide legal remedies to counteract private rights to purchase property outside of racially integrated neighborhoods, negative rights to be free from inherently unequal segregated schools are sacrificed. The only solution is to debunk the myth of naturalness and normalcy. Only then will the Court and the country be able to consider a conception of third-tier and fourth-tier positive rights that acknowledge the social and political realities creating our racially defined urban and suburban landscapes. A new conception of rights is necessary to change the current attitudes about racial relations, attitudes that these realities have helped perpetuate and accentuate.

A Historic Demonstration of the Four-Tiered Model

First-Tier Democracy

First-tier democracy existed in our country up until the Civil War and the passage of the Thirteenth, Fourteenth, and Fifteenth Amendments.[41] Under this conception of democracy, racial minorities (most obviously black slaves) had few to no legal rights. This conception is perhaps best captured by Chief Justice Taney in *Dred Scott v. Sandford.*

> [A] perpetual and impassable barrier was intended to be erected between the white race and the one which they had reduced to slavery, and governed as subjects with absolute and despotic power, and which they then looked upon as so far below them in the scale of created beings . . . [that certain] rights [were guaranteed] to the citizen [which could not be withheld]. [These rights] are of a character and would lead to consequences which make it absolutely certain that the African race were not included under the name of citizens of a State, and were not in contemplation of the framers of the Constitution when these privileges and immunities were provided for the protection of the citizen in other States.[42]

Under first-tier democracy, blackness became the proxy for a denial of the rights granted to whites. Race was taken into account very consciously for the purposes of perpetuating a white supremacist society where whites were given protected rights under the Constitution and blacks were denied these rights. Once one was declared to be black, one's rights ceased to exist, and one risked being thrown into slavery. Because blackness meant a denial of rights, most importantly the right to freedom, determinations about a person's race were heavily litigated. The numerous cases mapping the race line demonstrate the severity of the denial of rights sanctioned by a first-tier democratic society devoted to theories of racial inequality.

An important feature of first-tier democracy is the important role property rights played in perpetuating negative rights for both blacks and whites. Property rights defined the very essence of our unequal first-tier society. White slave owners defined their power and position in American slave society by exercising absolute ownership over black slaves as property.[43] As a means of increasing production of the slave owner's land, the most crucial right in slave property was the negative right to forbid others from using or, ironically, even abusing one's slaves.[44] White owners claimed exclusive dominion over their slaves and were able to sue for the exclusive right to use the person and labor of their slaves. The Fugitive Slave Law,[45] and the emotional battles it engendered,[46] is just one example of the importance white slave owners attached to their negative rights to slave property.

White property rights over black slaves also necessitated the total negation of rights for most African Americans. Because the white slave owner retained total and exclusive control over his slave property, the slave himself could have no rights at all. All rights inhered to the owner. Thus, white owners retained slaves' "rights" of contract and association, as well as their rights to property in their persons. Slaves were forbidden from contracting themselves out to other owners without the permission of their masters. Similarly, slaves were unable to make private choices of association: slaves could not legally marry and were even forbidden from challenging their owners' decision to separate them from their family members. To allow the slave to retain any rights at all, especially any negative rights excluding his owner from some aspect of his life or personhood, would threaten the "[t]he power of the master [which] must be absolute to render the submission of the slave perfect."[47]

Second-Tier Democracy
Because it is the predominant conception of democracy under which American society operates today, second-tier democracy needs only a

brief explanation. With the passage of the Civil War amendments, in particular the Fourteenth Amendment, racial minorities were officially guaranteed equal protection of the laws. This marks the beginning of second-tier democracy, which is characterized by the negative right to be free from the denial of equal protection under the law. As a formal matter, the passage of the Thirteenth, Fourteenth, and Fifteenth Amendments ushered in a revolution unparalleled in world history.

Though some second-tier advances were made after the Reconstruction,[48] minorities were still significantly denied the right to be free from discrimination. As Jim Crow laws were implemented in strong southern defiance of federal mandates, state-sponsored racial discrimination and inequality continued to exist unchallenged. Thus second-tier democracy, as proposed by this chapter, was not fully developed until *Brown v. Board of Education*. In this seminal case, a unanimous Supreme Court first articulated the principle of second-tier antidiscrimination in the form we acknowledge today. Termed by some as a "third constitutional moment," *Brown* revolutionized the way both the courts and American citizens would conceive of the right to racial equality. *Brown* solidified the principle of negative rights guaranteed by second-tier democracy with its firm pronouncement that racial equality requires the right to be free from government discrimination on the basis of race.

Brown developed a new conception of second-tier negative rights that quickly became an accepted part of both American legal doctrine and American democratic folklore. The rhetoric of negative-rights racial equality became the rhetoric of our constitutional democracy. New laws were fashioned on the basis of this understanding of American democracy and our Constitution. In case after case, the right to be free from discrimination, both by government and private actors, was upheld with conviction,[49] often trumping the more traditional rights of property and freedom of contract. The negative right to be free from racial discrimination also began to define the outer limits of other rights; for example, the right to freedom of association was interpreted to include the right to interracial marriage.[50]

Today, however, negative-rights, second-tier democracy is primarily used to attack affirmative action programs. Affirmative action is attacked as a violation of the non-beneficiary's liberty of contract, and as interfering with nonminority rights to property.[51] Negative-rights thinking is used to support a color-blindness rationale for criticizing affirmative action.[52]

Limiting the goal of *Brown* to a second-tier negative-rights conception of democracy ignores the social pressures containing the Court's explanation of its racial and democratic vision. It also ignores the very premise upon which *Brown* was laid: changing social situations require changing constitutional rules. An understanding of the historic reality and legal theory animating *Brown* helps to justify the position that *Brown's* ultimate mission cannot be halted at second-tier democracy. Given the new reality of our race relations today, we must move onward to third-tier and fourth-tier democracy.

Third-Tier Democracy

Third-tier democracy entitles racial minorities to a positive right to reparation for present inequalities caused by the negative denial of rights and racial equality in the past. Thus, race can be used as a factor in programs geared toward remedying past discrimination. Such programs entitle racial minorities to a preference in the allocation of resources or opportunities to which they have been denied access in the past. Justice Blackmun best explained this theory of racial equality in his separate opinion in *Bakke*. "In order to get beyond racism, we must first take account of race."[53] Justice Marshall also advocated third-tier democracy in his *Bakke* opinion, stressing the fact that racial inequality stemming from an extensive history of past discrimination is very much a part of society even today.[54]

Third-tier democracy has been legitimated to a certain extent in today's political world. This is largely because, in order to withstand strict scrutiny by the present Court, today's third-tier affirmative action programs must be very limited in nature and scope. Thus, part of affirmative action's legitimacy can be attributed to its relatively minimal interference with the traditional rights of property, contract, and association. Liberty of contract is necessarily implicated by affirmative action, but recent jurisprudence and politics ensure that any interference is minimal. Furthermore, the nature of existing affirmative action programs makes them applicable mainly to organizational and higher education arenas. Thus, property rights and freedom of association are generally not threatened. Third-tier affirmative programs that implicate property and free association are almost unheard-of. Outside of the school desegregation context, society seems incapable of examining the current ordering of racial geography largely resultant of unchallenged notions of private property and associational freedom.

Related to limits in scope and nature, and equally responsible for affirmative action's partial legitimacy in today's political and legal environment, is the negative aspect of the third-tier positive rights conferred by current legalized programs of affirmative action. Third-tier democracy attempts to enforce equal democratic participation by quantifying past denial and recognizing positive rights solely on the basis of provable past loss. Thus, today's affirmative action confers positive rights based upon a formal finding of past discrimination or disparate impact. The quantifiable denial alone justifies the right. The negative aspects of the positive right confer acceptability upon it. However, in reality, the loss suffered by past discrimination cannot accurately be determined. Therefore, any remedy based upon quantification would necessarily confer a positive right unconnected to a demonstrated loss in the past. This is precisely why quotas have been found objectionable: To extend minority jobs or scholarships based on a numerical figure that cannot be supported in negative, reparative terms creates a justiciable property right to diversity. Such a right is unacceptable in the current legal and social climate. Fears of creating a positive right to diversity also prevent the use of societal discrimination as a justification for affirmative action.[55] However, where past universal discrimination is well understood, even though not quantifiable, there is no reason to discourage affirmative action by requiring institutions to admit guilt to something the entire nation had a hand at imposing.

There is another example of third-tier democracy that has been considered at various times in our history. Monetary reparations, precisely because they can supposedly be quantified and thus limited, are another permissible remedy under third-tier democracy. As with affirmative action, monetary reparations do not significantly interfere with rights of property, contract, or association. Although reparations do implicate the nation's collective property rights to private income in that they must be paid out of tax dollars, our society does not generally conceive of government expenditures as violations of the right to private property.

The problem with monetary reparations as a manifestation of third-tier democracy is that any realistic attempt at putting a dollar figure on past racial harms is likely to yield an amount too large and politically infeasible. For instance, reparations allegedly due Mexican Americans under the Treaty of Hidalgo were rejected, supposedly on such grounds. American Indians under the Reorganization Act of 1934 have been given reparations in the form of mineral rights, but they remain one of the most impoverished groups in American society. Monetary recovery was granted in 1948, and again in 1988, to descendants of Asian Americans who were interned during World War II, but in both instances the amount of money awarded was minimal. In addition to the essential failure of such attempts at financial reparation, monetary compensation as a form of positive right for past wrongs does little to change societal attitudes about racial equality. Because of its remedial nature and its limited, one-shot effort, monetary reparation, like affirmative action justified by remediation only, will not necessarily have a lasting or meaningful effect on the attainment of racial equality. A truly racially equal democracy demands more than limited affirmative action efforts or token monetary compensation: it requires positive rights of lasting significance and a move toward fourth-tier democracy.

Fourth-Tier Democracy

Fourth-tier democracy is the most difficult to articulate because we have not come close to achieving it; it requires a conception of racial equality that has few, if any, precedents to legitimate it. Under fourth-tier democracy, race may be taken into account as a positive factor in the ordering of our legal and social worlds. Fourth-tier democracy promises all racial groups, whether minority or majority, the positive right to have their racial identity positively recognized and celebrated by both government and private individuals. It should be noted that fourth-tier "positive rights for positive goals" democracy is neither forced separatist pluralism nor forced assimilation.[56] Instead, it is a conception of racial equality that dignifies, legally recognizes, and actively encourages people's private choices to celebrate racial identity. In addition, through the promotion of diversity, fourth-tier democracy rewards those willing to share their racial identifications with others, through "trans-racial" associations.

Justice Stevens best expounds the theory of racial equality embodied by fourth-tier democracy in his dissent in *Adarand*. "Instead of merely seeking to remedy past discrimination, [affirmative action programs] intended to achieve future benefits in the form of . . . diversity" should be encouraged.[57] Other commentators on race relations have also suggested types of fourth-tier democracy. Calling for action that "goes beyond reparations and beyond recognizing victimhood"[58] and "attempts to attack the underlying structure of thought that supports inequality,"[59] Professor Aleinikoff advocates a model of race-consciousness that enables "dominant white society to come to a better understanding of itself by seeing itself through the eyes of a diverse range of nonmajority members of society."[60] Similarly, Professor Duncan Kennedy recognizes the need for greater minority scholarship in legal academia, not only to remediate past absences, but to "change the framework of ideological conflict within which issues in the race area [and] other areas are discussed."[61] Fourth-tier democracy not only advocates government and private entitlements that help satisfy these societal needs, but it offers needed changes in the framework of rights within which racial relations presently operate in society.

Because fulfillment of fourth-tier democracy requires changing conceptions of rights and the interaction of rights, the traditional rights to private property, contract, and association are all implicated and must be reconceptualized. This challenge to property, contract, and association is probably the greatest reason for the lack of many existing examples of fourth-tier democracy. Nonetheless, our legal and political experience is not completely void of foundational concepts that support and bolster the image of a fourth-tier, racially equal society.

For example, the government (or private actors) could actively recruit and preference candidates for scholarships or jobs on the basis of their ability to add a larger understanding of a certain racial culture. Preferenced candidates would possess identifications with a particular racial group whose voice is underrepresented in mainstream culture. Rights to contract would be implicated, but not unequally if administrators were careful to use objectifiable, nonarbitrary factors in the decision-making process. Authors Brest and Oshige offer what they have termed "salience" criteria, such as a group's numerical size and the extent to which its culture differs from the dominant culture, as a means of determining which applicants possess the desired racial identifications.[62]

Another example of how fourth-tier democracy could work is found in *Metro Broadcasting, Inc. v. FCC.*[63] In this case, the Federal Communications Commission (FCC) distributed positive licensing rights to racial minorities based on a determination that diversity in broadcasting was a positive good to which all society, not just the minority community, had a right. Property rights were clearly at issue in *Metro Broadcasting*, but again no injustice was done since applicants did not yet possess the licenses and had no legal entitlements to them. Furthermore, because communications legislation requires the FCC to distribute its licenses in order to enhance the public interest, license rights may legally be awarded only to a mix of applicants who can enhance that interest. If Congress chooses to define the public interest to require diversity, as it has, property rights of potential applicants unable to offer diversity are arguably not implicated since such applicants do not meet the necessary requirements for advancing the public interest.

Powell's *Bakke* opinion, suggesting diversity of views as a compelling justification under strict scrutiny, offers another example of a legally acceptable distribution of government entitlements as positive racially conscious rights.[64] Diversity in a student body broadens the marketplace of ideas from which society learns about itself to include non-majority perspectives. This brings all of society closer to achieving the goal of true racial equality envisioned by fourth-tier democracy.

Shaw v. Hunt,[65] a voting districting case upholding a majority-minority district that was reversed by the Supreme Court in 1996, suggests another way in which positive rights may be conferred upon racial minorities in a positive manner. In its formal reasoning, the district court in *Hunt* upheld the North Carolina majority-minority district under strict scrutiny because North Carolina created the districting scheme at issue in order to comply with the Voting Rights Act of 1965, a statute remedial in purpose (third-tier democracy). However, implicit in the very concept of majority-minority districting is the idea that in order to have a properly functioning democracy, we must first achieve racial equality. The only way to ensure such equality is to give racial minorities a positive right to have representation in American politics. Majority-minority districting challenges the right to free association in some senses because it takes voting power away from racially exclusive suburban communities historically able to manipulate district boundaries to preference themselves. On the other hand, majority-minority districting could be defended as a means of strengthening the right to association. By ensuring minorities an equal voice in politics regardless of their geographic location, it enhances freedom of association by allowing both minorities and nonminorities to live where they choose without implicating the strength of their racially identified vote. Fourth-tier positive-rights democracy advocates a legal scheme that accepts majority-minority districting as a means of ensuring a distinctive representation for minorities. Other comparable measures, such as cumulative or weighted voting, also envision a form of fourth-tier democratic rights.

Because fourth-tier democracy assumes that third-tier democracy positive-rights reparations have already been accomplished, the use of diversity as a goal is not a disingenuous means of achieving restorative justice. On the contrary, at the very heart of fourth-tier democracy is the legitimization of positive rights to racial identification for the purpose of increasing tolerance and, in fact, celebrating racial difference. As Martin Luther King Jr. explained in his "I Have a Dream" speech, tolerance is essential to our democracy because white freedom is inextricably linked to black freedom.[66] Thus, fourth-tier democracy requires not only reparative justice for racial minorities, but a more forward-looking integration of various racial cultures and acceptance of all racial identities as true equals.

In the final part of this chapter, a specific model of fourth-tier "positive rights for positive goals" democracy will be discussed. In this model, the positive rights addressed will be those to housing and education, but the examples should offer the reader a more concrete concept of how fourth-tier democracy might look and work in today's American society.

Third- and Fourth-Tier Positive Rights Democracy: A Solution to School Resegregation

The Supreme Court's complete acceptance of the dominance of negative rights to property, contract, and association over the negative rights to be free from racial discrimination in education makes necessary the formulation of an alternative construction of rights. Such a construction might cause the Court to pause before claiming judicial helplessness in the face of one of modern society's largest problems. This part attempts to offer a new framework of rights to racial equality based on third-tier and fourth-tier conceptions of democracy.

The *Gautreaux* case, in which the Supreme Court found both HUD and the Chicago Housing Authority guilty of intentional housing segregation in metropolitan Chicago, offers an example of a third-tier "positive rights for remedial purposes" approach to curbing the problems of residential segregation and thus improving opportunities for integrated schools.[67] In *Gautreaux*, the courts fashioned a remedy that was intended to combat discriminatory housing practices by encouraging minority members to take advantage of housing subsidies available in white suburban neighborhoods. In order to help expose minority members to housing opportunities in white markets, the settlement of the case created a program offering housing counseling, escort services, and moving assistance to black families. As noted in one commentary, the program "was designed to help blacks overcome their lack of knowledge of white housing markets and to help them overcome their fear of violence and intimidation from whites."[68] It was quite successful. Several hundred families used rent subsidy certificates to move from all-black, inner city public housing projects to suburban private units where their children were able to attend higher quality, more integrated schools. Thus, remedial efforts as simple as offering basic informational services may provide tremendous opportunities for minority members.

The most obvious solution to the problem of school resegregation involves the Supreme Court abandoning its misconceptions of suburban innocence and approving interdistrict remedies that involve suburban areas presently exempt from bearing a fair share of the burdens of school desegregation. The Court need not necessarily overrule *Milliken*, since, according to the actual language of *Milliken* and the Court's subsequent interpretation of that language in *Gautreaux*, whenever a city or state violation has had "any significant [interdistrict] segregatory effect," an interdistrict remedy is appropriate.[69] The Court need only recognize that the suburbs, and their predominantly white residents, have been the primary beneficiaries of an extensive history of federal and state-sponsored discrimination in housing, and this has left a distinctive geography of black cities surrounded by impenetrable white suburbs, a geography that causes significant interdistrict segregative effects in schools.

Lower courts, using precisely this logic, have implemented interdistrict desegregation orders that have been left undisturbed by the Supreme Court. For example, the Court of Appeals for the Seventh Circuit placed Indianapolis and its surrounding suburbs under a school desegregation order based on findings of discriminatory state action in housing, action that contributed to school segregation.[70] The appellate court devised a test, closely associated with third-tier notions of positive rights to reparation for past wrongs, to determine whether an interdistrict remedy was required. The court found that an interdistrict remedy is appropriate under four circumstances:

> 1. Discriminatory practices have caused segregative residential housing patterns and population shifts. 2. State action, at whatever level, by either direct or indirect action, initiated, supported, or contributed to these practices and the resulting housing patterns and population shifts. 3. Although the state action need not be the sole cause of these effects, it must have had a significant rather than a *de minimis* effect. 4. Even if the state discriminatory housing practices have ceased, it is shown that prior discriminatory practices have a continuing segregative effect on housing patterns and the school attendance patterns dependent on them.[71]

The Seventh Circuit approach is unremarkable as an adaptation of presently accepted third-tier affirmative action in the school segregation context. By understanding the nature of housing discrimination in our country's history and recognizing the lasting effects of this housing discrimination, the court conferred positive rights to racially equal education upon victims of the inseparably connected school segregation. The court concentrated more on the segregated students' rights to reparation for past discrimination than on the technicalities involved in separating and apportioning blame among the many state and private actors responsible for the present interdistrict segregative effects. As long as housing discrimination can be found to have existed at some level of state action, the court felt justified in ordering an interdistrict remedy, the only type of solution capable of remedying the school segregation between city and suburb.

Because all municipalities are mere agents of the state, courts should not hesitate to impute state housing discrimination to the suburbs, especially since they are the primary beneficiaries of the resulting residential and school segregation. Once the proper relationship between the state and its cities is understood, it becomes much easier to preference the positive right to racial equality over the traditional negative rights of property, contract, and association protected by suburban exclusionary policies. Furthermore, courts have plenty of legal precedents to justify this third-tier conception of positive rights and order reparations for past discrimination. In addition to Supreme Court precedent upholding congressional or state positive-right affirmative action programs designed to counteract effects of discrimination under federal law,[72] there is a considerable body of state law upholding positive-right third-tier affirmative action under state constitutional law.

New Jersey's far-reaching *Mt. Laurel* plan is one well-known example of reparative state law.[73] In 1975, the New Jersey Supreme Court ruled that a suburb could not enact exclusionary zoning policies that prevented low- and moderate-income housing from being built within the community as such exclusionary policies violated the state constitution.[74] Upon finding that similar exclusionary zoning regulations were preventing low- and moderate-income housing from being built in many suburban communities, the New Jersey Supreme Court ruled that each New Jersey community was required to provide a "fair share" of low- and moderate-income housing based on an assessment of the needs of the state as a whole. This famous remedial plan was based on a conception of rights grounded in third-tier democracy. By imposing an affirmative duty to provide affordable housing upon each New Jersey community, *Mt. Laurel* made housing in an economically, and often racially,[75] integrated community a positive right of all New Jersey citizens. Until the effects of past discrimination were eliminated and each community had housed its proportionate share of lower income residents, this positive right could not be diluted or infringed upon by private property owners in the suburbs. Wealthier white residents could no longer resort to the traditional negative powers conferred by ownership of property, such as the power over zoning boards, to escape integration.

Mt. Laurel's "fair share" requirements enabled housing developers to sue for exemptions from zoning regulations that had previously isolated segregated white communities from minority and poorer residents. As more minority members take advantage of this positive right to housing in integrated communities, public schools in these communities will become similarly integrated. Thus, New Jersey has developed a means of maintaining the ideal of local control of neighborhood schools based on property, contract, and association rights, while promoting positive rights to racial equality inherent in school integration.

Mt. Laurel and the New Jersey Fair Housing Act it engendered also offer an example of how third-tier democracy can lead to fourth-tier democracy. Under the New Jersey Fair Housing Act, municipalities are allowed to share *Mt. Laurel* obligations by entering into regional contribution agreements, subject to approval by the state's Council on Affordable Housing or the courts. The sharing provision of the act allows one municipality to transfer to another no more than 50 percent of its own fair share obligation, as long as the other municipality agrees. In order to accomplish this transfer, the first municipality must contribute funds to the other, presumably to make the housing construction possible and to eliminate any financial burden resulting from the receiving municipality's added fair share. The provision is intended to allow suburban municipalities to transfer a portion of their obligation to urban areas, thereby aiding in the construction of decent lower-income housing in the areas where a majority of lower-income households are already found.

Though this provision helps further the legislature's intent to encourage construction, conversion, or rehabilitation of housing in urban areas, it does not necessarily ease city burdens of housing and school desegregation. As it now stands, this feature of New Jersey's Fair Housing Act may undermine rather than accomplish the goals of housing and school integration. However, adding one further adjustment to the act demonstrates how third-tier democracy can be modified to lead to fourth-tier democracy. If transferring suburbs were required to offer minority city residents placements in their local schools in addition to a financial contribution, positive rights to school integration could be fostered at the same time that positive rights to improved housing in the neighborhood of one's choice were enhanced.

Under such a scheme, fourth-tier democracy is achieved because the right to racial equality, in the form of an entitlement to attend suburban schools, is a positive right. However, it is not a positive right in the negative, reparative sense of third-tier democracy. Instead, minority residents are given the positive right to join suburban schools, and thus avoid more segregated city schools, but they can choose whether or not to exercise that right. This element of choice makes the remedial, negative nature of the right more positive: should a minority citizen choose to make positive racial associations in predominantly minority neighborhoods and schools, that citizen has the right to do so. Furthermore, exercising the right to remain in a minority neighborhood does not implicate his rights to high-quality, affordable housing in that neighborhood nor the rights to high-quality, attractive schools in that neighborhood school district. Both housing and schools in the city must be shown to be comparable to housing and schools in the nonminority suburb. As long as the transferring system ensured that an unused minority placement in a suburban school would be compensated to the city by the amount of money necessary to educate one student in the suburban school, cities and suburbs would be able to negotiate for the optimum mix of suburban integration and improved city schools and housing. The market setting and the statutorily imposed equal-ization of city-suburb power bases would hopefully offer communities more freedom to determine, on a positive, fourth-tier basis, what mix of rights and entitlements best suited the preferences of their combined con-stituencies of residents.

Furthermore, such a system, if it worked, would lead to a more efficient use of resources. Instead of allowing further abandonment of inner city housing, the proposed *Mt. Laurel* adaptation would offer cities the in-centives and financial resources to rehabilitate city units for use by current minority and lower-income residents. Requiring suburbs to build newer units for lower-income residents may, in a number of cases, be more costly than rehabilitating older inner city structures. Given the ringed na-ture of suburban development and the filtering process whereby lower-income residents take over the older homes of wealthier residents who move further and further out, suburbs would likely find it most profitable to satisfy their new *Mt. Laurel* obligations by building bigger, higher-income units at the outer rings rather than building lower-income housing nearer to the city borders. Constructing these new, upper-income homes along the suburbs' outer ring in turn requires the construction of high-ways and other infrastructure necessary to service the new outlying homes. Furthermore, it develops rural land that otherwise might have remained preserved in a more natural state. This endeavor is quite expensive and is least likely to improve the living conditions of the lower-income people the system was devised to assist.

On the other hand, rehabilitating existing inner city units for use by current residents saves money by eliminating the need for new highways and new infrastructure and assists the lower-income residents such a plan is intended to help. Because the adapted *Mt. Laurel* system would require these more affordable, renovated units to be utilized by lower-income and minority residents, gentrification and displacement would not become a problem. Furthermore, when the school transfer or compensation requirement is added, the new renovated neighborhoods are given the choice to use suburban compensation funds to improve their own neighborhood schools. The combination of renovated homes and improved schools can contribute to an upward spiral of neighborhood development. As businesses become attracted by the stable, renovated neighborhoods and higher-quality education of the local job force, greater job opportunities and a greater sense of community empowerment should follow. Once city slums are transformed into stronger, more successful city neighborhoods, suburban isolationists motivated by racist stereotypes will be faced with positive examples of successful minority communities. This may help erode racism and lead to natural and normal integration efforts: White suburbanites and black city dwellers would move freely back and forth across the city-suburb boundaries, changing their city-suburb identities and making their own positive choices about which racial groups to associate with, where to purchase property, and where to send their children to school. A fourth-tier democracy would be achieved.

A similar incentive-based approach has already been experimented with in Ohio and Wisconsin. These states have special mortgage programs that provide financial incentives for families whose moves increase housing and school integration. By offering families special low-interest mortgage loans if they are willing to move into neighborhoods that help improve residential and school integration, these programs confer positive rights on both whites and blacks willing to choose neighborhoods for the purpose of facilitating integration. Although all of the current programs rely upon third-tier remedial justifications in order to pass legal muster, it is possible to conceive of mortgage assistance programs intended to improve racial integration without being connected to desegregation orders or required findings of past discrimination. If rights to racial equality are placed on an equal par with rights to property, contract, and association, low-interest mortgages could be conceived of as a property or contractual right that entitles beneficiaries to associate with an integrated community. Recipients of the special mortgages would all make personal decisions to live in integrated communities, with the understanding that their property and contractual rights would be defined by, as well as conditioned upon, the continuing interracial character of the community.

Thus, reciprocal restrictive covenants forbidding property owners from selling to families whose racial background would negatively affect the integrated composition of a neighborhood might be placed on properties financed by the special mortgages.[76] These covenants would then run with the land in order to ensure the continued vitality of the integrated character of the community. A certain percentage of minority and nonminority families, such as a percentage representing the annually calculated racial mix of the greater metropolitan area, could be required at all times.[77] Families would be able to sell their property freely up until the point where the percentages in the neighborhood would begin to differ significantly with the current population proportions. At that point, the restrictions would kick in.

In order to avoid the injustice of placing the burden of maintaining racial integration on the one family that happens to need to sell at the point where the racially integrated nature of the community would be significantly altered, a market system of non-disturbance certificates could be established. The mortgagee, or some other entity capable of acting as the initial lender and as the central bank for non-disturbance certificates, could establish initial prices for the certificates. The initial prices could represent the value to the mortgagee of not having the racially integrated nature of the community disturbed. This value could be determined by a variety of factors depending on the identity of the mortgagee. A government entity interested in meeting its constitutional or statutory duties to promote racial integration in either housing or schools might base the value on the alternative cost of compliance with such mandates. For example, if racial segregation costs a school district a certain amount per pupil in busing costs or compensatory programs each year,[78] the value of the non-disturbance certificates could be set at that same amount multiplied by the average number of school-age children per family in the district. On the other hand, if the mortgagee were a private institution, the value could be determined on the basis of a formula designed to reflect threats to the lender's risk-based capital portfolio posed by the possibility of the community becoming segregated.

Under such a certificate system, each family, in return for the special mortgage financing, would be contractually bound by the restrictive covenants not to sell to parties who significantly altered the racially integrated character of the neighborhood. If the seller still wished to go forward, this party would be required to purchase a non-disturbance certificate at market value in order to be relieved of the breach of the restrictive covenant. Families in the community might purchase certificates from the mortgagee before they were needed if they became worried that the mortgagee's price for the certificates was going to go up in the future.

Similarly, families could buy and sell non-disturbance certificates amongst themselves if they believed that the mortgagee's prices either undervalued or overvalued the desirability of continued racial integration. Assuming all members of this community initially made the conscious choice to purchase low-interest mortgages with an understanding of the integration restrictions, a market for the non-disturbance certificates would be established that appropriately reflected the participants' collective willingness to either forego or maintain racial integration. Because fourth-tier democracy envisions a society where racial equality is grounded in positive rights to make positive choices about one's racial preferences, market-based incentive programs help achieve fourth-tier goals. The most important caveat is that the market must initially place racial integration as a right on equal standing with traditional rights to property, contract, and association. Where a system of legal rights transforms rights to property, contract, and association into rights to racial equality, as does a market-based, non-disturbance, mortgage-financing plan, fourth-tier democracy is fulfilled.

Conclusion

This chapter began with a demonstration of the extensive legacy of official discriminatory action in housing, action that has led to today's racially segregated urban-suburban landscape. It then examined the ways in which state-sponsored residential segregation has detrimentally affected efforts at school desegregation. The frustration of school desegregation reflects our society's failure to fulfill the design for democracy promised by *Brown v. Board of Education*.

In order for racial equality in housing and education to exist in American society, we must be willing to abandon unworkable conceptions of negatively defined second-tier rights to property, contract, and free association in favor of more positively defined fourth-tier rights. These fourth-tier conceptions of rights must understand property, contract, and free association as dependent upon, rather than antithetical to, rights to racial equality. The Supreme Court's unwillingness to recognize obvious examples of state action promoting the housing discrimination responsible for school segregation highlights the need for a reconceptualization of American democracy and the rights it protects. Until rights to racial equality are made positive counterparts to rights to property, contract, and association, the Court will continue to claim helplessness in addressing so-called natural patterns of residential segregation. This helplessness will lead to a generation of minority children educated in inferior, segregated city schools.

Part 2 of this chapter offered a historical rationale, based on a four-tiered model of American democracy, to help legitimate a movement for a reconceptualization of rights. Its purpose was to provide a framework within which to reformulate our understanding of the rights contributing to widespread school and housing segregation. Part 3 of this chapter articulated several ways that legislators and the courts can help solve this unhappy reality. These solutions are dependent, however, on changed legal conceptions of protected rights. Fourth-tier democracy must be embraced before positive change can occur. It is now up to society and the courts to either accept or reject these proposals. My hope is that we are ready to accept them. Over forty years after *Brown*, it is high time that we move forward to the fulfillment of fourth-tier democracy and true racial equality.

Notes

1. 515 U.S. 70 (1995).

2. Ibid., 118 (Thomas, J., concurring) (quoting *Freeman v. Pitts*, 503 U.S. 467, 495 (1992)).

3. *Plessy v. Ferguson*, 163 U.S. 537, 551 (1896) overruled by *Brown v. Board of Education*, 347 U.S. 483 (1954) (emphasis added).

4. *Jenkins*, 515 U.S. at 95.

5. *Plessy*, 163 U.S. at 551.

6. After the Supreme Court's decision in *San Antonio Independent School District v. Rodriguez*, 411 U.S. 1 (1973), segregated black communities with lower tax bases than white neighborhoods have no constitutional right to have state educational funds redistributed to eliminate severe disparities in the ratio between tax burdens and school expenditures. Without state redistribution of educational funds, segregated white suburban schools inevitably become superior to segregated black inner city schools.

7. *Jenkins*, 515 U.S. at 90.

8. For the purposes of this chapter, African American segregation, because it is most severe, will be focused on. Thus, terms such as "minority," "black," and "African American" will be used interchangeably. However, it is important to understand at the outset that the problems of segregation addressed by this article are suffered by other minority groups, such as Asians, Hispanics, and Native Americans. See, e.g., *Gong Lum v. Rice*, 275 U.S. 78 (1927) (school segregation of Asians); *Keyes v. School District No. 1*, 413 U.S. 189 (1973) (school segregation of Mexican Americans and African Americans).

9. See, e.g., Douglas S. Massey and Nancy A. Denton, *American Apartheid: Segregation and the Making of the Underclass* (1993); William J. Wilson, *The Truly Disadvantaged: The Inner City, the Underclass, and Public Policy* (1987); Michael H. Schill and Susan M. Wachter, "The Spatial Bias of Federal Housing Law and Policy: Concentrated Poverty in Urban America," 143 *U. Pa. L. Rev.* 1285 (1995); Reginald L. Robinson, "The Racial Limits of the Fair Housing Act: The Intersection of Dominant White Images, the Violence of Neighborhood Purity, and the Master Narrative of Black Inferiority," 37 *Wm & Mary L. Rev.* 69 (1995).

10. See, e.g., *Hills v. Gautreaux*, 425 U.S. 284 (1976) (finding both Chicago Housing Authority and United States Department of Housing and Urban Development guilty of housing discrimination); *United States v. Yonkers Board of Education*, 624 F. Supp. 1276 (S.D.N.Y 1985) (finding the City of Yonkers and City of Yonkers Community Development Agency liable for housing segregation).

11. U.S. Kerner Commission, *Report of the National Advisory Commission on Civil Disorders*, 2 (1968).

12. 245 U.S. 60 (1917).

13. 299 F. 899 (D.C. Cir. 1924), appeal dismissed, 271 U.S. 323 (1926).

14. *Corrigan v. Buckley*, 271 U.S. 323, 329–30 (1926).

15. Kenneth T. Jackson, *Crabgrass Frontier: The Suburbanization of the United States*, 203 (1985).

16. Massey and Denton, *supra* note 9, at 53; *see also* Arnold R. Hirsch, "With or without Jim Crow: Black Residential Segregation in the United States," in *Urban Policy in Twentieth-Century America*, 84–85 (Arnold R. Hirsch and Raymond A. Mohl, eds., 1993) ("For the first 15 years of its existence, the FHA Underwriting Manual . . . 'read like a chapter from Hitler's Nuremberg Laws'").

17. Massey and Denton, *supra* note 9, at 59.

18. 334 U.S. 1 (1948).

19. Massey and Denton, *supra* note 9, at 56.

20. 42 U.S.C. §§ 3601–3619 (1999).

21. U.S. Commission on Civil Rights, *Twenty Years after Brown*, 114 (1977).

22. *Hills v. Gautreaux*, 425 U.S. 284, 287–88 (1976) (citing *Gautreaux v. Chicago Housing Authority* 296 F. Supp. 907 [N.D. Ill. 1969]).

23. 837 F.2d 1181 (2d Cir. 1987).

24. Ibid., 1194.

25. 628 F. Supp. 1037 (E.D. Tex. 1985).

26. See *Walker v. U.S. Department of Housing and Urban Development*, 734 F. Supp. 1289, 1290 (N.D. Tex. 1989).

27. See Class Action Complaint, *Thompson v. HUD* (D. Md. filed Jan. 31, 1995) (No. MJG 95–309).

28. Ibid., 17.

29. See *Liddell v. Board of Education*, 491 F. Supp. 351 (E.D. Mo. 1980). *Liddell* serves as a good example of judicial willingness to undertake a coordinated effort to solve school and housing segregation. White flight has not been a big problem in St. Louis.

30. As the Supreme Court recently explained in the context of race-based voting districting, laws that deliberately distinguish between citizens on the basis of their race are "odious to a free people whose institutions are founded upon the doctrine of equality, because they threaten to stigmatize persons by reason of their membership in a racial group and to incite racial hostility." *Shaw v. Reno*, 509 U.S. 630, 631 (1993).

31. See, e.g., *Dred Scott v. Sandford*, 60 U.S. (19 How.) 393 (1856).

32. See, e.g., *Plessy v. Ferguson*, 163 U.S. 537 (1896).

33. See, e.g., *Giles v. Harris*, 189 U.S. 475 (1903) (refusing to remedy acknowledged violation of Fifteenth Amendment).

34. See, e.g., *Pace v. Alabama*, 106 U.S. 583 (1883) (justifying greater punishment for interracial adultery by claiming it affects blacks and whites equally and thus does not violate Fourteenth Amendment, though clear motivation of law is discriminatory animus towards blacks).

35. *Regents of the University of California v. Bakke*, 438 U.S. 265, 402 (1978) (Marshall, J., dissenting).

36. The problems presented by the use of rights theories as a mode for understanding notions of equality have been anticipated in Professor Horwitz's insightful article on rights in American legal culture. See Morton J. Horwitz, "Rights," 23 *Harv. C.R.-C.L. L. Rev.* 393 (1988). In his discourse on the history of rights theory, Professor Horwitz reveals the "double-edged sword" presented by rights theories in legal scholarship. Id. Rights theories for the greater part of our Constitutional history "have been associated with the protection of property against a more just distribution of wealth and privilege." Id. at 405–6. However, recently, rights theories have been used to promote the interests of minorities, the marginal, and the scorned. See id. at 394. Professor Horwitz concludes that the only way to reconcile the inherent tension between these two strands of rights theory in favor of the latter is to ground rights theory in a substantive conception of a society committed to equality. In order to do this, he posits a need to recognize the social construction of all rights and duties and the production of values as the result of collective social choice. See id. at 404.

37. See *Bakke*, 438 U.S. at 315–19 (race can be used as a factor in affirmative action programs geared to remedying past discrimination); *Green v. County School Board*, 391 U.S. 430 (1968) (freedom-of-choice plan as means of desegregation not sufficient; more affirmative measures designed to eliminate the effects of de jure segregation are required).

38. See *Metro Broadcasting, Inc. v. FCC*, 497 U.S. 547, 566–68 (1990); *Bakke*, 438 U.S. at 310–13 (both implying that diversity is a positive right of racial equality in and of itself).

39. See, e.g., Duncan Kennedy, "A Cultural Pluralist Case for Affirmative Action in Legal Academia," *1990 Duke L. J.* 705, 721–26 (1990) (justifying race-conscious affirmative action in legal academia based on need to infuse minority perspectives into current frameworks of legal debate); T. Alexander Aleinikoff, "A Case for Race-Consciousness," 91 *Colum. L. Rev.* 1060 (1991) (advocating race-consciousness as a means of empowering minorities rather than solely a means of remedying past discrimination); Iris Marion Young, *Justice and the Politics of Difference*, 156–91 (1990) (proposing institutional mechanisms ensuring positive political recognition and representation of distinct voices and perspectives of minority groups).

40. See, e.g., *Village of Arlington Heights v. Metropolitan Housing Development Corp.*, 429 U.S. 252 (1977).

41. U.S. Const., Amend. 13 (abolishing slavery), Amend. 14 (prohibiting states from denying due process and equal protection of laws on the basis of race), and Amend. 15 (prohibiting states from denying the right to vote on the basis of race).

42. *Dred Scott v. Sandford*, 60 U.S. (19 How.) 393, 409, 422 (1856).

43. As a formal matter, it is important to recall that not all blacks were slaves during the period of American slavery defined here as first-tier democracy.

44. An abused or injured slave would be less productive. Thus, laws were developed, and strictly enforced, which prohibited the "destruction of another's property" by injuring or maiming a slave owned by someone else. See R. Cover, *Justice Accused: Antislavery and the Judicial Process*, 45 (1975).

45. Act of September 18, 1850, 9 Stat. 462 (1985). See generally S. Cambell, *The Slave Catchers: Enforcement of the Fugitive Slave Law*, 1850–60 (1970).

46. See generally T. Morris, *Free Men All: The Personal Liberty of the North, 1780–1861* (1974) (describing legal reaction in the North to the Fugitive Slave Law—the enactment of so-called personal liberty laws that prohibited local officials from carrying out the federal Fugitive Slave Law); see also *Prigg v. Pennsylvania*, 41 U.S. 539 (1842) (federal government lacked authority to compel state officials to assist with returning fugitive slaves).

47. *State v. Mann*, 13 N.C. 263 (1829).

48. See *Strauder v. West Virginia*, 100 U.S. 303 (1879) (holding that law limiting jury service to white males violated Fourteenth Amendment); *Yick Wo v. Hopkins*, 118 U.S. 356 (1886) (striking down law administered in a racially discriminatory manner on Fourteenth Amendment grounds); *Buchanan v. Warley*, 245 U.S. 60 (1917) (invalidating law requiring racial segregation as violation of Fourteenth Amendment).

49. See, e.g., *South Carolina v. Katzenbach*, 383 U.S. 301 (1966) (upholding provisions of Voting Rights Act that protected minorities from discrimination in exercising the right to vote); *Loving v. Virginia*, 388 U.S. 1 (1967) (anti-miscegenation laws struck down as violation of right to be free from government discrimination under Fourteenth Amendment); *Griggs v. Duke Power Co.*, 401 U.S. 424 (1971) (employment tests with racially disproportionate impact were discriminatory in violation of Title VII).

50. See *Loving*, 388 U.S. at 1. The negative right to be free from racial discrimination was crucial to this new definition of the boundaries of the freedom of association. When racial discrimination is not at issue, the right to associate freely is much more limited. See, e.g., *Village of Belle Terre v. Boraas*, 416 U.S. 1 (1974) (Fourteenth Amendment does not protect right of unrelated students to associate freely with one another).

51. See *Adarand Constructors, Inc. v. Pena*, 515 U.S. 200 (1995) (affirmative action program that resulted in white applicant's loss of government contract, thus impeding his freedom of contract, invalidated).

52. Justice Harlan, the elder, first introduced the idea of color blindness in his passionate and prescient dissent in *Plessy v. Ferguson*. See *Plessy*, 163 U.S. at 554–55 (Harlan, J., dissenting). Today, as Professor Duncan Kennedy has demonstrated, color blindness, at least in the context of academia, has become the basic set of ideas through which "meritocratic fundamentalism," the conservative reaction to affirmative action, defines itself. See Kennedy, *supra* note 39, at 709–10.

53. See *Bakke*, 438 U.S. at 407 (Blackmun, J., concurring in part and dissenting in part).

54. Ibid., 400–401 (Marshall, J., concurring in part and dissenting in part).

55. See *Bakke*, 438 U.S. at 370–71 (Brennan, J., concurring). Critics attack the theory of remediating minority members for societal discrimination by claiming it would be too difficult, given our history of discrimination against many white immigrant groups as well as more traditionally defined minorities, to determine which groups were entitled to affirmative action. See Justice Antonin Scalia, "The Disease as Cure," 1979 *Wash. U. L.Q.* 147, 152–53 (1979) (mockingly suggesting that a Restorative Justice Handicapping System be applied to all members of modern society). This critique ignores the reality that most intelligent Americans, and certainly a congressional or state legislative committee entrusted with the task, can identify which groups in society have suffered invidious racial discrimination. For example, Brest and Oshige undertook a study identifying American Indians and blacks as two groups for whom affirmative action is justified on the basis of achieving diversity, corrective justice, and redistributive justice. See Paul Brest and Miranda Oshige, "Affirmative Action for Whom?" 47 *Stan. L. Rev.* 855 (1995).

56. The Dawes Act of 1877, c. 119, 24 Stat. 388 (codified as amended in scattered sections of 25 U.S.C.), which attempted to "acculturate" American Indians by forcing upon them mainstream education, means of production, and culture, is a good example of forced assimilation.

57. *Adarand*, 115 S. Ct. at 2127 (Stevens, J., dissenting).

58. Aleinikoff, *supra* note 39, at 1109.

59. Ibid., 1110.

60. Ibid., 1094.

61. Kennedy, *supra* note 39, at 729.

62. Brest and Oshige, *supra* note 55, at 873. Note that using salience as the determining factor accepts the fact that even wealthy blacks approach life with a different, and thus culturally valuable, view of the world as a result of racism in our country.

63. 497 U.S. 547 (1990). Though *Metro Broadcasting* applied intermediate scrutiny and has now been overruled by *Adarand* to the extent that it did not apply strict scrutiny, Justice Stevens pointed out in *Adarand* that the program at issue in *Metro Broadcasting* would still pass constitutional muster under the current test since broadcast diversity is a compelling state interest. See *Adarand*, 515 U.S. at 258 (Stevens, J., dissenting).

64. See *Bakke*, 438 U.S. at 265, 315–19.

65. 861 F. Supp. 408 (E.D.N.C. 1994) rev'd 517 U.S. 899 (1996).

66. Martin Luther King Jr., "I Have a Dream Speech," in *I Have a Dream: Writings and Speeches that Changed the World,* 101–06 (James Melvin Washington, ed., 2d ed., 1992).

67. *Hills v. Gautreaux*, 425 U.S. 284 (1976).

68. Gary Orfield et al., *Dismantling Desegregation*, 326 (1996).

69. *Gautreaux*, 425 U.S. at 294; *Milliken v. Bradley*, 418 U.S. 717, 745 (1974).

70. *United States v. Board of School Commissioners of City of Indianapolis*, 637 F.2d 1101, 1116 (7th Cir. 1980), cert. denied, 449 U.S. 838 (1980) (Indianapolis Board of School Commissioners).

71. Orfield, et al., *supra* note 68, at 322 (citing *Indianapolis Board of School Commissioners*, 637 F.2d at 1109).

72. See, e.g., *United Steelworkers of America v. Weber*, 443 U.S. 193 (1979) (upholding Title VII affirmative action requirements intended to address past workplace discrimination); *Regents of the University of California v. Bakke*, 438 U.S. 265 (1978) (declaring that states may use race as affirmative positive factor in order to make up for past discrimination by state university). See generally *supra* Part II. B. 3.

73. See *Southern Burlington County NAACP v. Township of Mt. Laurel*, 336 A.2d 713 (N.J. 1975) (*Mt. Laurel I*); *Southern Burlington County NAACP v. Township of Mt. Laurel*, 456 A.2d 390 (N.J. 1983) (*Mt. Laurel II*).

74. See *Mt. Laurel I*, 336 A.2d at 724–25.

75. Many of the low-income residents who sought to not be excluded by wealthier suburbs were blacks. In Mt. Laurel itself, the minimum lot requirements were designed to block the sprawl of nearby Camden, a predominately black community, into predominantly white Mt. Laurel. See *Mt. Laurel I*, 336 A.2d at 718. Today, Mt. Laurel is much more racially integrated.

76. Given *Shelley v. Kraemer*, 334 U.S. 1 (1948) (striking down government enforcement of racially restrictive covenants), and the current Court's apparent commitment to second-tier antidiscrimination principles, court enforcement of such restrictive covenants might been seen as a violation of the Fourteenth Amendment.

77. Under our current legal regime where rights are defined somewhere between second-tier and third-tier democracy, this percentage requirement would likely be struck down as an impermissible racial quota under *Bakke*. See *Regents of the University of California v. Bakke*, 438 U.S. 265 (1978).

78. *Milliken II* programs, such as magnet schools, are compensatory programs that are designed to improve the quality of segregated city schools where interdistrict desegregation is impossible in light of the ruling in *Milliken I*. See *Milliken II*, 433 U.S. 267 (1977).

Chapter 4

The Persistence of Segregation: Links Between Residential Segregation and School Segregation

Nancy A. Denton

Parents, researchers, courts, and others interested in school desegregation issues for the last four decades have noted almost unanimously that school segregation and residential segregation are inextricably entwined. This connection is grounded in the preeminence of the concept of neighborhood schools in the United States. As Reynolds Farley said twenty years ago, "If parents desire that their children attend neighborhood schools and if the nation's Constitution requires racially integrated schools, then neighborhoods must be integrated."[1] The violent reaction to busing in many urban areas further demonstrates the important relationship between neighborhood segregation and school segregation.[2]

It is appropriate, then, to examine the status of residential segregation as a prelude to a discussion of school segregation. As long as the traditional, geographic idea of neighborhood schools continues to hold sway, neighborhood segregation will naturally determine school segregation. Trends in residential segregation during the past four decades are very clear. To put it bluntly, neighborhood segregation, particularly that between neighborhoods of African Americans and neighborhoods of non-Hispanic whites, has been high, continues to be high, and can be expected to remain high in the foreseeable future.[3] This is particularly true in large cities of the Northeast and Midwest with large African American populations, where, not coincidentally, school segregation also remains very high.[4] While there is evidence of a decline in residential segregation in many places, the magnitude of these declines is small.[5]

One need not delve exhaustively into the research on school desegregation to find acknowledgment of the important effect of residential segregation on school segregation. Yet researchers studying residential segregation have not tended to give school segregation the important role it deserves. No doubt some of this asymmetry comes from the lack of data on schools in the population and housing census, the data source researchers use most often in studying residential segregation. But if we acknowledge that progress in reducing segregation in both neighborhoods and schools has stalled or slowed,[6] then considering the two issues jointly may shed light on both.

In this chapter, part 1 documents the current status of research into the levels and trends of residential segregation in the urban areas of the United States. To the extent that neighborhood schools remain important to U.S. citizens, discussions of policy to desegregate schools must be rooted in up-to-date information about residential segregation. I then review various explanations for the levels and trends in residential segregation. In part 2, I argue that many people frequently explain residential segregation with intuitively appealing but erroneous rationales that I call "myths," and that these myths about residential segregation in turn distort discussions of school desegregation. In part 3, I describe commonalities between school and residential segregation. At the neighborhood level, I discuss refinements in the study of neighborhood change needed to account for the importance of school segregation as a factor in neighborhood racial change. At the metropolitan level, I explore how metropolitan boundary fragmentation affects efforts to desegregate both schools and neighborhoods. I conclude in part 4 with a discussion of my own research on multiethnic neighborhoods. I suggest that such neighborhoods should become a centerpiece of policy initiatives for citizens and communities concerned about the issues of school and housing segregation in the mid-1990s.

Persisting Residential Segregation

Research over the last four decades unequivocally shows that in the large urban areas of the United States, African Americans are highly residentially segregated from non-Hispanic whites.[7] In 1990, more than 75 percent of African Americans in northern metropolitan areas and more than 65 percent of those in southern metropolitan areas would have had to move to different neighborhoods if they were to be distributed evenly across the neighborhoods as compared to non-Hispanic whites.[8] While levels of segregation have declined overall, this decline has not been uniform; the greatest declines have been in the South and West, in newer metropolitan areas, and in areas with smaller absolute or proportionate African American populations.[9] At the rates of change seen between 1980 and 1990, it would take another seventy-seven years for segregation in northern metropolitan areas to reach moderate levels, and about half that time for areas in the South.[10] All of this is not to deny progress but to emphasize the *high level* and *slow change* of African American residential segregation.

In 1980, the pattern of residential segregation for African Americans in some metropolitan areas was so extreme that Douglas Massey and I coined the term "hypersegregation."[11] By hypersegregation we mean that no matter how one conceptualizes segregation, African Americans score very high: they are *unevenly distributed* across neighborhoods; they are highly *isolated* within very racially homogenous neighborhoods; their neighborhoods are *clustered* to form contiguous ghettos, *centralized* near central business districts and away from suburban schools and jobs, and *concentrated* in terms of population density and spatial area compared to white neighborhoods. Together, these five concepts (evenness, isolation, clustering, centralization, and concentration) comprise five distinct dimensions of segregation. In 1980, African Americans in Baltimore, Chicago, Cleveland, Detroit, Milwaukee, and Philadelphia were highly segregated on *all five* of these dimensions; blacks in Gary, Indiana, Los Angeles, Newark, and St. Louis were highly segregated on four of the five dimensions.

This means that we classified a total of ten metropolitan areas as hypersegregated.[12] By 1990, hypersegregation had not greatly decreased. Only two cities had dropped from our list and African Americans remain hypersegregated in the remaining metropolitan areas.[13]

Between 1980 and 1990, the absolute magnitude of change for the five dimensions of hypersegregation was very small. Over those ten years, the average changes never even reached 0.05 (or five points on a 0 to 100 scale). Indeed, the average isolation, clustering, and concentration indices actually *increased* between 1980 and 1990. If we separate the average changes into those that are positive and those that are negative, the average increase is larger than the average decrease for all the dimensions except evenness.[14] Thus the kindest interpretation one can put on this analysis of residential segregation in these hypersegregated metropolitan areas is one of stability; certainly there is little to indicate any significant improvement in the residential segregation of African Americans in these large metropolitan areas of the Northeast and Midwest.

When we move beyond these large northeastern and Midwestern metropolitan areas, the situation in 1990 showed a continuation of the trends observed from 1970 to 1980. Analyzing data from 1980 to 1990 for African Americans, Farley and Frey found a pervasive pattern of modest declines; the average index of dissimilarity fell from 69 in 1980 to 65 in 1990.[15] The number of moderately segregated metropolitan areas more than doubled (from 29 in 1980 to 68 in 1990), indicating declines in segregation in many areas that were formerly severely segregated. The average score for the fifteen least segregated places in 1990 was only 42, less than half the degree of segregation in the fifteen *most* segregated places in that year.[16] As was the case in 1980, the large majority of metropolitan areas with comparatively low black-white segregation scores were in the South and West.

The historical impetus for school desegregation was clearly linked to improvement of educational opportunities for African Americans,[17] and both school and residential segregation studies share a focus on comparisons between blacks and whites. However, U.S. urban areas are clearly populated by more than these two groups. Fortunately, the nation's other two large minority groups, Hispanics and Asians, have not experienced the same pattern of *extreme* residential segregation as have African Americans.[18] Furthermore, while the continued immigration of new members of these groups might have been expected to increase their segregation, trends between 1980 and 1990 showed mainly stability or only modest increases. In Farley and Frey's research, the average segregation score for Hispanics and Asians was twenty points lower than the average for blacks,[19] and clearly in the moderate range as segregation scores are normally interpreted.[20] Furthermore, there is some tendency for black-white segregation to decline more in metropolitan areas with more multiethnic populations.[21]

Looking at the residential patterns of these broadly defined groups, however, fails to account for real intragroup variation. Research suggests the presence of a color line within these groups as well.[22] Among Hispanics, those who racially identify as black or as Spanish are more segregated than those who identify as white.[23] Cities with a Hispanic population largely or historically Puerto Rican have higher Hispanic versus non-Hispanic white segregation scores than those dominated by Mexicans or Cubans.[24] Similarly, darker-skinned Asians from the Indian subcontinent are more residentially segregated than lighter-skinned Chinese and Japanese.[25] Thus, while the uniqueness of the segregation of African Americans cannot be overemphasized, as we become a more diverse society we need to watch for an expanding color line.[26] There is little evidence that the residential situation of Hispanics and Asians will ever be as segregated as that of African Americans, but it is important to follow the residential and school patterns of all groups.

Thus, the current levels and trends of residential segregation in American cities do not indicate positive trends in school integration, particularly for African Americans in the large northern metropolitan areas. These trends have been remarkably consistent over the last few decades and the results have been consistent across researchers. Unevenness, isolation, clustering, concentration, and centralization cumulate in their effects on neighborhoods. While it may be possible to combat one or two factors, their additive effects exacerbate the difficulty of changing neighborhood patterns by attracting whites back to the cities and areas of cities they have left. Thus, while it is intuitively true that school integration should follow neighborhood integration, the persistence of severe residential segregation, particularly in the large northern metropolitan areas, does not bode well for school desegregation.[27] We must now ask what causes and maintains these patterns of severe residential separation.

Myths and Other Explanations for Residential Segregation

Three Myths

Research on the residential segregation of African Americans shows such a uniform pattern of high levels and slow change that a number of what I call myths have arisen to explain segregation. Because these myths superficially and intuitively seem to account for the reality that most people, regardless of race, see around themselves every day, the myths are quite easy to believe. These myths are most often used to explain the segregation of African Americans, but occasionally are used for other groups as well. Like their more individual psychological counterpart, stereotypes, these myths contain small grains of truth that make them believable, yet wrong.

Myth One: Segregation Has Always Been with Us

Travel to city after city, talk to many different people and to older people, and it seems that blacks have always lived in separate neighborhoods. But historical research into neighborhood patterns reveals this common view to be false. Despite severe prejudice, discrimination, poverty, and the existence of separate and unequal schools, African American residential patterns at the beginning of this century were nowhere near as segregated as those we see now.[28] True, there were areas in cities that were known for their black residents, but those areas were not *all* black and not *all* blacks in the city lived in them.[29] Homogeneously black neighborhoods containing nearly all of the black population in a city are a twentieth-century development in the United States, and this has never been experienced by any other group in this country.[30] The danger of this myth is that it is very difficult to see the possibility or even the need to change things that have always been that way.

Myth Two: Residential Segregation in Cities Is Natural

Severe and persisting residential segregation is not a normal part of the development of cities. The intensification of segregation of African Americans in the North occurred at the same time as a great period of growth in northern cities, but segregation was not a normal or natural part of this growth. A host of private, public, and governmental actors deliberately created residential segregation.[31] The real estate industry, banks, appraisers, and insurance agents translated private prejudice into public action ultimately sanctioned by the federal government in Federal Housing Administration (FHA) loan policies and the federal highway program.[32] As a result, the post–World War II suburban growth was for whites; blacks remained in the cities.

The rise of the suburbs corresponded in time with black migration to the North, but the residential segregation of African Americans increased *faster* than one would expect from their population growth alone.[33] In reflecting on the links between school and residential segregation, I am often struck by the fact that just as we started to implement *Brown v. Board of Education*,[34] we also started building the highways and suburban developments that would allow whites to escape the city into the suburbs.

Myth Three: Housing Discrimination Is Illegal, So It Must Not Be a Problem

It is an easy enough assumption that the 1968 Fair Housing Act,[35] which outlawed discrimination in the sale and rental of housing, effectively ended discrimination in housing. At a more general level, this myth involves an appeal to law as a justification for shrugging off problems we see in society: It is against the law to discriminate, so segregation must be the result of other factors. This is a myth because research confirms the persistence of widespread discrimination in the sale and rental of housing; relative to whites, blacks and Hispanics are likely to encounter unfavorable treatment roughly one-half of the time.[36] This discrimination is sometimes subtle (what Gary Orfield has called "discrimination with a smile"), but the actions and consequences are real: Blacks and Hispanics see fewer units of housing, are quoted unfavorable terms and conditions, and generally must search harder to find housing comparable to that of whites with similar means.

It may seem unbelievable that discrimination remains this high given official public disapproval, but one must remember that there is a wide discrepancy between white attitudes on segregation *in principle* compared to *in practice*.[37] White attitudes toward the idea that blacks should be able to purchase a house wherever they can afford have become increasingly favorable over the years, but nearly half of the white population would still vote against laws that would implement and enforce desegregation in housing.[38] This led Doug Massey and myself to conclude that ultimate responsibility for the persistence of racial segregation rests with white America. On issues of race and residence, white America continues to be fundamentally hypocritical and self-deceiving. Whites believe that people should be able to live wherever they want to regardless of skin color, but in practice they think that people—at least black people–should want to live with members of their own race.[39]

More Sophisticated Explanations for Residential Segregation

As a result of the salience and seeming facial validity of these three myths to much of the American population, many individuals, both white and black, see residential segregation as a natural or inevitable part of the social structure of United States society. To say that something is part of the social structure implies that it is beyond the control of the individuals affected. Paradoxically, however, people often refer to individuals' characteristics when attempting to explain away segregation. Nowhere is this clearer than in the less mythical explanations for patterns of residential segregation to which I now turn. Unlike the three myths discussed above, these explanations have some empirical validity. But to the extent that they are offered as *sole* causes of continuing segregation, ignoring discrimination, they can neither justify nor explain away continuing patterns of severe black-white residential segregation in contemporary cities.

Income differentials and voluntary segregation are the most frequent, more sophisticated explanations for residential segregation.[40] It is clear that African Americans, and to an extent, Asians and Hispanics, are generally poorer than their non-Hispanic white counterparts.[41] If income, however, were the driving force behind residential segregation, we would expect residential segregation to decline as income, occupational status, or educational status improved.[42] Research using 1980 data has shown precisely such a decline for Hispanics and Asians, but almost no decline for African Americans.[43] While comparable analyses using 1990 data have not yet been completed, the overall segregation trends, combined with documented income polarization, suggest that not much has changed.[44] The segregation of African Americans is not as responsive to income or other measures of human capital as is the segregation of other minority groups. Put another way, African Americans are not as able to translate their social capital accumulations into spatial location as well as other groups. Estimates of the amount of segregation attributable to income vary and are the subject of scholarly dispute; however, the most common estimates suggest that income differentials account for no more than one-third of the residential segregation of African Americans.[45]

This leaves the argument that segregation is voluntary, a position increasingly adopted by both blacks and whites, though often for different reasons. For many whites, the belief that blacks prefer to live with blacks eliminates whites' responsibility for the segregated neighborhoods around them. It also implies that blacks are responsible for their own segregation, and that whites are giving them what they want by allowing it. Nowhere is this belief more clear than in the often-made comparison between white ethnic groups and blacks, implying that if the former were able to work their way up, so should the latter.[46] In reality, however, public opinion surveys reveal far more white reluctance to live with blacks than black reluctance to live with whites.[47] For some blacks, however, voluntary segregation has become associated with black empowerment, the importance of black culture, black self-help goals, and the rhetorical point that if all-white neighborhoods are not bad, why should all-black ones be bad?[48] Thus, voluntary segregation is the toughest explanation to discuss, for it strikes deeply at the political motivations of both groups. However, it is important that we at least try to understand how the current debate about separatism could be the *result* of generations of American apartheid rather than the *cause*.[49]

To explore this point, let me begin by saying that I do not doubt that some number of blacks choose to live in all-black neighborhoods, a choice that deserves respect. The need for such a choice is well-documented. Middle-class blacks experience a considerable number of overt racist incidents,[50] in addition to continued discrimination in real estate rental and sales and in employment.[51] In this context, a segregated neighborhood can be a retreat from the daily racism in the larger society.

However, one must question whether feeling the need for a retreat, and wanting to escape racist harassment and harm, constitutes truly voluntary action. Voluntary implies a free choice between at least two options, without compulsion or obligation; it connotes a positive choice. Thus, the issue is not whether some blacks prefer to live in all- or mainly black neighborhoods, for as a group, African Americans have varied opinions on this issue.[52] Rather, the issue really is whether such a choice can be called voluntary if it results from a need to escape racism and racists. It is worth remembering that no other minority group in the United States has preferred to live such that between 80 percent and 90 percent of its members would have to move to be evenly distributed in major northern cities.

The argument for the self-segregation of African Americans is also sometimes framed positively: Such segregation improves the ability to share and pass on culture, as well as to develop institutions. While this idea has some appeal, it ignores the fundamental issue of *power*. In much of society (and especially in industries connected to the provision, development, marketing, and location of housing), whites continue to have much more power than blacks.[53] This power means that all-white neighborhoods do not generally suffer the decreases in services, property value, maintenance, school quality, and other amenities that all-black neighborhoods do. It is, of course, possible to defuse this point by arguing that the problem is not only a matter of neighborhood integration but of equity in resource allocation.[54] This argument has facial validity, but sidesteps the issue that not all resources are allocated through established systems of legal power. Private investment follows public investment: A well-maintained neighborhood with attentive public services, appreciating property values, and good schools attracts industry and other amenities while discouraging crime and other disseminates.

Thus far, efforts by the government to ensure equitable treatment of black neighborhoods have encountered limited or, at best, short-term success.[55] While we certainly need to invest some money in housing in all-black areas (if only because these areas developed as a result of social policy), such reinvestment cannot be the main focus of housing policy. One needs only to remember that at one time *all* of our public housing was new and was viewed positively by many tenants: "When we moved in, it was nice. You didn't see all this graffiti, we had telephones in front, we had grass, we had fences."[56] Public housing was of much higher quality, with more light, space, and amenities than the tenement housing it replaced.[57] Buildings identical to those that are being dynamited are still occupied in many cities.[58] But these factors were not enough to overcome the social consequences of isolation and warehousing of the poorest of the poor, that is, segregation by race and class.[59]

Residential segregation, whether imposed or voluntary, is thus an important component of what John Yinger calls the "discrimination system," which also includes racial and ethnic disparities in the labor market and public schools and which interacts with racial-ethnic prejudice to reinforce and amplify the negative effects of each component.[60] Similarly, Melvin Oliver and Thomas Shapiro note that blacks accumulate less actual wealth compared to whites with comparable incomes, in part because their houses do not appreciate in value as much as houses owned by whites.[61] Neighborhoods are thus more than just places to live; they also can be very important in determining a person's possibilities for employment and wealth accumulation, as well as one's friends, personal safety, and the schools one's children attend. Neighborhoods are an integral part of the systems that structure peoples' lives. Segregation, which is ultimately grounded in racial and ethnic discrimination, can only exacerbate that discrimination. As Yinger notes, "Prejudice against minorities thrives when minorities and whites tend not to live together and when minorities achieve less success than whites, on average, in school and in work. Moreover, prejudice feeds back into the system . . . [and] is a key cause of discrimination by landlords, real estate agents, lenders, and others."[62]

Comparing all-white to all-black neighborhoods to justify why segregation might be good thus ignores the social context in which segregated neighborhoods were created and persist. The comparison would only be valid in a society with equitable power distribution across the races and no racism, hardly a description of contemporary United States society. This is not to say that all-black neighborhoods are intrinsically bad, but rather to point out that all-black neighborhoods, because of the social context of the white power structure in which they are embedded, face a harder time in gaining equitable resource allocation than all-white ones.[63] Those who assert that all-black neighborhoods are justifiable can make logical and even compelling points. However, the separatist position, like the argument that segregation is due to individual *choice*, ignores the practical and historical facts of racism, power, and economic domination.

In the end, all of the myths and other explanations I have discussed fail to account for historical and contemporary patterns of segregation. The high levels of racial segregation in the contemporary United States have not always been with us; segregation is not the result of some natural process of urban growth; segregation was not solved by the Fair Housing Act[64] nor by other civil rights laws; and segregation cannot be explained away by black-white income differences or by a resort to ban indefensible notions of personal choice. Residential segregation is the direct and continuing result of racism. This racism is both private and public and has become institutionalized in government and business as well as in individuals' conduct. That this institutionalization is complete is manifest in the fact that segregation is now being hailed as a better option by some of its own victims.[65] While it is easy to understand blacks who feel a need for refuge from daily racism, separation means that *whites get what they want*, and it condemns blacks to further economic hardship and deprivation. No matter how much African Americans increase their income or personal power, the social structure of segregation means that they do not realistically have the same residential opportunities as whites.

If we give them credence, these three myths and the two more sophisticated explanations of segregation (income differentials and voluntary segregation) have strong implications for our understanding of the relationship between school and residential segregation, as well as our commitment to remedy them. Most directly, these myths serve to remove racial segregation from the responsibility or the control of whites.[66] If segregation has always been here and if it is a natural outgrowth of city development as we know it in the United States, then there is little we can do about it. School desegregation, if it is to happen, must take place *within* the boundaries of residential segregation patterns. By treating the two issues as separate we make it impossible to solve either, while still feeling that we are making an effort. It is in this context that advocates for desegregation have attempted to link housing and schools in the courts.[67] Thus it is vitally important to consider the *links* between school and neighborhood segregation.

Theoretical Links Between Residential and School Segregation

Treating residential segregation and school segregation as separate problems has enabled courts to rule that neighborhood segregation is outside the realm of what schools can address or be responsible for.[68] This is understandable, given that the NAACP (National Association for the Advancement of Colored People) and other advocates initially fought school segregation in the context of state-sponsored separate facilities. But while overt state sponsorship of segregation has been struck down, segregation attributable to neighborhoods and districts has proven much harder to combat. Neighborhood segregation has become the contemporary way of keeping schools segregated. By treating school and neighborhood segregation as separate, we ignore the fact that the original bases for neighborhood segregation were state sponsored and state approved,[69] though not as overtly as in the case of schools.

Let us begin by thinking about school and residential segregation from the point of view of an individual neighborhood. At the neighborhood level, the degree of residential integration is simply a function of the relative number of members of different racial-ethnic groups residing there.[70] Segregation in a neighborhood school, however, is more than a function of the races/ethnicities of the attending students because it is influenced by the relative ages of a community's racial-ethnic groups and the rate of private school attendance, as well as the racial-ethnic composition of the neighborhood.

For this reason, empirical studies of the effect of neighborhood segregation on school segregation have frequently used the racial proportions of the resident student population, rather than the total population, as the relevant variable for studying school desegregation efforts.[71] But if the aim is to find out how the two types of segregation are linked, then it is best to include all persons on the neighborhood side of the equation. Assuming only two racial-ethnic groups, we can formally summarize this analysis with two equations:

Neighborhood segregation = a function of (number of group 1, number of group 2)

School segregation = a function of (neighborhood segregation, private school use, school age of group 1, school age of group 2)

By specifying the dynamic in this way, we can begin to explore the process through which school and neighborhood segregation work together. For example, if both populations are the same age and there is no use of private schools, then school segregation mirrors neighborhood segregation. Private schools, if affordable by parents, provide an outlet for groups to live together while not sharing schools. They can function to make the schools less integrated than the neighborhood if the private schools are not used equally by all racial-ethnic groups. Note that equal use by racial groups is less likely the more the private schools cost, given the higher poverty rates of blacks. Age can function in a similar way: If whites do not mind having black neighbors but do not want their children socializing or attending school with them, then whites can live in integrated neighborhoods before or after child-rearing. An analogous result occurs when urban schools are of lower quality than suburban schools, thus leading whites to avoid them and their neighborhoods if they have school-age children.[72]

Moving to a more dynamic perspective, we can think about how segregation changes over time. From our neighborhood equation, we see that segregation (by definition) changes with the relative numbers of different groups in a neighborhood. The neighborhood segregation literature reveals that there are very few integrated neighborhoods, though the number is increasing.[73] By and large, blacks live in heavily black neighborhoods and whites in heavily white ones. If this situation begins to change, and some blacks move into a previously white neighborhood, what kind of neighborhood will it be? Given the income differences between blacks and whites, as well as the persistent discrimination faced by blacks, we might expect blacks to move into older, established neighborhoods with lower housing values.[74] But these neighborhoods may very well be occupied by older whites who no longer have school-age children. Thus, the impetus that school integration can receive from neighborhood integration is constrained by the age of the adults in the neighborhood.

Thinking about school and neighborhood segregation as interrelated processes at the neighborhood level offers two advantages over thinking of them separately. First, it suggests new research topics at the neighborhood level. For example, using only census data, researchers could examine private school attendance and population age structure differences in the context of black and white mobility into neighborhoods. If one has both school and neighborhood data for a particular neighborhood, then one can look at the process of neighborhood change modeled with the dynamic of school change included. Second, thinking about these two issues simultaneously raises the serious theoretical issue of whether residential and school population changes are mutually reinforcing (both schools and neighborhoods integrate, as would be the case in new housing marketed without discrimination), or working in opposition to each other (as might happen if a neighborhood is gentrified by young whites who do not have children in schools). Clearly, more progress will be made on both fronts if the former is true, but I suspect that the latter case is actually more common; that is, the processes of school and neighborhood changes are more often working against each other than in a complementary fashion.

In addition to the theoretical commonalities between school and residential segregation at the neighborhood level, it is also helpful to think of the broader metropolitan context. The stagnation of progress in both residential and school segregation in the large metropolitan areas of the North is complicated by the same structural factor: metropolitan fragmentation.[75] Metropolitan fragmentation refers to the fact that in the North, and in older industrial metropolitan areas, governmental and school district boundaries tend to be numerous and closely linked to the center city-suburban division. This is in direct contrast to the situation in the South and in newer, smaller urban areas, where metropolitan areas have been able to repeatedly annex land (allowing the tax bases of the central cities to keep up with population spread) and where school districts are often county-wide rather than subdivided within municipalities or counties.

This political fragmentation limits the effectiveness of even favorable judicial judgments regarding either school or housing to the boundaries within which the suit took place. It is exactly this political fragmentation that the plaintiffs in *Milliken v. Bradley*[76] attacked, to no avail.[77] Commentators have long noted not only that *Milliken* made school desegregation more difficult,[78] but that the Court's decision had profound effects on residential desegregation as well. Once *Milliken* made school district boundaries inviolable, suburbs could more easily remain all-white enclaves.[79] Political boundaries serve to inhibit the location of low-income housing and discourage city-suburban mobility even in the few suburban areas that have actually formed public housing authorities. In northeastern metropolitan areas, for example, there can be hundreds of public housing authorities.[80] Keeping track of these various boundaries and making separate applications to all of them for assisted housing is hard work for even the most motivated inner city mover who wants to use the portability of Section 8 certificates.[81] Suburban residential stratification has been well documented in a series of articles by two of my colleagues, John Logan and Richard Alba.[82] Their research shows that even suburban blacks get less in terms of spatial goods[83] than whites with comparable socioeconomic characteristics.[84] Governmental fragmentation thus affects ability of both schools and neighborhoods to desegregate,[85] and courts can provide only limited relief as long as their remedies only apply to specific suburbs.[86]

These two phenomena thus reinforce each other: The processes by which neighborhoods and schools actually change feed into and from the proliferation of municipal boundaries. This interaction negatively impacts all African Americans through its segregative effects. But no people are as strongly affected as the members of the group known colloquially as the urban underclass. In our recent book, *American Apartheid: Segregation and the Making of the Underclass*,[87] Douglas Massey and I argue that segregation is the linchpin of the underclass.[88] Discussions of the underclass too often focus on the behaviors of the residents, many behaviors of which society disapproves, such as dropping out of school, children having children, lack of labor force attachment, and drug use. While these issues are too complicated for a chapter of this length, the negative effects of segregation on poor African Americans are abundantly clear.[89] It is equally clear that poor public housing residents do *well* if they move to better areas,[90] but because African Americans at *all* income levels are restricted in their choice of residence, the whole group pays the price of segregation.[91] In addition, Joe Feagin and Melvin Sikes note the costs of segregation to whites: "This social isolation will become even more of a serious handicap for whites as the United States moves into the twenty-first century during which whites will eventually become a minority in the United States population. Even today, living in all-white enclaves does not prepare white Americans for dealing with a world that is composed mostly of people of color."[92]

At the simplest level, metropolitan segregation and the percentage of African Americans in central city school districts are strongly and positively related. Thus, as metropolitan segregation goes up, the average percentage of blacks in the center city school district rises. The uneven distribution of persons in the metropolitan area is thus a crucial determinant of the challenges that center city districts face in desegregating schools. Modeling this relationship more precisely is beyond the scope of this chapter, especially given the increasing complexity pointed out by other researchers.[93] There are dramatic regional differences in segregation, in part because of differences in how well school districts have desegregated, but also because of the different political boundaries that define those districts. County-wide boundaries in the South are quite selective in this regard.[94] It is also noteworthy that the correlation between black-white segregation and the proportion of African Americans in center city school districts is strongest in the Midwest and the South, regions where there is less ethnic diversity than in the Northeast and West.

In summary then, residential and school segregation are interrelated both theoretically and empirically in contemporary U.S. society. While a correlation does not necessarily imply mutual causation, it does suggest that in our efforts to combat either type of segregation we would be well advised to pay attention to the effects of the other. While I leave a full model of the complexity of these interrelationships to further research, it is beneficial to explore some policy options, the subject to which I now turn.

Combating Residential Segregation and School Segregation Together

The literature on residential and school segregation shares a focus on the situation of African Americans, a focus which reflects both the *Brown* decision and the civil rights movement of the 1960s generally. However, population data reveal that metropolitan areas in the United States are increasingly becoming multiethnic,[95] and projections reveal that by the year 2050, the United States as a whole will only barely be a white majority.[96] Therefore, efforts to desegregate either schools or neighborhoods will occur in a more multiethnic framework than was true in the past. What are the implications of this multiethnicity? In a recent study, Bridget Anderson and I examined the patterns of neighborhood transition in five metropolitan areas between 1970 and 1990: Philadelphia, Miami, Chicago, Houston, and Los Angeles.[97] We chose these five cities to reflect different regions and different combinations of racial-ethnic groups, in order to provide five mini-laboratories for detailed examination of the process of neighborhood change.[98] Neighborhoods occupied by a single group were relatively uncommon throughout the years studied, with two dramatic exceptions: white-only neighborhoods were substantial in Philadelphia (55 percent in 1970, declining to 34 percent in 1990); and in Chicago white-only and black-only neighborhoods were 31 percent and 11 percent of the total, respectively, in 1970, but declined to 6 percent and 19 percent, respectively, by 1990. The most common type of two-group neighborhoods contained whites and Hispanics only: 63 percent of Miami's neighborhoods in 1970 were of this type, as were 42 percent of Los Angeles', 33 percent of Houston's, and 29 percent of Chicago's.

Over time, however, two-group neighborhoods declined in importance. Three- and four-group multiethnic neighborhoods became the norm: white-Hispanic-Asian, white-black-Hispanic, or white-black-Hispanic-Asian. The presence of Asians in the city appears to determine how often the four-group type of neighborhood can emerge. Thus, nearly half of Los Angeles' neighborhoods contained all four groups by 1990, whereas in Philadelphia (with a much smaller Asian population), only 11 percent did. We found similar results in the New York metropolitan area over the same time period.[99] Further analysis revealed that these multiethnic neighborhoods are not confined to center cities only,[100] that they were generally formed by the entry of minorities,[101] and that their white population did not decline precipitously on average.[102]

While more detailed study of the stability of these new multiethnic neighborhoods remains to be done, their existence in substantial numbers offers a new possibility to proponents of both school and neighborhood integration. Historically, integrated neighborhoods have often turned back toward resegregation: public policy has enhanced resegregation by condoning real estate steering and financial discrimination.[103] This process was further enhanced by municipal fragmentation, thereby facilitating the availability of all-white enclaves. To the extent that these all-white enclaves are diminishing in number and to the extent that multiethnic neighborhoods can be preserved, this new kind of neighborhood change could support integrated schools as well as the creation of integrated neighborhoods.

To capitalize on the growth of multiethnic neighborhoods requires that we begin to tie together social policy designed to desegregate schools and neighborhoods. First, it is necessary to establish formal institutional ties between organizations fighting school segregation and those fighting neighborhood segregation, with a specific focus on these neighborhoods. Such cooperation is easy to suggest, of course, while the organizations involved in combating both types of segregation are frequently underfunded, understated, and overworked. Organizations that focus on specific neighborhoods, however, could promote creative policies, such as eliminating busing requirements for schools already serving integrated neighborhoods.[104] This would reestablish the importance of neighborhood schools while simultaneously promoting residential integration.

Focusing on multiethnic neighborhoods in linking school and neighborhood desegregation efforts also provides the opportunity to actively promote specific examples of *successful* schools and neighborhoods. Too often we focus only on conflict or on failures, thus increasing the sense of despair frequently pervading discussion of these issues.[105] While there is evidence of the positive effects of metropolitan-wide school desegregation in reducing housing segregation patterns,[106] changing demographics are not accepted by the courts as a cause of school segregation and that must be attacked. There are many arguments for the continued importance of integration,[107] even while there is concern for the difficulties inherent in doing so.[108] The importance of having experience with members of other race and ethnic groups from an early age is vital to the increasingly multiethnic society that the United States is becoming[109] and as we increasingly interact closely in a world where most of the people are not white.

In addition to focusing on multiethnic neighborhoods to revise and strengthen both school and neighborhood desegregation policies, other cross-linkages exist as well. First, we could link the building of new schools or the remodeling of old schools to the building of racially and economically integrated housing. A new school is a boon to developers trying to sell houses, and Florida has had success in allowing developers to build, but only if they meet certain housing requirements.[110] Second, we could link the building of housing to particular schools, for example, by offering incentives to builders to improve neighborhoods with reasonably good schools in danger of decline due to demographic changes. There are, of course, obstacles to such linkages, and state and federal housing and education departments remain both institutionally separated and shackled by obsolete policies and constraining case law. Identifying the linkages between housing and school segregation, and the *possibilities* for cooperation and reform, however, are necessary steps in breaking down these institutional and political barriers to change.

Conclusion

We are at a time when racism seems to have become more open[111] and when major leaders are quite discouraged about future progress.[112] Yet the dream lives on that by being together as equals, particularly from a young age before stereotypes and racial distrust have hardened, we can learn to appreciate and understand each other.[113] Research continues to show benefits to race relations from interracial contact,[114] particularly for whites,[115] and also shows that a better neighborhood environment improves outcomes for blacks.[116] While the policy recommendations I suggest are hardly enough, and face both legal and practical difficulties, they do represent a different approach from the past.

The need for a different approach from the past is well exemplified in a book by Jennifer Hochschild entitled *Facing Up to the American Dream*.[117] Hochschild demonstrates, using meticulous analysis of survey data by race and class and precise arguments, both the continuing power of and the internal inconsistencies in the American Dream. She argues that since the American Dream focuses on individuals rather than structures, the seeds for the discontent currently seen among the estranged poor are part and parcel of the dream itself.[118] Yet the dream remains salient among many poor of both races.[119] Hochschild thus concludes that the alternatives to the dream—white denial and black separatism—would be unfortunate for the fabric of the nation.[120]

As Joe Feagin and Hernan Vera note at the end of their volume, *White Racism*, whites support the cause of equality and justice for blacks only when it is in their interest to do so. [121] The difficult and necessary task, in our view, involves bringing whites to a recognition that the destruction of racism is in their interest. Since people of all races care deeply about both their neighborhoods and the education of their children, perhaps the strategy of combating both school and neighborhood segregation simultaneously in a multiethnic neighborhood context will be in everyone's interest. The limited success seen in the two spheres of residential segregation and housing segregation separately makes approaching them together even more challenging. But as long as these two systems of segregation mutually reinforce each other, it may prove easier and indeed *necessary* to combat them together. And combat them we must.

Notes

1. Reynolds Farley, "Residential Segregation and Its Implications for School Integration," in *The Courts, Social Science, and School Desegregation,* 164, 164 (Betsy Levin and Willis D. Hawley, eds., 1975).

2. See Susan Olzak and Suzanne Shanahan, "School Desegregation, Interracial Exposure, and Antibusing Activity in Contemporary Urban America," 100 *Am. J. Soc.* 196, 217 (1994) (describing antibusing protests including meetings, rallies, picketing, boycotts, and riots). See generally Jennifer Hochschild, *The New American Dilemma: Liberal Democracy and School Desegregation* (1984) (examining how incrementalism and popular control work to desegregate schools); D. Garth Taylor, *Public Opinion and Collective Action: The Boston School Desegregation Conflict* (1986) (showing that although a great majority of white Bostonians are not racist on most questions, most of the non-racist majority is against busing in Boston).

3. See Douglas S. Massey and Nancy A. Denton, *American Apartheid: Segregation and the Making of the Underclass,* 57, 77, 114, 221–23 (1993).

4. See Gary Orfield, "School Desegregation after Two Generations: Race, Schools, and Opportunity in Urban Society," in *Race in America: The Struggle for Equality,* 234, 239 (Herbert Hill and James E. Jones, eds., 1993) (providing a table showing levels of desegregation by region during the period 1968–1988); Steven G. Rivkin, "Residential Segregation and School Integration," 67 *Soc. Educ.* 279, 289 (1994) (providing a table showing exposure index for school districts in 40 large cities).

5. Massey and Denton, *supra* note 3, at 222; Reynolds Farley and William H. Frey, "Changes in the Segregation of Whites from Blacks during the 1980s," 59 *Am. Soc. Rev.* 23, 30 (1994); Roderick J. Harrison and Claudette E. Bennett, "Racial and Ethnic Diversity," in 2 *State of the Union: America in the 1990s, Social Trends,* 141, 161 (Reynolds Farley, ed., 1995).

6. Massey and Denton, *supra* note 3, at 223; Rivkin, *supra* note 4, at 291.

7. See Massey and Denton, *supra* note 3, at 47, 68, 222; Karl E. Taeuber and Alma F. Taeuber, *Negroes in Cities,* 28–68 (1965); Reynolds Farley, "Neighborhood Preferences and Aspirations among Blacks and Whites," in *Housing Markets and Residential Mobility,* 161, 179–83 (G. Thomas Kingsley and Margery Austin Turner, eds., 1993); Farley and Frey, *supra* note 5, at 23; Harrison and Bennett, *supra* note 5, at 161–62. See generally Annemette Sorenson et al., "Indexes of Residential Segregation for 109 Cities in the United States, 1940–1970," 8 *Soc. Focus* 125 (1975).

8. Massey and Denton, *supra* note 3, at 222.

9. Farley and Frey, *supra* note 5, at 23; Douglas S. Massey and Nancy A. Denton, "Trends in the Residential Segregation of Blacks, Hispanics, and Asians: 1970–1980," 52 *Am. Soc. Rev.* 802, 812, 814 (1987).

10. Massey and Denton, *supra* note 3, at 221, 223. Researchers generally measure levels of segregation on a 100-point scale, with a score around 60 generally considered moderate. A score of 60, for example, indicates that 60% of a particular group in the area studied would have to move in order to reach the number expected if racial-ethnic groups were evenly distributed.

11. Douglas S. Massey and Nancy A. Denton, "Hypersegregation in U.S. Metropolitan Areas: Black and Hispanic Segregation along Five Dimensions," 26 *Demography* 373, 373 (1989).

12. Ibid., 381–82. We later added Buffalo, Indianapolis, Kansas City, New York, Atlanta, and Dallas to our list of hypersegregated cities, for a total of sixteen. We measure hypersegregation using indices of segregation, all of which range from 0 to 1.0. The average segregation scores for each dimension for sixteen metropolitan areas in 1990 were 0.78 for evenness, 0.72 for isolation, 0.59 for clustering, 0.84 for concentration, and 0.86 for centralization. All of these are still well above our cutoff score of 0.6 with the exception of clustering, which falls just below it because of the inclusion of Atlanta and Dallas, cities that we no longer classified as hypersegregated in 1990. Nancy A. Denton, "Are African Americans Still Hypersegregated?" in *Residential Apartheid: The American Legacy*, 49, 57 (Robert D. Bullard et al., eds., 1994). Since we defined hypersegregation as four or five segregation indices greater than 0.6, actual changes of the values of the indices must be examined to ensure that having the same cutoff point in both years does not mask considerable improvement. This would be the case, for example, if the values were all close to 1.0 in 1980 but close to 0.6 in 1990. Massey and Denton, *supra* note 3, at 76.

13. The cities dropped from the list of hypersegregated metropolitan areas—Atlanta and Dallas—are both southern cities. Denton, *supra* note 12, at 57.

14. Ibid., 60.

15. Farley and Frey, *supra* note 5, at 30. The index of dissimilarity ranges from 0 to 100. It is generally interpreted as the percent of either group (African Americans and whites in this case) that would have to move in order for the two groups being compared to be distributed evenly across the neighborhoods in the city.

16. Ibid., 33.

17. See *Brown v. Board of Education*, 347 U.S. 483, 493 (1954) (stating that the question presented in the case is whether "segregation of children in public schools . . . deprive[s] the children of the minority group of equal educational opportunities").

18. Farley and Frey, *supra* note 5, at 32; Harrison and Bennett, *supra* note 5, at 162.

19. Farley and Frey, *supra* note 5, at 32.

20. That is, around 60 on a 100-point scale.

21. Farley and Frey, *supra* note 5, at 38.

22. My research on the individual Hispanic and Asian groups that make up these umbrella categories is planned but has not yet been completed for 1990.

23. Nancy A. Denton and Douglas S. Massey, "Racial Identity among Caribbean Hispanics: The Effect of Double Minority Status on Residential Segregation," 54 *Am. Soc. Rev.* 790, 803 (1989).

24. Douglas S. Massey and Nancy A. Denton, "Residential Segregation of Mexicans, Puerto Ricans, and Cubans in Selected U.S. Metropolitan Areas," 73 *Soc. and Soc. Res.* 73, 79 (1989).

25. Douglas S. Massey and Nancy A. Denton, "Residential Segregation of Asian-Origin Groups in U.S. Metropolitan Areas," 76 *Soc. and Soc. Res.* 170, 172 (1992).

26. Indeed, Gary Orfield has pointed out recently that Hispanic students rapidly are becoming segregated in terms of the average number of non-Hispanic whites in their classrooms. Orfield, *supra* note 4, at 235.

27. In many cities, the school desegregation potential is severely limited by the few whites remaining in the school system. David R. James, "City Limits on Racial Equality: The Effects of City-Suburb Boundaries on Public School Desegregation, 1968–1976," 54 *Am. Soc. Rev.* 963, 975 (1989); Rivkin, *supra* note 4, at 285; see also Farley, *supra* note 1, at 192 (concluding that residential segregation makes school integration more difficult to accomplish because, as the proportion of black students increases, it becomes necessary to bus more children longer distances to achieve integration of schools).

28. Massey and Denton, *supra* note 3, at 17–26; Henry Louis Taylor Jr., "City Building, Public Policy, the Rise of the Industrial City, and Black Ghetto-Slum Formation in Cincinnati, 1850–1940," in *Race and the City: Work, Community, and Protest in Cincinnati, 1820–1970*, 156, 159 (Henry Louis Taylor Jr., ed., 1993). Taylor notes, "The structure of the commercial city kept black ghettoes from forming. The population had no choice but to mix. Lack of adequate transportation systems, mixed patterns of land use, and the ubiquity of cheap housing led to the dispersal of both the immigrant and black populations. Cincinnati's experience was not unique. Throughout the nineteenth century, in both the North and South, blacks lived in biracial residential areas; even in the most segregated locations blacks and whites lived adjacent to one another or shared the same dwellings." Id. at 159.

29. See generally Thomas Lee Philpott, *The Slum and the Ghetto: Neighborhood Deterioration and Middle-Class Reform, Chicago, 1880–1930*, 131 (1978) ("An ethnic enclave was not a district in which all the inhabitants were of the same ethnic group and in which all of the people of that ethnic group lived").

30. Massey and Denton, *supra* note 3, at 57–59.

31. See Massey and Denton, *supra* note 3, at 26–57, 83–114 (suggesting that the spatial isolation of black Americans was achieved by a conjunction of racist attitudes, private behaviors, and institutional practices that disenfranchised blacks from urban housing markets and led to the creation of the ghetto); see also Kenneth Jackson, *Crabgrass Frontier: The Suburbanization of the United States*, 190–230 (1985) (stating that there are many ways in which government largesse can affect where people live, such as housing administration, loan subsidies, and the tax code); Gregory D. Squires, *Capital and Communities in Black and White: The Intersections of Race, Class, and Uneven Development*, 48–56 (1994) (stating that uneven development, in terms of the industrial and spatial configuration of cities and the outcomes of this process as it affects class, race, and gender groups within cities, has been the predominant feature of the revolution of metropolitan areas in the United States in recent decades).

32. Kenneth Jackson writes: "In 1955 Columbia Professor Charles Abrams pointed a much stronger accusatory finger at FHA for discriminatory practices. Writing in 1955, the famed urban planner said: 'A government offering such bounty to builders and lenders could have required compliance with a nondiscrimination policy. Or the agency could at least have pursued a course of evasion, or hidden behind the screen of local autonomy. Instead, FHA adopted a racial policy that could well have been culled from the Nuremberg laws. From its inception FHA set itself up as the protector of the all white neighborhood. It sent its agents into the field to keep Negroes and other minorities from buying homes in white neighborhoods.'" Jackson, *supra* note 31, at 214.

33. Stanley Lieberson, *A Piece of the Pie: Blacks and White Immigrants since 1880*, 291 (1980).

34. 347 U.S. 483 (1954).

35. 42 U.S.C. §§ 3601-3631 (1994).

36. Margery Austin Turner and Ron Wienk, "The Persistence of Segregation in Urban Areas: Contributing Causes," in *Housing Markets and Residential Mobility*, *supra* note 7, at 193, 199. For a more general discussion of all aspects of this research, see Michael Fix and Raymond Struyk, eds., *Clear and Convincing Evidence: Measurement of Discrimination in America* (1993).

37. Cf. Theodore M. Shaw, "Equality and Educational Excellence: Legal Challenges in the 1990s," 80 *Minn. L. Rev.* 901, 904 (1996) ("[T]his fight is not accepted with grace, nor is it welcomed by the majority in this country, not in practice, maybe in policy or in principle, but not in practice").

38. See Howard Schuman et al., *Racial Attitudes in America: Trends and Interpretations*, 97 (1985) (providing a table showing the attitudes of whites toward the principle of free residential choice and open housing laws).

39. Massey and Denton, *supra* note 3, at 212–213.

40. A five article exchange between W.A.V. Clark and George Galster on whether contemporary discrimination needs to be included with income and personal preferences to understand contemporary residential segregation can be found in 5 *Population Res. and Pol'y Rev.* 95 (1986); 7 *Population Res. and Pol'y Rev.* 93 (1988); 7 *Population Res. and Pol'y Rev.* 113 (1988); 8 *Population Res. and Pol'y Rev.* 181 (1989); and 8 *Population Res. and Pol'y Rev.* 193 (1989).

41. Reynolds Farley, "The Common Destiny of Blacks and Whites: Observations about the Social and Economic Status of the Races," in *Race in America: The Struggle for Equality,* 197, 206–07 (Herbert Hill and James E. Jones Jr., eds., 1993); Harrison and Bennett, *supra* note 5, at 176; Frank Levy, "Incomes and Income Inequality," in 1 *State of the Union: America in the 1990s, Economic Trends,* 1, 41–43 (Reynolds Farley, ed., 1995).

42. Harrison and Bennett, *supra* note 5, at 162.

43. Nancy A. Denton and Douglas S. Massey, "Residential Segregation of Blacks, Hispanics, and Asians by Socioeconomic Status and Generation," 69 *Soc. Sci. Q.* 797, 802–05 (1988).

44. Levy, *supra* note 41, at 23–26. Between 1979 and 1989, family income adjusted for family size grew by about 2 percent in the bottom quarter of the distribution and by 15 to 20 percent in the top quarter. Id. at 26.

45. "Since the mid-1970s, the race-class debate has gone on without definitive resolution with respect to a variety of socioeconomic outcomes: employment, wealth, family stability, education, crime. But when one considers residential segregation, the argument is easily and forcefully settled: race clearly predominates. Indeed, race predominates to such an extent that speculation about what would have happened if black economic progress had continued becomes moot. Even if black income had continued to rise throughout the 1970s, segregation would not have declined: no matter how much blacks earned they remained spatially separated from whites. In 1980, as in the past, money did not buy entry into white neighborhoods of American cities." Massey and Denton, *supra* note 3, at 85; see also John E. Farley, "Race Still Matters: The Minimal Role of Income and Housing Cost as Causes of Housing Segregation in St. Louis, 1990," 31 *Urb. Aff. Rev.* 244, 252 (1995) (asserting that as economic barriers to housing choices decrease, race has an even greater effect on differences in housing locations).

46. See Lieberson, *supra* note 33, at xi–xii (describing the common belief that if late immigrants from central, east, and south Europe were able to improve their social position, blacks should be able to do so as well).

47. Farley, *supra* note 7, at 168, 173.

48. A good overview of thinkers and issues surrounding the idea of self-segregation for blacks can be found in Bernard R. Boxill, *Blacks and Social Justice,* 173 (rev. ed., 1992).

49. Similarly, Dr. Kenneth Clark writes that the "rise of the black separatist movement in the 1960s manifested blacks' identification with the reasoning of their

oppressor. Black separatists internalized the reasoning of the proponents of racial separation." Kenneth B. Clark, "Beyond *Brown v. Board of Education*: Housing and Education in the Year 2000," 80 *Minn. L. Rev.* 745, 747 (1996).

50. *See* Joe R. Feagin and Melvin P. Sikes, *Living with Racism: The Black Middle-Class Experience*, 37–77 (1994); Joe R. Feagin, "The Continuing Significance of Race: Antiblack Discrimination in Public Places," 56 *Am. Soc. Rev.* 101, 104 (1991). In addition, both the popular media and activist groups such as the Southern Poverty Law Center and numerous fair housing agencies continue to document incidents of harassment, firebombing, ostracizing, and otherwise bad treatment of blacks. Feagin and Sikes, id., at 249–67.

51. *See generally* Fix and Struyk, *supra* note 36.

52. Farley, *supra* note 7, at 172; *see also* John Yinger, *Closed Doors, Opportunities Lost: The Continuing Costs of Housing Discrimination*, 215 (1995) (stressing the need to provide opportunities for integration for minorities who choose to integrate and to revitalize minority communities for those who do not).

53. Evidence of this phenomenon can be seen in the continuing racial disparities in incomes, occupational status, and control of management in many of these arenas.

54. *See, e.g.*, John O. Calmore, "Spatial Equality and the Kerner Commission Report: A Back-to-the-Future Essay," 71 *N.C. L. Rev.* 1487, 1495 (1993) (asserting that opportunities in housing should be seen as including the "choice to overcome opportunity-denying circumstances while continuing to live in black communities"); John O. Calmore, "Fair Housing vs. Fair Housing: The Problems with Providing Increased Housing Opportunities through Spatial Deconcentration," 14 *Clearinghouse Rev.* 7, 15–17 (1980) (arguing that decentralization of low-income housing should be slowed to allow resources in housing to be distributed).

55. *See* Joe R. Feagin and Robert Parker, *Building American Cities: The Urban Real Estate Game,* 144–48, 254 (2d ed., 1990) (detailing the failure of government programs to improve inner-city housing that, due to a series of disinvestment-investment cycles, results in deteriorated housing for minorities and luxury housing for whites); Squires, *supra* note 31, at 112–15 (describing the short-lived revitalization efforts in Boston and Chicago).

56. Studs Terkel, Race: *How Blacks and Whites Think and Feel about the American Obsession,* 107 (1992) (quoting Peggy Byas, a resident of the Ida B. Wells homes, a public housing complex in Chicago).

57. Camilo Jose Vergara, *The New American Ghetto,* 42 (1995).

58. Ibid., 60.

59. Ibid., 42–65 (discussing how efforts to improve public housing failed because of continued discrimination against minority groups).

60. *See* Massey and Denton, *supra* note 3, at 47, 68, 222; Taeuber and Taeuber, *supra* note 7, at 28–68; Farley, *supra* note 7, at 179–83; Farley and Frey, *supra*

note 5, at 23; Harrison and Bennett, *supra* note 5, at 161–62; Sorenson et al., *supra* note 7, at 125.

61. Melvin L. Oliver and Thomas M. Shapiro, *Black Wealth, White Wealth: A New Perspective on Racial Inequality*, 119, 147–52 (1995).

62. Yinger, *supra* note 52, at 158.

63. Cf. Shaw, *supra* note 37, at 905 ("There is nothing inherently wrong with an all-black institution. There is something inherently wrong with all-black institutions that are created and maintained by a predominately white power structure and that do not have the resources because the resources are withdrawn as white folks flee.").

64. 42 U.S.C. §§ 3601–3631 (1994).

65. See generally Andrew Weise, "Neighborhood Diversity: Social Change, Ambiguity, and Fair Housing since 1968," 17 J. *Urb. Aff.* 107 (1995) (providing a summary and examples of the tension within the fair housing movement between pro-integration and non-discrimination [free-choice] camps). The forces of the Great Migration, redlining, block busting, and real estate discrimination combined to limit white demand for housing in a neighborhood once blacks entered it. As a result, pro-integration programs reach out affirmatively to whites as well as blacks, something that can appear as an insult to blacks who clearly face the bulk of the discrimination in the housing market. Id. at 118. Furthermore, there is the issue of comfort. "Being black in America is hard enough without having to live in a setting where one feels constantly on display." Id. at 125. Thus, "[t]hat many have chosen to build segregated communities now that alternatives exist is surely a symbol of growing freedom among the black middle class. It is also a reflection of frustration with the slow pace of change for all African Americans since the mid-1960s." Id. at 126. For an explicit argument against separatism, see generally Kofi Buenor Hadjor, *Another America: The Politics of Race and Blame* (1995).

66. For example, if segregation has always been with us, is a natural part of city growth, and at any rate is illegal, then why do whites need to even think about it, much less take responsibility for it or seek to change it? If one pushes the illegality rationale a bit further, then it has been eliminated by laws, so there is no need for whites to try to do anything about it.

67. Orfield, *supra* note 4, at 249–53; see generally Michael H. Sussman, Discrimination: A Pervasive Concept, chapter 8 of this volume.

68. See *Milliken v. Bradley*, 418 U.S. 717, 740–41 (1974) (rejecting the "assumption that the Detroit schools could not be truly desegregated . . . unless the racial composition of the student body of each school substantially reflected the racial composition of the population of the metropolitan area as a whole"); see also Sussman, *supra* note 67 (discussing *United States v. Yonkers Board of Education*, which held the city of Yonkers liable for racial segregation, and stating that politicians in Yonkers realized and intended that school segregation would result from segregation in public housing).

69. See Massey and Denton, *supra* note 3, at 17–59; Squires, *supra* note 31, at 48–52; Robert L. Green, "Desegregation," in *Metropolitan Desegregation*, 1 (Robert L. Green, ed., 1985).

70. See Nancy A. Denton and Douglas S. Massey, "Patterns of Neighborhood Transition in a Multiethnic World: U.S. Metropolitan Areas, 1970–1980," 28 *Demography* 41, 44 (1991). Note that this leaves aside for the moment the fact that the location of a particular neighborhood in the metropolitan context may be influenced by the demography of nearby neighborhoods.

71. Rivkin, *supra* note 4, at 282

72. Again, this assumes that whites, on average, have greater residential mobility than African Americans. Given the unquestionable income differential and the evidence of continuing discrimination in housing, this is not a difficult assumption.

73. Richard D. Alba et al., "Neighborhood Change under Conditions of Mass Immigration: The New York City Region, 1970–1990," 29 *Int'l Migration Rev.* 625, 641–43 (1995); Denton and Massey, *supra* note 70, at 46.

74. While I do not know of any research that directly studies the housing value in neighborhoods into which blacks move, this statement can be inferred from data showing lower housing values in neighborhoods with greater integration (Turner and Wienk, *supra* note 36, at 206) and also from data showing greater housing value and newer housing in neighborhoods that are less integrated (Margery Austin Turner and John G. Edwards, "Affordable Rental Housing in Metropolitan Neighborhoods," in *Housing Markets and Residential Mobility, supra* note 7, at 125, 131–34) and finally from discussions of how the filtering process works for African Americans (Phillip L. Clay, "The (Un)Housed City: Racial Patterns of Segregation, Housing Quality, and Affordability," in *The Metropolis in Black and White: Place, Power, and Polarization*, 93, 101 (George C. Galster and Edward W. Hill, eds., 1992).

75. Gregory R. Weiher, *The Fractured Metropolis: Political Fragmentation and Metropolitan Segregation*, 190–95 (1991); James, *supra* note 27, at 975; Rivkin, *supra* note 4, at 285.

76. 418 U.S. 717 (1974).

77. Ibid., 744–45. The Court in *Milliken* refused to allow school desegregation to take place across school district boundaries, though it did specify the conditions under which such a remedy would be allowed by the courts.

78. James, *supra* note 27, at 965; Orfield, *supra* note 4, at 241; Rivkin, *supra* note 4, at 291.

79. Gregory Weiher has documented the many ways this proliferation of boundaries enhances segregation. Weiher, *supra* note 75, at 45, 87–115.

80. Philip D. Tegeler et al., "Transforming Section 8 into a Regional Housing Mobility Program," in *Housing Mobility: Promise or Illusion?* 103, 106–07 (Alexander Polikoff, ed., 1995).

81. Section 8 certificates (or vouchers) are an individual family-based form of housing assistance given to poor families who then search for housing in the private market. 24 C.F.R. § 982.1 (1995). They are administered and distributed by PHAs (Public Housing Authorities), many of which have long waiting lists. HUD allocates them to metropolitan areas based on need, but in determining the sub-metropolitan area allocation to PHAs, older assisted housing in the city also counts. Therefore, cities may get less than their share of Section 8 certificates even though their higher poverty proportions raised the total number given to the metropolitan area as a whole. In recent years there has been considerable discussion about the relative lengths of waiting lists in cities and suburbs, the PHA requirement that one must live within the PHA boundaries in order to apply, and the difficulties with "portability" (using a Section 8 certificate from one PHA in another PHA), something that is technically allowed but in practice is sometimes difficult. See generally Tegeler et al., *supra* note 80 (providing a full discussion of these issues).

82. Richard D. Alba and John R. Logan, "Minority Proximity to Whites in Suburbs: An Individual-Level Analysis of Segregation," 98 *Am. Jour. Soc.* 1388, 1394–95 (1993); John R. Logan and Richard D. Alba, "Locational Returns to Human Capital: Minority Access to Suburban Community Resources," 30 *Demography* 243, 248 (1993)

83. By "spatial goods" I mean better tax bases, better schools, lower crime rates, better quality housing, better city services, greater housing appreciation, etc. All of these are related to both income of residents and the percentage of residents who are white.

84. Logan and Alba, *supra* note 82, at 259–63.

85. Weiher, *supra* note 75, at 190–95.

86. Farley and Frey, *supra* note 5, at 39.

87. Massey and Denton, *supra* note 3.

88. Ibid., 147. Some have suggested that the term "underclass" is pejorative, but it has been widely used in the literature to denote spatially concentrated, high-poverty areas where dropping out of school, teen pregnancy, drug use, and unemployment are very high. I use it in this sense.

89. Ibid., 148–85.

90. Mary Davis, "The Gautreaux Assisted Housing Program," in *Housing Markets and Residential Mobility, supra* note 7, at 243, 247–49; James E. Rosenbaum et al., "Can the Kerner Commission's Housing Strategy Improve Employment, Education, and Social Integration for Low-Income Blacks," 71 *N.C. L. Rev.* 1519, 1555 (1993).

91. See Scott J. South and Glenn D. Deane, "Race and Residential Mobility: Individual Determinants and Structural Constraints," 72 *Soc. Forces* 147, 161 (1993).

92. Feagin and Sikes, *supra* note 50, at 271.

93. See, e.g., Reynolds Farley et al., "School Desegregation and White Flight: An Investigation of Competing Models and Their Discrepant Findings," 53 *Soc. Educ.* 123, 124, 136 (1980); Christine H. Rossell, "The Carrot or the Stick for School Desegregation Policy?" 25 *Urb. Aff. Q.* 474, 481 (1990); Franklin D. Wilson, "The Impact of School Desegregation Programs on White Public School Enrollment, 1968–1976," 58 *Soc. Educ.* 137, 138, 142, 145 (1985); Franklin D. Wilson, "Patterns of White Avoidance," 441 *Annals Am. Acad. Pol. and Soc. Sci.* 132, 139 (1979).

94. Orfield, *supra* note 4, at 239; Gary Orfield, "Segregated Housing, Educational Inequality, and the Possibility of Urban Integration," 16 (1988) (paper prepared for the Urban Institute Symposium on Residential Mobility and Minority Incomes, on file with the author).

95. Farley and Frey, *supra* note 5, at 38.

96. Harrison and Bennett, *supra* note 5, at 141.

97. Nancy A. Denton and Bridget Anderson, "A Tale of Five Cities" (1995) (paper presented at the meeting of the Population Association of America, on file with the author).

98. Ibid. This research uses a classification scheme of 100 African Americans, Hispanics, Asians, or non-Hispanic whites to indicate a group's presence in a neighborhood and defines neighborhoods as census tracts.

99. Alba et al., *supra* note 73, at 625, 641–44.

100. Ibid., 640.

101. Ibid., 643.

102. Ibid., 638–39.

103. Massey and Denton, *supra* note 3, at 200–205.

104. See Rossell, *supra* note 93, at 480–83 (giving many examples of combinations of magnet and voluntary school desegregation plans, especially those that allow within-district variations across schools to improve black-white exposure, even though a few schools remain segregated).

105. J. S. Fuerst and Roy Petty, "Quiet Success: Where Managed School Integration Works," 10 *Am. Prospect* 65, 65, 72 (1992).

106. Joe T. Darden, "Neighborhood Racial Composition and School Desegregation in New Castle County, Delaware," in *Metropolitan Desegregation, supra* note 69, at 123, 124; Diana Pearce, "Beyond Busing: New Evidence on the Impact of Metropolitan School Desegregation on Housing Segregation," in *Metropolitan Desegregation, supra* note 69, at 97, 102–03.

107. See, e.g., Fred Freiberg, "Promoting Residential Integration: The Role of Private Fair Housing Groups," in *Housing Markets and Residential Mobility, supra* note 7, at 219, 240–41; George C. Galster, "The Case for Racial Integration," in

The Metropolis in Black and White, supra note 74, at 270, 272–77; Leslie Inniss, "School Desegregation: Too High a Price?" *Soc. Pol'y*, 6, 16 (winter 1993); Mary Haywood Metz, "Desegregation as Necessity and Challenge," 63 *J. Negro Educ.* 64, 64–65, 74–75 (1994).

108. See, e.g., Mittie Olson Chandler, "Obstacles to Housing Integration Program Efforts," in *The Metropolis in Black and White, supra* note 74, at 286, 300–302; Juliet Saltman, "Maintaining Racially Diverse Neighborhoods," 26 *Urb. Aff. Q.* 416, 429 (1991); Richard A. Smith, "Creating Stable Racially Integrated Communities: A Review," 15 *J. Urb. Aff.* 115, 128–31 (1993).

109. Harrison and Bennett, *supra* note 5, at 141, 147–53.

110. See Orfield, *supra* note 4, at 252 ("Developers were told that they could have a neighborhood school, which would greatly help in the marketing of their housing, only if they developed a plan to market it to an integrated market and thus create a naturally integrated community").

111. Joe R. Feagin and Hernan Vera, *White Racism: The Basics*, 25 (1995).

112. Kenneth Clark states: "Reluctantly, I am forced to face the likely possibility that the United States will never rid itself of racism and reach true integration. I look back and shudder at how naive we all were in our belief in the steady progress racial minorities would make through programs of litigation and education, and while I very much hope for the emergence of a revived civil rights movement with innovative programs and dedicated leaders, I am forced to recognize that my life has, in fact, been a series of glorious defeats." Kenneth B. Clark, "Racial Progress and Retreat: A Personal Memoir," in *Race in America: The Struggle for Equality*, 3, 18 (Herbert Hill and James E. Jones, eds., 1993); see also Derrick Bell, *Faces at the Bottom of the Well: The Permanence of Racism*, 21 (1982); Shaw, *supra* note 37, at 909 ("I tend to be susceptible to anger. I have to fight bitterness, because bitterness is corrosive and destructive. I may not be as optimistic as some . . . about where we are on race in this country").

113. Metz, *supra* note 107, at 64.

114. Christopher G. Ellison and Daniel A. Powers, "The Contact Hypothesis and Racial Attitudes among Black Americans," 75 *Soc. Sci. Q.* 385. 396 (1994).

115. Lee Sigelman and Susan Welch, "The Contact Hypothesis Revisited: Black-White Interaction and Positive Racial Attitudes," 71 *Soc. Forces* 781, 781, 792 (1993).

116. See Rosenbaum et al., *supra* note 90, at 1529, 1533–39 (noting statistical improvement in educational achievement and job prospects, among others).

117. Jennifer L. Hochschild, *Facing Up to the American Dream: Race, Class, and the Soul of the Nation* (1995).

118. Ibid., 252–53.

119. Ibid., 157–83.

120. Ibid., 259–60.

121. Feagin and Vera, *supra* note 111, at 191.

Chapter 5

Metropolitan School Desegregation: Impacts on Metropolitan Society

Gary Orfield

Recently the Supreme Court handed down a number of decisions that authorized the dismantling of school desegregation plans. In *School Board of Oklahoma City v. Dowell*,[1] *Freeman v. Pitts*,[2] and *Missouri v. Jenkins*,[3] the Court permitted a return to segregated neighborhood schools, at times questioning the feasibility and democratic foundation for desegregation. I will argue that desegregation of schools is both feasible and an expression of our democratic norms. I will also show that the most extensive forms of desegregation not only may be the most successful in the long run, but also may lead to a broader form of democracy in school policy. This examination will be informed by our changing urban metropolitan demographic as well as forty years of experience with various desegregation efforts.

Since *Brown*,[4] there have been remarkable changes in the composition of our population and its distribution within metropolitan areas. Central cities, now often referred to as the "inner city," became the home of growing racial minorities as whites and, more recently, middle-income minorities fled to the suburbs. Although these changes profoundly affect the feasibility of various forms of desegregation and have occurred in all parts of the country, they have been either ignored or misunderstood by the courts. Even as the courts began to focus attention on these changes, they often blamed the changes, described as "white flight," on desegregation itself, using this as a basis for ending desegregation orders. The courts have not considered, however, the possibility that their own limited remedies may have substantially contributed to the racial sorting that has occurred in this country over the last forty years.

School desegregation policy arose out of a decision that the Constitution required striking down legal barriers to interracial education. Not until twenty-seven years after *Brown*, in 1971, however, did the Supreme Court hand down its first decision explicitly addressing the issues of urban desegregation.[5] Nothing was decided about desegregating the urban North until *Keyes v. School District No. 1* in 1973.[6]

Then, a year later in *Milliken*, the Supreme Court found that even though the Detroit schools had been segregated intentionally by the state, a remedy could not include the suburbs. The Court based its decision on the theory that autonomy of the suburbs represented a basic constitutional value effectively limiting the rights of Detroit's black students.[7] Justice Potter Stewart, the swing vote against including suburbs in desegregation plans, expressed puzzlement about how the suburbs had become so extremely segregated.[8] Housing segregation, he said, came from "unknown or perhaps unknowable factors."[9] Thurgood Marshall predicted in his dissent that attempting to desegregate public schools wholly from within the city of Detroit would be an exercise in futility and would cause white flight.[10] History has proven him right. Detroit was the second most segregated metropolitan area in the United States in 1992 and 1993.[11] Since 1974, the Supreme Court has done nothing positive about the metropolitan dimension of school segregation, despite the fact that more than three-fourths of the population and about nine-tenths of minority students reside in metropolitan areas.[12] Virtually all of our big-city school districts have large majorities of minority students, whether or not those districts instituted busing.

Various desegregation plans have been adopted since 1971. Today, therefore, we are in a position to compare the long-term effects of various desegregation plans ranging from unchanged neighborhood schools to small voluntary plans, to mandatory transfers inside central cities, to racial balance mandates across entire metropolitan areas.

Metropolitan-wide desegregation, rather than the fragmented plan ordered by the Court in Detroit, has been the most successful and stable. In the rural South early desegregation efforts that followed the metropolitan-wide plan have been the most successful. These remain the most integrated school districts today in the United States.[13] By contrast, desegregation efforts have stalled in the urban North and West where fragmented individual district plans were adopted.

Consider the very different scenarios presented by cities affected by the first Supreme Court decisions on urban desegregation. The very first urban case, *Swann v. Charlotte-Mecklenburg Board of Education*,[14] dealt with mandatory desegregation across the city and suburbs of Charlotte, which had been combined into one large, county-wide school district before the case arose. This metropolitan plan has been operating successfully for a quarter century. Two years later, the next major case desegregated a central-city district in Denver.[15] Legislators passed the Poundstone Amendment, a state constitutional amendment cutting off Denver's school district from further expansion. This amendment guaranteed that further growth in the school-age population would be outside the reach of the desegregation order.[16] Also in 1973, the Supreme Court upheld a lower court order blocking the desegregation of metropolitan Richmond, an area then about the same size as metropolitan Charlotte.[17]

By the early 1990s, Richmond had an overwhelmingly black city system with almost no desegregation.[18] Denver won a release from court supervision in 1995 for what had become a heavily minority school district.[19] Charlotte, however, continued its county-wide desegregation, years after the federal court's supervision ended. In the mid-1990s, its county-wide district was gaining more white students both numerically and proportionally. In 1995, Charlotte voters overwhelmingly defeated candidates supporting partial dismantling of desegregation.[20]

These outcomes suggest that the more extensive the desegregation plan, the better—precisely the opposite of the widely shared assumption that the smallest plans are the least disruptive, most stable, and most likely to succeed. This analysis further suggests that the current trend toward resegregation through a return to neighborhood schools is based on simple-minded and inaccurate assumptions. Those who believe that returning to neighborhood schools can reverse metropolitan demographic changes ignore the fact that such changes have been taking place for decades in cities that already have neighborhood schools.

Initial Propositions on School Desegregation

White Flight

Since the early 1970s, the courts have moved backwards in their understanding of metropolitan communities. The first urban desegregation decisions showed a sensitivity toward complex interactions between segregated schools and segregated housing. They also reflected an awareness that cities continually change and that the expansion of identified minority areas due to discrimination and fears of ghetto growth largely shapes that change. Later decisions, however, do not reflect this awareness. The remedies are static and ignore the relationship between educational and housing discrimination. Most recently, while approving resegregation, some courts have suggested that the resumption of segregated neighborhood schooling may stabilize enrollment. Those decisions, however, fail to examine the record of school districts that have already implemented neighborhood schools.

When the Supreme Court first ordered desegregation of schools in American cities outside the South, it found that school segregation in those communities was the result of a complex interaction between educational and housing discrimination. The Court found that practices such as faculty discrimination, gerrymandering, and selection of segregated building sites had marked certain schools as black schools, and such marking in turn affected the willingness of whites to move into or stay in neighborhoods with such schools. Over time, these trends marked entire parts of cities as ghettos or barrios and eventually transformed entire central cities into an almost all non-white public school district. Residential segregation was so extensive that many schools would remain segregated even if the specific problems identified by the Court were eliminated. The Court concluded that residential segregation itself was not something that just happened. Rather, segregation was the product of the long-term effects of school segregation on the structure of the community and of other governmental actions in housing and urban development. In the first northern school case, *Keyes v. School District No. 1*,[21] the Court concluded that segregation of "neighborhood" schools could influence enrollment in other schools and that racial "earmarking" of schools "may have a profound reciprocal effect on the racial composition of residential neighborhoods within a metropolitan area, thereby causing further racial concentration within the schools."[22]

The assertion that school racial patterns could affect housing was not limited to the Burger Court; it was also expressed by leading critics of desegregation plans in the antibusing movement. The antibusing groups, as well as the experts that school districts hired to fight school desegregation plans, contended that transferring students to integrated schools affected housing decisions. The advocates of the white flight theory, beginning with James Coleman's 1975 article,[23] argued that mandatory desegregation plans in city school districts induced whites to move away from those cities. The Supreme Court itself agreed with this theory in the 1995 decision, *Missouri v. Jenkins*.[24] The white flight theory clearly rested on the belief that changing the racial composition of schools changed residential decisions of families.

White support for school integration has increased greatly in the past two generations.[25] However, the evidence suggests that although most whites support desegregation up to about the 50 percent minority level, few wish to have their children in schools with whites as the minority population.[26] Perhaps white families move for fear that racial transition in schools would isolate white children. White resistance also may be related to overwhelmingly non-white schools with high levels of poverty and social problems. Neighborhood schools along racial boundaries tend to experience rapid racial transition, often exacerbated by a concurrent residential transition. Many city desegregation plans reassign white students to heavily minority schools, leaving all-white middle-class schools in nearby suburbs completely untouched. If the fear of racial transition and racial and class isolation affects residential choice, then the most wide-ranging desegregation plans must distribute desegregation across an area broad enough to create a stable middle-class white majority in virtually all schools. Under such circumstances, the benefit of flight declines, since there are no nearby all-white alternatives. The motivation for flight also declines, since there is little threat that whites will become isolated minorities in virtually all-black schools. Desegregation plans that cover entire urbanized counties have produced the highest levels of desegregation and the nation's most stable districts in their percentage of white enrollment.[27] White flight is more likely to occur in a fractured intradistrict plan that isolates schools with a majority of low-income and minority students.

County-Wide Desegregation as a Social Experiment

Metropolitan school integration, one of the most important urban experiments during the last quarter century, has been ignored, despite its proven feasibility and durability in a number of large U.S. metropolitan areas. This experiment has affected hundreds of thousands more students than such widely discussed issues as vouchers, Afrocentric schools, or contracting management of schools to private firms, but it largely has been ignored in civil rights policy debate since the Supreme Court defended suburban autonomy in the 1974 Detroit litigation.

Unlike housing desegregation policies, such as the Clinton administration's Moving to Opportunity program,[28] which affects only a few thousand households, or small-scale programs matching city residents with suburban jobs, metropolitan school desegregation is a radical and far-reaching policy affecting all schools within some metropolitan areas and nine-tenths of all young people growing up in such areas.

Metropolitan school desegregation plans have operated for twenty-five years in a number of large and rapidly growing Sunbelt metropolitan areas. More than a million students attend the school districts listed below in table 1, all in the seventy-five largest systems in the United States and most of which have had city-suburban desegregation plans in place for at least the last twenty years. This experience should be considered a primary subject for urban policy analysis.

Some of the areas where this experiment is operating are the nation's most educationally integrated communities and rapidly growing metropolitan economies. Metropolitan desegregation tends to produce far more stable and extensive desegregation in predominantly middle-class schools, yielding the greatest benefits for minority students and minimizing threats to white neighborhoods.[29] As importantly, it counters the trend toward multiple school districts within a given metropolitan area deeply separated by race, class, and politics. The children of the most powerful and least powerful sectors of the community must depend on the same large institution, and all races and classes have a vital interest in its success. This, in turn, can affect the decisions families make about housing, neighborhoods, and business. People have very little incentive to make residential choices on the basis of a school's racial concentration, since none of the schools are segregated or threaten to become segregated soon and none are isolated and all-white. All schools then would be supported by the same tax base. Local employers cannot pick and choose among school districts; the local school system must work. Business does not have the incentive to flee to another nearby school district without leaving the

Table 1 Large School Districts with Metro Desegregation, 1990

District	Number of Students
Broward County (Ft. Lauderdale)	161,000
Clark County (Las Vegas)	122,000
Nashville-Davidson County	68,500
Jacksonville (Duval County)	111,000
Tampa	123,900
St. Petersburg	94,400
Jefferson County (Louisville)	91,500
Indianapolis[a]	48,100
Charlotte-Mecklenburg Wilmington (4 districts)	77,100
Orlando (Orange County)	103,000
Palm Beach County	106,000

[a] The Indianapolis plan also includes many independent suburban districts which are mandated to receive and educate minority students from the city.

metropolitan community entirely. Economic development throughout the metropolitan area requires the school district to function effectively and to be seen as a community asset.

Policy makers often ignore school issues in urban housing research. The Carter administration attempted to address school issues with the creation of a joint school and housing desegregation litigation section in the Justice Department's Civil Rights Division[30] and by initiating research and policy proposals within HUD.[31] The Reagan administration quickly abandoned these initiatives, which have never been resumed. Given that cities continue to decline, however, and that funds for direct federal urban interventions are likely to be small and diminishing for the foreseeable future, an educational policy with the potential to positively affect urban conditions deserves careful scrutiny by both the courts and the elected branches of government.

Philosophic Rationales for Area-Wide Metropolitan Districts

In one of the greatest classics of American political thought, the *Federalist Papers,* James Madison wrote that the best way to cure the evil of narrow factions pursuing narrow interests undermining the interest of the broader community is to expand the scope of the community.[32] By bringing a wider diversity of interests into a larger government, he said, there would be less likelihood of the tyranny of a narrow majority and greater likelihood of a full debate leading to the pursuit of broader community-wide interests. Madison reasoned that "the smaller the society" deciding a policy, the more likely that a local majority, not balanced by other forces and considerations, will "concert and execute their plans of oppression."[33] In arguing for the creation of the federal government, he said that a bigger polity would make more probable both genuine freedom and effectiveness.[34] Even though the United States was then an overwhelmingly rural society with limited need for a federal government, Madison argued that the costs of extreme localism were great.[35]

When the Founding Fathers thought about the problems of governing the country, they tried to reason from the history of other societies. When we think about the problems of providing public education within metropolitan communities, we have something much better: examples of both fragmented and unified metropolitan approaches to desegregation. Among multiple-district metropolitan areas, there are almost no examples of communities with significant minority populations able to provide substantially desegregated schools and obtain access to middle-class schools for most minority children. In many such areas, the central-city school system is the target of intense public discussion, almost all of it negative. Since the early 1980s, most states have enacted education reforms that impose some form of state-wide testing and require publication of comparative results.[36] When these results are published, they show the very low achievement levels of central-city schools relative to suburban schools. They often show that some of the worst achieving schools in the state are in big cities that are spending more than the state average on students. These data tend to produce ongoing attacks on urban school systems and their leaders, who are often the most visible minority educators in the region.

Typically the blame is placed on the central-city bureaucracy, and the response is to tighten state requirements and to encourage alternatives to the existing system, such as transfers, charter schools, private contracting for control of public schools, vouchers to use private schools, radical decentralization to the school level, taking over the public school system in the central city, and so forth. In central cities, where even minority middle-class children no longer use the schools, local elected officials often join the attack on the city school system. New York's Rudolph Giuliani, Richard M. Daley of Chicago, and Mayor Raymond Flynn of Boston were among those following this strategy recently.[37] Some minority mayors also have adopted this tactic.[38]

If unequal performance is actually rooted in the social and educational isolation of city students and not in the administration of the city schools, such attacks are likely to be extremely counterproductive, weakening and demoralizing the city school staffs without producing gains for children. Such attacks also accelerate middle-class departure from schools and communities and continuously weaken the political base for attracting additional assistance from the outside. Since schools and the quality of the local labor force are vital factors in determining the location of businesses, negative beliefs can intensify the economic decline of central cities; this, in turn, produces more middle-class departures and deepens the problems of local families, feeding the vicious cycles.

As the city population becomes increasingly dominated by aging, low-income families with no children in the schools, the possibility of local tax increases declines even as leverage for assistance from other levels of government deteriorates. The result is a continuously deteriorating central-city system providing the only option for the children who need education most urgently. The fact that this system will be overwhelmingly non-white only reinforces racial stereotypes. Often minority administrators end up with the job of imposing cuts and being blamed for low achievement.

School Segregation Differences Related
to Size of Districts

The Supreme Court's 1974 decision in the Detroit case, *Milliken v. Bradley*,[39] which limited desegregation orders to single districts except in extraordinary conditions,[40] meant that whether or not minority students could be desegregated depended to a substantial degree on how their state happened to organize its school districts. In New England, where tiny towns dated back to colonial days and where a city like Boston had been cut off from expansion long before the automobile age, a given school district included only a small fraction of the students in the urban community. Boston, for example, had only one-eleventh of the students in the Boston metropolitan area, but served the greatest concentration of black students. Thus under *Milliken*, the vast majority of Boston's middle class was beyond the reach of the city's desegregation plan. Florida, on the other hand—a state with a much higher proportion of black students— was totally organized in county-wide systems, most of which included both the central city and its suburbs in a single district. In Orlando, Jacksonville, and Tampa, whites and blacks were in the same big district and could be desegregated by a single court order.

One rough measure of the impact of school district organization is the relationship between the size of the average school district in a state and the level of segregation of that state's students. As table 2 shows, among the states with the largest average size of school districts, often meaning school district organizations at the county level, no state reports much more than one-third of its black students in intensely segregated schools. Among the states with the smallest districts, on the other hand, those with large black populations tend to be dramatically segregated. All of the states with the highest levels of segregation for black students had relatively small school districts and fragmented district patterns.

None of the states with the largest school districts is located in the North. The fact that county government was historically much more important in the southern and border states and in parts of the West meant that these regions often met the federal desegregation challenge with county-wide school districts containing enough of the local housing market and large enough white populations to make long-term and comprehensive desegregation much more viable. Unfortunately, the states where a large majority of Hispanics were enrolled—California, Texas, New York, Illinois—had small, fractured districts and the most segregated schools.

The level of segregation for African American and Hispanic students attending schools in large central cities is several times higher than that

Table 2 Average Size of School Districts and Level of Segregation, States with Largest and Smallest Districts, 1991–1992

Largest Districts	Median Enrollment	Black Students in Intensely Segregated Schools (%)
Alabama	3,905	36.8
Delaware	3,479	0.0
Florida	12,028	24.9
Louisiana	6,526	34.4
Maryland	13,165	36.7
Nevada	3,184	0.0
North Carolina	4,838	6.2
South Carolina	3,592	17.7
Tennessee	3,235	37.3
Virginia	3,571	6.4

Smallest Districts	Median Enrollment	Black Students in Intensely Segregated Schools (%)
Arkansas	687	8.2
California	1,396	33.7
Colorado	521	0.1
Connecticut	1,827	36.2
Illinois	795	59.3
Indiana	1,906	25.9
Massachusetts	1,821	12.5
Michigan	1,674	58.5
Missouri	556	26.2
Nebraska	37	0.0
New Jersey	971	54.6
New York	1,431	57.5
Ohio	1,768	12.9
Oklahoma	355	14.4
Texas	801	30.2
Wisconsin	924	16.6

Source: National Center for Education Statistics, *Directory of Public Elementary and Secondary Education Agencies*, 1991–92, Table 6.
Note: States with less than 5 percent African American students have been omitted.

found in smaller communities. Segregation is lowest in the places once considered most resistant to racial change: small towns and rural areas. As table 3 shows, this heightened isolation is not merely racial; it is also reflected in isolation by poverty and by inferior schooling along many dimensions. Although racial attitudes were most negative in the rural and small-town South, those areas achieved much higher levels of desegregation because their districts were likely to include both whites and blacks in the area.

Table 3 Segregation Patterns by Type of Community School Segregation of Blacks and Hispanics, 1991–1992

| School | Large Metros | | Small Metros | | Towns | | Rural |
Race (%)	City	Suburbs	City	Suburbs	25,000+	Small	Areas
90–100% Minority							
Blacks	63.9	21.5	27.4	14.6	12.2	9.3	17.3
Hispanics	56.2	22.4	32.8	13.7	4.2	20.0	19.3
50–100% Minority							
Blacks	92.4	57.9	62.9	43.0	45.5	44.9	45.8
Hispanics	93.8	63.9	70.4	51.4	44.0	60.5	46.5
Majority White							
Blacks	7.6	42.1	37.1	57.0	54.5	55.1	54.2
Hispanics	6.2	31.1	29.6	48.6	56.0	39.5	53.5

Source: Gary Orfield, *The Growth of Segregation in American Schools: Changing Patterns of Separation and Poverty since 1968.* Alexandria, Va.: National School Boards Association, 1993, 20–21.
Note: Large metros have a central city with a population over 400,000. Likewise, small metros have a central city with a population under 400,000.

In 1986, the twenty-five largest central-city systems contained 30 percent Hispanic students, 27 percent blacks, and 3 percent whites. This extremely unequal distribution of students shows the inefficacy of the Supreme Court's efforts to desegregate within these districts. Comparing the largest city and county-wide districts in the early 1990s, table 4 shows that the latter start out with almost twice the percentage of white students. They have vastly better possibilities of both enrolling minority students in majority white, middle-class schools and maintaining desegregation long enough to make a significant impact.

Table 4 Racial Composition of Central City and County-Wide School Districts in Metropolitan Areas over 1,000,000 Population, 1991–1992

	White (%)	Black (%)	Hispanic (%)
Central city	28.9	35.6	28.6
County-wide	51.1	26.2	20.7

Source: Computations were gathered from the U.S. Department of Education, *Common Core of Education Statistics* (Washington, D.C., 1992).

Table 5 Most Stable Large School Systems, 1967–1986
Decline in Percent of White Students

School System	White Students (%)
Broward County, FL	9
Palm Beach County, FL	9
Greeneville, SC	7
Albuquerque, NM	6
Jordan, UT	5
Mobile, AL	4
Pinellas County, FL	4
Cobb County, GA	4
Ann Arundel County, MD	3
Polk County, FL	2

Note: Washington, D.C., was omitted from this because its white percentage in 1967 was only 8 percent.

Another sign that the scale of a district matters can be found in data on the stability of the racial proportions in school systems, a fundamental issue in the white flight literature. A study of racial change over a nineteen-year period found that among the nation's sixty largest school districts, a majority of the ten districts with the least decline in percentage of white students (9 percent or less) had county-wide desegregation plans in place.[41] Three of the four others had the advantage of being county-wide systems, though they lacked overall desegregation plans, and two had very few minority students. In contrast, most of the ten with the largest declines in percentage of white students were in central-city systems with no mandatory student reassignments.[42] A number of the county-wide school districts had less of an increase in percentage of minority students than the entire country experienced from changing birth rates and immigration patterns—forces obviously independent of desegregation plans.

The Value of District Consolidation

Recent Creation of County-Wide Districts Without Court Orders

The economic cost of central-city school systems that are in serious decline has recently led several communities in the South to merge their city and suburban school districts into single county-wide systems. Following the great success of metropolitan Charlotte and Raleigh, two of the South's most economically buoyant areas that merged their school districts a generation ago, decisions have been taken to merge school systems in Chattanooga and Knoxville, Tennessee,[43] as well as Durham and Greensboro, North Carolina.[44] The North Carolina state government put considerable pressure on localities to consolidate into county-wide districts. This was not done for desegregation purposes but, instead, because the state believed broader districts were more efficient and effective.[45]

North Carolina's and Tennessee's efforts can be seen as part of a larger trend toward school district consolidation in the twentieth century. The United States went from 108,579 districts in 1942 to 67,355 in 1952 and 34,678 in 1962.[46] The numbers continued to decline rapidly to 15,781 in 1972, but then virtually stalled.[47] In 1992, there were still 14,600 districts.[48] Consolidation was pushed hard by state governments during much of the twentieth century in the belief that larger, more comprehensive school systems would provide stronger educational programs. The movement faltered, however, when it moved from rural and small town consolidation to metropolitan areas. The initiatives in these two southern states, however, are a welcome sign that the trend toward consolidation continues.

Desegregation Possibilities and Support in Merged Districts

Support for desegregation on a county-wide level was strongly reaffirmed in 1995 elections in both Raleigh and Charlotte. In both counties supporters of integration won school board elections, and in Raleigh the local chamber of commerce endorsed continuing the desegregation plan. In Charlotte, desegregation supporters won all of the district seats and two-thirds of the at-large seats.[49] Superintendent John Murphy, who had worked with the business community to cut back desegregation, resigned following the election and did not find another superintendency.[50] These positive outcomes came at the same time that many areas with plans limited to central cities were moving to dismantle desegregation. One of the reasons Raleigh and Charlotte voters endorsed continuing desegregation was that both districts were experiencing reverse white flight. In striking contrast to the national enrollment picture and the trends in almost all large urban districts, both the number and percent of white students were increasing as shown in table 6.[51]

Metropolitan school districts also bring about concrete differences in educational possibilities. The norm in multidistrict metropolitan areas is intense isolation of students by both race and income. There is a concentration of more affluent children in the schools with the highest completion

Table 6 Wake County Public Schools (Metropolitan Raleigh)

Year	Total Enrollment	Minority Enrollment	Minority (%)
1976	55,649	16,025	28.8
1987	59,687	17,885	30.0
1988	60,985	17,366	28.5
1989	62,462	17,725	28.4
1990	64,243	17,588	27.4
1991	66,915	18,108	27.1
1992	70,052	18,495	26.4
1993	73,192	18,865	25.8

1976 to 1993: Minority enrollment change   +17.7%
               White enrollment change   +37.1%
               Total enrollment change   +31.5%
Source: Wake County Public School System data.

and achievement levels, the richest curriculum, and the best connections to college. Normally, minority children, particularly low-income minority children, have little or no access to the schools and teachers that most successfully prepare students for college. In single-district metropolitan areas, by contrast, desegregation ends or greatly reduces high-poverty minority schools and opens the best schools to non-white students. Affluent white children grow up in interracial schools with real exposure to working-class and poor people rather than in the isolation of white, upper-class suburbia. This is a major change in the most important public institution provided by American society. It clearly and dramatically changes the possibilities for many minority students, and it denies higher-income whites their normal status of almost total isolation in homogeneous schools with few if any non-white or low-income students.

The possibilities of desegregation, of course, are not always realized. Whether or not the full benefits are obtained depends on fair treatment within the receiving school, the preparation and attitudes of the teachers, grouping and tracking policies, and other factors.[52] Nonetheless, moving from a failing school to a far more successful school greatly increases possible benefits.

The Interaction of Education and Housing

Impacts on Residential Integration

The first study to link metropolitan school desegregation to housing was conducted in 1980 by Diana Pearce.[53] Her research for the National Institute of Education showed that in areas without metropolitan desegregation plans, housing advertisements were replete with racial signals.[54] Schools mentioned in advertisements were white schools, often in areas where people might not know the racial composition of the region without a school reference.[55] Minority schools were never mentioned.[56] Such racial signals were absent, however, in the metropolitan areas with areawide desegregation.[57] Realtors tended to promote areas more equally, and deemphasized the importance of schools and, implicitly, of race. Other factors such as length and convenience of work commutes became more important.[58] Segregated schools made it possible to identify the racial composition of a neighborhood, and for realtors to perpetuate beliefs about the desirability of a neighborhood based on race.[59]

A subsequent paper by Pearce and Robert Crain suggested that city-wide desegregation plans increased residential desegregation from 1970 to 1980 in the cities studied.[60] A study now underway shows that residential segregation declined much more sharply from 1970 to 1990 in districts with county-wide desegregation plans than in similar metropolitan areas without such plans. Preliminary data suggest that metropolitan desegregation is related to twice as large an average decline in the residential segregation index during this two-decade period.

There are several other possible intersections between metropolitan school desegregation and housing. What, for example, is the effect on an African American family's housing knowledge and choices when their children go to suburban schools and the family becomes involved in the life of a suburban school community? When children go to school across race and class lines, does it affect their housing preferences as adults?

On both these issues there are some intriguing findings. In Milwaukee, where the state government funded voluntary transfers of city minority students to cooperating suburban school districts and now supports an expanded program under a consent decree, research shows that many of the minority families involved developed a strong interest in the possibility of moving to the suburbs.[61] Black and white adults who had attended integrated schools were more likely to live in integrated neighborhoods.[62] A fifteen-year longitudinal study comparing similar groups of minority students in Hartford who did or did not transfer to the suburbs under a voluntary desegregation program showed that those attending suburban schools were considerably more likely to live in integrated communities as adults.[63] It may be that educational experience strongly affects housing preferences by affecting levels of comfort with, and toleration for, interracial neighborhood contact. Preliminary data from the twenty-year study noted above support this conclusion.

Opponents of school and housing desegregation policies often argue that segregation cannot be defeated because the steady spread of ghettos is built into the incompatible housing preferences of whites and blacks. Because the average American household moves every six years, neighborhoods must continuously replace their populations. If, according to a theory articulated by Thomas Shelling[64] and examined empirically by Reynolds Farley and others,[65] blacks move into an area in greater concentrations than most whites prefer, the housing market will shift and the area will become more and more black, even though both races are willing to accept some level of integration. The basic claim is that by the time a neighborhood becomes comfortable for blacks, it is no longer acceptable to whites, rendering interracial neighborhoods highly unstable.[66] The policy implication that may be drawn from this is that since neighborhoods are inherently unstable, school desegregation is not feasible without constant changes in plans. The theory has also been used to attack housing desegregation efforts as exercises in futility. In many recent school desegregation cases, including the 1992 Supreme Court decision *Freeman v. Pitts*,[67] this argument was very important in supporting the proposition that housing preference structures produce a natural process of spreading segregation that the school systems cannot change, and therefore school districts should simply be allowed to return to segregated neighborhood schools. Surveys have been conducted by expert witnesses for school district defendants in a number of localities to try to create evidence to convince courts of these propositions.

Preferences grow out of experience and they change. Research is needed on ways in which experiences in interracial schools, particularly in the kind of integrated schools made possible by a city-suburban desegregation plan, change preferences in ways that make it easier to achieve widespread desegregation of housing.[68] Without metropolitan school desegregation plans, the concentration of minority housing on the boundaries of existing minority areas means that the only whites who will experience significant contact with non-whites in their neighborhoods or neighborhood schools are less affluent families living near ghettos. Usually that contact is brief and negative because it occurs during a racial transition often overlaid with severe social tensions and resentments. Much of the natural school integration occurring in cities without desegregation plans takes place in a situation of rapid white displacement. Usually the school resegregates much faster than the neighborhood because newcomers are younger, have more school-age children, and rely more heavily on public schools than the whites they replace.

In thinking about housing-school relationships, it is critically important to realize that the thousands of segregated minority schools in New York, Los Angeles, Chicago, Detroit, and many other cities were all interracial at some point but became resegregated, mostly through neighborhood transition. However, this entails not the limitation of desegregation, but the flaw of a fractured approach such as neighborhood schools. It is school integration at the neighborhood level that is unstable.

Under the typical city-only desegregation plan formulated after the Supreme Court blocked the path to city-suburban integration in *Milliken v. Bradley*,[69] suburban whites are largely isolated from any desegregation, except in suburbs where a sizable minority community forms. Whites choosing to live in the city, on the other hand, could well face an integration plan that places all white children in schools with large non-white majorities and high numbers of educationally disadvantaged low-income children. A white child in Cleveland, for example, might face assignment to a school that was integrated at the 80 percent African American level with 60 percent poor children, while three miles into the suburbs a similar child would go to a 99 percent white school with very few, if any, low-income children. Such differences are not unusual, and they reinforce the long-established suburbanization trend. They also spur out-migration of minority middle-class families.

A return to neighborhood schools in such a setting, often advocated by those fighting to preserve a white, middle-class population for the city, likely would not work. Central cities with neighborhood schools still house disproportionate numbers of minority and low-income children. Minority residential areas and schools continue to expand on their peripheries, producing racial and class change neighborhood by neighborhood and rarely producing a school that can compete with suburban schools.

One need only study the demographics of many central cities without busing plans, such as Chicago, Los Angeles, and Atlanta, to see the way in which neighborhood schools have failed to hold white families. After Atlanta's black leaders worked out a compromise in 1973 to drop a desegregation case in return for black control of the school administration, city leaders hoped it would stop white flight.[70] Atlanta schools, however, have had one of the nation's most dramatic declines in white enrollment, followed by a massive departure of the black middle-class to a sector of suburbia.[71]

Metropolitan desegregation plans alter conditions and incentives for families in key respects. The right of affluent families to attend homogeneous, high-status schools is built into beliefs about housing markets in many urban communities, where land-use and housing policies make residence by less affluent families impossible and where traditions of private discrimination exclude blacks. The right to attend such schools is commonly understood and marketed as part of buying an expensive house in an exclusive community—almost a property right. Although Americans strongly support the goal of equal educational opportunity for all, they also support—without recognizing the contradiction—the reality of far better educational opportunity for those who both have the money to buy it and do not face housing market discrimination. Metropolitan school desegregation partially detaches the best school opportunities from housing wealth and significantly lowers the intense class stratification of schools within metropolitan areas.

Given that desegregation plans change the experience of children and families, it is reasonable to think these changes would impact the residential choices families make. Area-wide desegregation would make city neighborhoods more viable and suburban communities somewhat less alluring, since white families moving within the area would be assured of integrated, rather than segregated, schools.

Subsidized Housing and Segregated Schools

Just as there have been few serious looks at the impact of school desegregation on housing integration, there has been little systematic study of the impact of subsidized housing on school integration. Housing policies have clearly contributed to the national problem of segregated schools. The only HUD-funded studies of this problem were conducted a decade and a half ago, and they showed dramatic relationships between subsidized housing and segregated schools in metropolitan St. Louis, Columbus, Phoenix, Denver, and Dallas.[72] In some communities, different placement and tenanting of subsidized housing could have eliminated much of the need for busing to produce integrated schools. Other HUD studies of the location and tenancy of subsidized housing suggest the likelihood of similar problems in many metropolitan regions.[73] A study of one of the most rapidly growing urban counties of the 1980s, Florida's Palm Beach County, showed a serious subsidized housing contribution to segregation there.[74]

Many of the census tracts with the highest levels of concentrated poverty and with the schools having the highest dropout rates are in communities where large numbers of the students live in federally subsidized housing.[75] The first city in the United States to return to neighborhood elementary schools with federal court approval, Norfolk, Virginia, instantly created schools where the students were nearly all African American and poor; some of these schools were dominated by students in subsidized housing.[76]

The Need for Better Housing Survey Research

One reason why there has not been more research on the school-housing relationship has been that surveys on housing choice often have not shown schools to be a serious consideration. There have been many surveys of why people choose homes and neighborhoods, but they tend to show that schools are a relatively unimportant feature compared to price, location, physical attributes, and other factors.[77] Questions asked in many housing choice surveys may be deeply misleading because they do not tap the ways in which home-seekers *define* communities before even beginning the process of searching in a community and choosing a particular unit. In the surveys, a very important prior question is omitted: "Why don't you consider looking for housing in the central city and certain parts of the inner suburbs or satellite cities?" If one were to visit real estate offices or sample relocation services in major metropolitan areas, it would become apparent that whites of higher economic and social status are almost never shown or asked to see homes in areas with heavily nonwhite schools.[78] This fact is so deeply built into the housing search process for many home-seekers, and there are so many other unattractive beliefs about urban neighborhoods (concerning violence and other problems), that the possibility is not considered. As political scientists have noted, sometimes the most important decisions to understand are nondecisions; the most important questions are those whose answers are so deeply predetermined that the question is not even posed.[79]

If white, suburban parents around Detroit or Newark or other older central cities were asked whether or not they would consider buying in an area where their children would have to attend city schools, the responses would doubtless contradict the impression of low concern about schooling that one might receive from the housing search literature. Since most of these studies were conceived with housing as a central focus and without considering schools, the responses tell much less than may be apparent. Polls show a sharp rise in white resistance to school integration, given the possibility of their children attending a majority non-white school (even among families perfectly willing to accept substantial integration). Such resistance should be one of the issues explored in future research.

In many cities, middle-class whites with children, and a growing number of middle-class minority families, will not even look in the city for housing. Desirable neighborhoods that have never decayed, or historically interesting communities that have gentrified, typically are occupied by young families, singles, gays/lesbians, empty-nesters, or affluent users of private schools.[80] Often families move from such neighborhoods when their children reach school age unless there is a local school or magnet school that is integrated and predominantly middle class in student background.[81]

If these relationships are true, there should be substantial and measurable differences in urban residential patterns of families with and without school-age children. Those patterns should show the varying effects of different types of schools provided within those communities under various forms of desegregation plans or neighborhood school arrangements. This is clearly a case where better surveys, probing more deeply into the stages of housing choice, are needed. Likewise, more serious analysis of actual behavior, based on migration trends for families with school-age children, is also necessary. The degree to which such differences are apparent will, of course, depend also upon the overall migration trends into metropolitan areas, the nature of the housing stock that exists in the city, and other factors. Everything else being equal, however, research should reveal an impact on the decisions of young families, given that a good metropolitan desegregation plan diminishes the incentive to flee from the central cities and move to newer suburbs.

Urban Policy and School Data
Urban decision-makers who shape the nature of the local private housing markets with transportation, infrastructure, zoning, and land-use policies typically do not use school data and have no relationship with school officials in their planning processes. In thinking about social issues, urban policy tends to rely overwhelmingly on census data and to make little or no use of public school data. As a result, urban policy decisions typically are made with little or no understanding of their impact on schools, on the quality and nature of schooling offered where the development takes place, or on the potential of using different school policies to help shape development or redevelopment. HUD, for example, in seeking to avoid segregation in public housing, has relied on out-of-date census data on minority population concentrations. This data often leads to approving new housing or locating families in areas that appeared to be diverse in 1990 but currently have virtually all-minority, all-poor schools with very low levels of educational achievement. Needless to say, either investing in such communities or using housing policy in ways that resegregate integrated schools is likely to be highly counterproductive for the children living in those communities.

Most debate about urban policy and the underclass concludes that only a small percentage of minority residents live in situations of concentrated poverty, although the percentage is growing.[82] A vastly higher proportion of minority youths but extremely few whites, however, attend schools with high concentrations of impoverished students.[83] In other words, the negative conditions strongly associated with concentrated poverty are much more severe in our educational institutions than they are in our residential communities. Schools comprised of greater than 90 percent black and Hispanic students are more than fourteen times as likely as white schools to have a majority of children living in poverty.[84] Focusing on contacts among young people rather than on the overall population may be much more important in analyzing the impact of poverty on youth. If HUD and local governments wish to stabilize neighborhoods and improve educational mobility, these issues need to be considered.

Since black and Hispanic children show much more extreme isolation by both race and income, it is certainly critical to understand the impact on these populations of metropolitan school desegregation plans that disrupt the bleak patterns predominant in central city districts. Nearly a third of black and almost half of Hispanic children in the nation's largest urban school districts attend schools with more than 50 percent poor students. Large numbers are in almost totally impoverished schools. All the urban data suggest these trends will intensify.[85] Since the percentage of poor children in a school is an extremely strong predictor of inequality in educational outcomes,[86] these data deserve the attention of researchers on urban poverty. Data that show metropolitan school districts with less poverty are particularly important.

There has been only one federal case where the relationship to housing and school was fully developed. Late in the Carter administration there was a short-lived effort to relate school and housing desegregation issues. A Ford Foundation report demonstrated the total absence of such coordination. HUD, for example, often approved subsidized housing that directly undermined a school desegregation plan.[87] During the Carter years, the Justice Department's Civil Rights Division combined its school and housing sections and began to develop comprehensive litigation strategies to ask for coordinated remedies in the *Yonkers* case.[88] *Yonkers* led to a sweeping victory in Yonkers, New York; it remains the only case, fully developed by the Justice Department, that reflects the housing-school relationship. The Justice Department was actively considering other major cases in areas such as Phoenix.[89] However, with the advent of the Reagan administration, school and housing sections were reseparated within the Justice Department, and no more suits of this type were considered. This was unfortunate; combining these issues enables a systemic strategy for considering how various types of governmental agencies interact to foster metropolitan-wide segregation. Separating the issues is more consistent with a passing-the-blame strategy, where each institution puts the onus of responsibility on private attitudes and the actions of other institutions, thereby limiting its own accountability.

Near the end of the Carter administration, one of the last regulations HUD published required that housing decisions be made in ways that supported school integration.[90] Such consideration would have brought about significant changes in housing decisions, but the regulation was rescinded in the first days of the Reagan administration.[91] In its final year under President Carter, HUD commissioned exploratory research on school-housing interactions and sponsored conferences bringing together school and housing officials in Dallas and Denver.[92] The Denver session stimulated a number of local initiatives and experiments, including a successful effort to develop the last major vacant land in the city as an intentionally integrated community with a naturally integrated neighborhood school.[93] Since that time there has been no serious analysis of these issues and no substantial effort to coordinate policy.

The White Flight Controversy

The only research on school desegregation funded during the Reagan and Bush administrations concerned white flight. Nothing was done to study positive effects of metropolitan plans. The only federally funded studies included a study funded by the U.S. Commission on Civil Rights and another funded by the Department of Education, both undertaken by investigators who had testified for school districts *against* mandatory desegregation orders.[94] These studies essentially agreed with James Coleman's 1975 paper that had ignited controversy by positing a relationship between school desegregation and white flight.[95] Claiming that implementing busing plans accelerated the loss of white students from school districts, Coleman's study received intense national attention because of his stature as the director of the study of desegregation mandated by Congress in 1964.[96] The study lent academic substance to a very unpopular policy: busing.[97] It seemed as if a prominent academic with credibility in the field was saying that urban desegregation was a futile effort.

Coleman's linking of urban desegregation and declining white enrollments launched numerous studies and countless courtroom battles. Researchers compiled data relating desegregation to enrollment changes, and specialists in analyzing such data emerged and appeared in courts across the country purporting to show the futility of school desegregation orders.[98] During the Reagan and Bush administrations, federal civil rights officials adopted the white flight theory and sponsored research by leading witnesses against desegregation plans intended to provide proof for this theory.[99] Some key federal court decisions on desegregation relied directly on evidence from studies commissioned by school districts to document white flight. The first federal court order permitting the dismantling of an existing desegregation plan came in Norfolk, Virginia, and relied on white flight testimony by David Armor,[100] even though the decline in white enrollment had ended several years before the elementary desegregation plan was partially rescinded. As it happened, the percentage decline in white enrollment resumed a few years later, after a partial return to neighborhood schools.[101]

While many issues in this debate are still unsettled, there are some agreements. Mandatory desegregation plans limited to central cities with large minority enrollments speed up the decline in white enrollment, at least in the beginning.[102] Virtually all central cities, however, have experienced a continuing decline in the percentage of white students for many years, and declines have been sharp in many cities, whether or not they had a desegregation plan.[103] In cities that have dismantled all or part of their plan, the white enrollment decline continues. In other words, the basic forces that are producing white enrollment decline go far beyond the school desegregation plan, although the plan can accelerate this decline. On the other hand, an analysis of the largest school systems in the United States shows that half of those with the greatest stability of enrollments by race between the 1960s and the mid-1980s had mandatory metropolitan desegregation plans. The large 1987 study for the U.S. Civil Rights Commission by Finis Welch and Audrey Light concluded that mandatory metropolitan plans produced very large increases in desegregation with "much less enrollment loss" than more limited plans.[104]

Possible Uses of Housing Policy to Reduce Metropolitan School and Housing Segregation

While this chapter endorses metropolitan school desegregation plans as the most effective way to overcome problems plaguing city-district desegregation, such plans need not and ought not exclude housing initiatives. Some districts have responded to the pressures of court-ordered school desegregation through housing policy. With pro-integration housing policies, more integrated schools are produced. Eventually, such an approach may permit the return of neighborhood schools in some sectors.[105] After the desegregation of the metropolitan Louisville area in 1975, with the merger of the city and its suburban county, the Kentucky Human Relations Commission initiated a policy of using Section 8 programs to reduce school segregation.[106] This policy was implemented primarily with the following measures: (1) counseling and escort service were provided to Section 8 certificate holders searching for housing; (2) families making pro-integration moves were exempted from busing; and (3) a return to neighborhood schools was instituted for those neighborhoods that became integrated. The school district was able to move a number of schools from its mandatory assignment plan. Denver undertook a scattered-site housing plan, working with realtors on integrating neighborhoods and negotiating a deal to build a new school for a major development only on the condition that the housing be strongly marketed as integrated. The Palm Beach County School Board attempted to respond to charges that it had built schools in a way that intensified segregation by the following requirement: Developers wanting new schools in outlying areas had to sign agreements about the development of residentially integrated communities.[107]

The situation to date has been one of policy experimentation in response to local conditions without national support, research, or assistance. There should be a serious effort to determine what works under what conditions to create and sustain lasting integration of schools and housing. From an educational perspective, a basic reason for housing integration follows from the substantial evidence that school integration works more efficiently and creates greater benefits when students live in integrated neighborhoods. A study of children in Omaha by Cornelius Jackson found, according to Meyer Weinberg, that "[c]hildren in the residentially desegregated schools . . . related more positively to their schools."[108] Parents in these areas also had more positive attitudes toward the schools. The author attributed it to "their having been classmates longer and having shared memberships in churches and social organizations."[109] Robert Green's study of the metropolitan Wilmington plan reached a similar conclusion.[110] James Rosenbaum's research on the educational experience of the students in the *Gautreaux* plan also suggests large benefits from school desegregation growing out of housing policy changes.[111] Certainly, these issues deserve very careful attention since they both respond to a fundamental criticism of desegregation orders ("the real problem is housing") and point toward a way to eventually end much of the coercion involved in school desegregation without recreating systems of separate and unequal schools.

Recent Approaches to Metropolitan
School Desegregation

There have been several mergers of city and suburban school systems in the last two decades, two under federal court order: Louisville and Wilmington.[112] In Indianapolis, a large-scale metropolitan desegregation plan was ordered involving only one-way busing from the city rather than a merger of the city and suburban school districts.[113] Federal courts ordered the merger of segregated suburban districts in the suburbs of St. Louis and Pittsburgh,[114] and a state court rejected an effort to split a district in New Jersey in a way that would increase segregation. Instead, a study of regional approaches was ordered in the latter case.[115]

There also have been two plans providing relatively large-scale transfers from city to suburban schools under federal court settlement agreements in metropolitan St. Louis[116] and in Milwaukee.[117] In St. Louis, more than one-fourth of the city's African American students attend suburban schools.[118] Boston also sends several thousand of its students on voluntary transfers under the METCO program, which has been operating for almost thirty years.[119] Finally, plaintiffs succeeded in a major metropolitan case filed in Hartford, Connecticut, in 1996 where the Connecticut Supreme Court found that the extreme racial and ethnic isolation of public school students in Hartford was a violation of Connecticut's state constitution;[120] and metropolitan desegregation policy goals recently were adopted in Minnesota.[121]

The destiny of these metropolitan areas and their school districts should be compared to those that took no action and allowed themselves to be transformed by demographic change. Metropolitan Richmond, Virginia, provides a good example of the latter. Civil rights lawyers sued for a merger and desegregation of Richmond and its two adjacent suburban counties, Henrico and Chesterfield, in the early 1970s, but the initiative was blocked by a four-four tie vote in the Supreme Court.[122]

The basic reality of multidistrict metropolitan areas is one of segregated patterns of student assignment, creating separate and unequal worlds of educational opportunity. The privileged sectors in those areas deny responsibility for, or common interest with, the school systems that serve the most disadvantaged students. Blame for the fate of such systems is shifted to urban institutions and communities. When the poor sectors face disastrous change, the changes are seen not as objects of general concern, but as sorry examples of the inability to be fiscally responsible.

The entire central-city system has been written off as unsuitable for middle-class white children and irrelevant to the white community in a good many metropolitan areas; in some, the minority middle class has also reached the same conclusion. The condemnation is so universal that ranking political party leaders who received the majority of the city's minority votes could send their children to private schools without facing any serious negative criticism. As New York, Cleveland, Washington, Los Angeles, and other large city districts face drastic cutbacks in local budgets, there is no initiative for a tax increase or an increase in state or federal grants to prevent a major cutback in school budgets. In fact, suburban pluralities in state legislatures often move to change the distribution of funds in their direction. At the same time, they lobby for higher inner city school standards, such as more difficult tests and other barriers to graduation and college access, policies based on the assumption that city schools are not overwhelmed but willfully negligent. Metropolitan school districts, in stark contrast, are viewed very differently; even when they include depressed inner city communities, metropolitan school districts are more apt to be perceived as powerful and influential centers of state economic policy and as magnets for, rather than obstacles to, business investment.

Conclusion

Since comparative systematic research to date has been so limited, this chapter can only spell out a theoretical argument and focus on a few comparisons that can be drawn from existing data sources concerning the linkages between housing and education. The data presented suggest powerful and important relationships, but this chapter is far from a definitive analysis of the issues. It does suggest that HUD's Moving to Opportunity policy, emphasizing expansion of the housing choices for low-income subsidized families and therefore school choices as well, could be an important, positive component of a broader policy. Such a policy also might include support for voluntary city-suburban school transfer and desegregation programs and assistance to regions desiring to learn from metropolitan areas with consolidated systems.

This chapter explores the possible operation of metropolitan school desegregation as a powerful element in reshaping the conception of a community of interests in educating all the children of a region and as a tool for changing beliefs about the probable future of various regions and communities within the metropolitan area. In such plans, all neighborhoods can have quality, largely middle-class schools, and central-city housing may be more desirable and pass much less rapidly from the white market to the minority submarket. Integrated neighborhoods may be less vulner-

vulnerable when they have the support of an integrated, rather than rapidly changing, school and when there is no incentive for whites to flee to another school district.

There are strong reasons to think that metropolitan school districts with strong desegregation plans can develop powerful and effective local schools well linked to major institutions, thus offsetting some of the racial and economic polarization existing in metropolitan America. A single district, instead of many systems that are separated by race and class and are turned against one another, can achieve some of the key benefits that James Madison pointed to in his argument for creation of the federal government. Many more interest groups of the larger society are represented and there is much less risk of tyranny from one locally dominant faction. Such a solution also aids democracy in other critical respects—a metropolitan district is far more visible and thus more susceptible to democratic control in an era in which the public relies on the mass media for its political information. Since the price of exit from the school district is greatly increased by its broad scope, there is much greater incentive for people to invest in improving the system rather than simply leaving for a better one. Learning how and under what conditions these area-wide districts work and exploring possibilities for mutually supportive educational, housing, and urban policies could lead to important contributions to the development of a workable metropolitan system for a highly urbanized and rapidly changing multiracial nation.

Notes

1. 498 U.S. 237 (1991).

2. 503 U.S. 467 (1992).

3. 515 U.S. 70 (1995).

4. *Brown v. Board of Education*, 347 U.S. 483 (1954).

5. *Swann v. Charlotte-Mecklenburg Board of Education*, 402 U.S. 1 (1971) (holding that limited use of mathematical ratios of white to black students constituted an equitable remedy for segregation where the school board failed to introduce an acceptable plan of its own).

6. 413 U.S. 189 (1973) (holding that findings of intentionally segregative school board actions created a prima facie case of unlawful segregation in urban school system).

7. *Milliken v. Bradley*, 418 U.S. 717, 741–42 (1974) (holding that interdistrict busing in Detroit exceeded the scope of permissible desegregation plans and could only be justified when racially discriminatory acts of the school districts substantially caused the interdistrict segregation).

8. Ibid., 756 n.2 (Stewart, J., concurring).

9. Ibid.

10. Ibid., 783, 802 (Marshall, J., dissenting)(noting the district court's finding that a Detroit-only decree, the only permissible remedy, would not desegregate Detroit's schools).

11. Computations by the author from U.S. Department of Education data tapes.

12. In 1993, only 10.9% of black students and 5.1% of Hispanic students attended nonmetropolitan public schools. U.S. Department of Education, National Center for Education Statistics, *The Condition of Education, 1995*, 120 (1995). Of the total United States population, 77.5% lived in metropolitan areas in 1990. U.S. Census Bureau, *Statistical Abstract of the United States, 1992*, 29, table 33 (12th ed., 1992).

13. Gary Orfield, *The Growth of Segregation in American Schools: Changing Patterns of Separation and Poverty since 1968*, 20–21 (National School Boards Association, 1993).

14. 402 U.S. 1 (1971).

15. *Keyes v. School District No. 1*, 413 U.S. 189 (1973).

16. Colorado Constitution, art. XIV, § 3, and art. XX, § 1. Article XX of the Colorado Constitution, titled "Home Rule Cities and Towns," was adopted on Novem-

ber 5, 1974. The amendment gives each suburban county a veto over any further annexations by Denver, effectively ending the city's ability to expand. Id. This meant, at the time of its passage, that the Denver school board, just then implementing desegregation, could not capture any of the suburban white growth as it had in the past, thereby ensuring that it would steadily become increasingly minority and less representative of the metropolitan population.

17. *Bradley v. School Board*, 462 F.2d 1058 (4th Cir. 1972), aff'd per curiam, 412 U.S. 92, and reh'g denied, 414 U.S. 884 (1973).

18. Computations by the author from U.S. Department of Education data tapes.

19. *Keyes v. School District No. 1*, 902 F. Supp. 1274 (D. Colo. 1995).

20. Neil Mara and C. J. Clemmons, "School Board in Hands of Backers of Reforms District-Based Board Has 4 Carryovers," *Charlotte Observer*, Nov. 8, 1995, at A1.

21. 413 U.S. 189 (1973).

22. Ibid., 202.

23. James S. Coleman et al., *Trends in School Segregation, 1968–73*, 76–80 (Urban Institute Paper No. 722–03–01, 1975).

24. 515 U.S. 70, 92 (1995).

25. Gary Orfield, "Public Opinion and School Desegregation," 96 *Tchrs. C. Rec.* 654, 654–57 (1995).

26. Gary Orfield, *Must We Bus? Segregated Schools and National Policy*, 109 (1978).

27. Gary Orfield and Franklin Monfort, *Racial Change and Desegregation in Large School Districts: Trends through the 1986–1987 School Year*, 22–23 (National School Boards Association, 1988); Finis Welch and Audrey Light, *New Evidence on School Desegregation*, 6 (U.S. Commission on Civil Rights Clearinghouse Pub. No. 92, 1987).

28. Congress authorized HUD in 1992 to fund a demonstration project known as "Moving to Opportunity" in five metropolitan areas. Housing and Community Development Act of 1992, § 152, Pub. L. No. 102–550, 106 Stat. 3716–3717 (1992). The program generated major conflict only in Baltimore. "Outcry Stalls Access to Housing in Baltimore Suburbs," *NIMBY Rep.*, Sept./Oct. 1994, at 1–2.

29. See generally Robert L. Crain and Rita E. Mahard, "Minority Achievement: Policy Implications of Research," in *Effective School Desegregation: Equity, Quality, and Feasibility*, 55–77 (Willis D. Hawley, ed., 1981) (discussing the educational benefits of desegregation).

30. See Martin E. Sloane, "Federal Housing Policy and Equal Opportunity", in *A Sheltered Crisis: The State of Fair Housing in the Eighties*, 133, 140–41 (1983) (describing the Reagan administration's policy on fair housing as "retrenchment").

31. Ibid., 139 (discussing HUD's ineffective fair-housing marketing regulations).

32. E. H. Scott, ed., *The Federalist No. 10*, 58–60 (James Madison) (1894).

33. Ibid., 59.

34. Ibid. Madison argued: "Extend the sphere, and you take in a greater variety of parties and interest; you make it less probable that a majority of the whole will have a common motive to invade the rights of other citizens. . . . Besides other impediments, it may be remarked, that where there is a consciousness of unjust or dishonorable purpose, communication is always checked by distrust, in proportion to the number whose concurrence is necessary." Id.

35. In fragmented government, "enlightened statesmen" would "rarely prevail over the immediate interest which one party may find in disregarding the rights of another, or the good of the whole." Scott, *supra* note 32, 56. "Improper or wicked" policies would be "less apt to pervade the whole body of the Union, than a particular member of it; in the same proportion as such a malady is more likely to taint a particular county or district, than an entire State." Id. at 60.

36. Gail Sunderman, "The Politics of Reform: The Educational Excellence Movement and State Policymaking" (Ph.D. diss., University of Chicago, 1995).

37. See, e.g., Peter Applebome, "Education Mayors: Political Hands Reach for the Schools," *New York Times*, Sept. 17, 1995, at E1, E16 (discussing increases in influence of big-city mayors on school systems); see also James Barron, "Cortines Says He's Quitting after Battles with Mayor over Control of Schools," *New York Times*, June 16, 1995, at A1 (detailing resignation of New York City Schools Chancellor Ramon C. Cortines after disagreement with Mayor Rudolph Giuliani); Joseph A. Kirby and John Kass, "Gardener Tries Tossing a GOP Label at Daley," *Chicago Tribune*, Feb. 14, 1995, at 2 (noting Mayor Daley's support for the privatization of the management of the Chicago public schools); "Boston High Schoolers Protest Plans to Privatize Program," *Chicago Tribune*, Mar. 26, 1993, at 4 (noting Mayor Raymond Flynn's proposal to privatize a vocational education program at a local high school).

38. Alan Ehrenhalt, "Neighborhood Schools May Be Idea Whose Time Has Returned," *Commercial Appeal* (Memphis, TN), Feb. 25, 1996, at B3 (noting that the African American mayors of Cleveland and St. Louis have expressed an interest in ending school busing programs in preference for emphasizing neighborhood schools); Patrice M. Jones and Scott Stephens, "Hard Work Ahead for Schools: White Urges All to Cooperate with Order, Blames Parrish," *Cleveland Plain Dealer*, Mar. 5, 1995, at A1 (noting Cleveland Mayor White's criticism of a departed superintendent).

39. 418 U.S. 717 (1974).

40. Ibid., 745 ("it must be shown that racially discriminatory acts of the state or local school districts . . . have been a substantial cause of interdistrict segregation").

41. Orfield and Monfort, *supra* note 27, at 13.

42. Ibid., 12–13.

43. The Chattanooga merger was stimulated by a report of the Chattanooga Area Chamber of Commerce in 1992. Chattanooga Area Chamber of Commerce, "Opportunities: Improving Education in Chattanooga/Hamilton County" (1992). Merger was approved in the fall of 1994 and $7.5 million in donations were obtained to plan an improved county-wide system. Meg Summerfeld, "Grants to Aid Merger of Chattanooga, County Districts," *Education Week,* June 14, 1995, at 3.

44. Ann Bradley, "Beyond City Limits," Education Week, Aug. 2, 1995, at 33–39; Anna Varela, "Magnets Leave Some Waiting, Race Issue Afflicts Magnet Plans," *Greensboro News and Record,* Aug. 15, 1995, at B1–B2; Edward F. Hanes Jr., "Durham City and County School Merger" (unpublished paper, Harvard University, 1996, on file with author).

45. John N. Bridgman, *A Manual for Mergers* (Raleigh, N.C., Department of Public Instruction, 1987).

46. "Disappearing Districts," *Education Week*, Mar. 3, 1993, at 3 (citing U.S. Census Bureau statistics on dropping number of independent school districts).

47. Ibid.

48. Ibid.

49. Personal communication to the author from Roslyn Mickelson, Professor, University of North Carolina at Charlotte (Jan. 12, 1996).

50. Adrienne D. Coles, "People," *Education Week*, Jan. 17, 1996, at 5.

51. Metropolitan Raleigh's district was substantial, comparable to 1990 enrollments of Washington, D.C., 80,700; Cleveland, 70,000; San Francisco, 61,700; Atlanta, 60,800; and Boston, 60,500. "Enrollment of the 100 Largest Public School Districts: Fall 1990," *Education Week*, May 16, 1993, at 8 (compiled by the National Center for Education Statistics, U.S. Department of Education).

52. Willis D. Hawley et al., *Strategies for Effective Desegregation: Lessons from Research*, 118–47 (1983) (discussing the need for additional organizational changes within desegregated schools).

53. Diana M. Pearce, "Deciphering the Dynamics of Segregation: The Role of Schools in the Housing Choice Process," 13 Urban Review 85, 88 (1981).

54. Ibid., 90–91.

55. Ibid.

56. Ibid.

57. Ibid., 90, 98.

58. Ibid., 97.

59. Ibid., 98.

60. Robert L. Crain et al., "Lessons Not Lost: The Effects of School Desegregation in Large Central Cities" (working paper, Program in Sociology and Education, Teachers College, 1995, on file with author).

61. Lois M. Quinn et al., *Relationships Between School Desegregation and Government Housing Programs: A Milwaukee Case Study* (1980).

62. Robert L. Crain and Carol S. Weisman, *Discrimination, Personality, and Achievement: A Survey of Northern Blacks*, 166 (1972).

63. Robert L. Crain, *The Long-Term Effects of Desegregation: Results from a True Experiment* (1986).

64. Thomas C. Schelling, "A Process of Residential Segregation: Neighborhood Tipping," in *Racial Discrimination in Economic Life*, 157–84 (Anthony H. Pascal, ed., 1972).

65. See Reynolds Farley et al., "'Chocolate City, Vanilla Suburbs': Will the Trend toward Racially Separate Communities Continue?" 7 *Soc. Sci. Res.* 319, 333–38 (1978) (discussing the results of a study aimed at discovering how much residential integration whites would accept).

66. Reynolds Farley, "Neighborhood Preferences and Aspirations among Blacks and Whites," in *Housing Markets and Residential Mobility*, 161–91 (G. Thomas Kingsley and Margery A. Turner, eds., 1993).

67. 503 U.S. 467 (1992).

68. A fascinating contrast to Farley's data on the incompatibility of housing attitudes in Detroit came in a survey in metropolitan Indianapolis, the metropolitan region with the highest level of school desegregation in the Midwest after city-suburban desegregation. When asked to choose between several kinds of communities ranging from all white or black to mostly one group or an even mix, 68% of blacks and 48% of whites said that an "even mix" would be their preference. "Blacks and Whites: Can We All Get Along? Responses to the Poll," *Indianapolis Star*, Feb. 24, 1993, at A8. Whites in Indianapolis were much more willing to live in the kind of communities considered ideal by blacks but seen as unacceptable by Detroit whites. See generally Linda Graham Caleca, "Residents Find Area's Diversity Is Appealing," *Indianapolis Star*, Feb. 24, 1993, at B1.

Research on stable interracial neighborhoods in Chicago suggests that it is much more the belief about the future of the neighborhood that affects the stability of integration. Richard Taub et al., *Paths of Neighborhood Change*, 38–118 (1984) (discussing racial integration in several Chicago neighborhoods). Such beliefs may well be related to successful interracial experiences.

69. 418 U.S. 717 (1974) (refusing to impose a multidistrict remedy for single district de jure segregation).

70. Gary Orfield and Carole A. Ashkinaze, *The Closing Door*, 103–12 (1991).

71.   Ibid., 104–5.

72.   See generally *Scott Cummings, Racial Isolation in the Public Schools: The Impact of Public and Private Housing Policies* (1980); Gary Orfield, *The Housing Issues in the St. Louis Case* (1981) (report to the federal district court in St. Louis); Gary Orfield and Paul Fischer, *Housing and School Integration in Three Metropolitan Areas: A Policy Analysis of Denver, Columbus, and Phoenix* (1981).

73.   See Robert Gray and Steven Tursky, "Local and Racial/Ethnic Occupancy Patterns for HUD-Subsidized Family Housing in Ten Metropolitan Areas," in *Housing Desegregation and Federal Policy*, 235, 249 (John M. Goering, ed., 1986) (finding that HUD-subsidized rental housing in 10 metropolitan areas was concentrated in a relatively small number of minority-occupied census tracts).

74.   Gary Orfield, "Building an Integrated Community: Racial Trends and Community Choices in Palm Beach County" (unpublished report to Project Mosaic, 1991, on file with author) (reporting on statistics compiled from HUD files).

75.   See Orfield, *supra* note 72; Gray and Tursky, *supra* note 73 (discussing the results of a study that revealed that HUD rental housing subsidy programs were concentrated mainly in minority census tracts); Orfield, *supra* note 74.

76.   See Christina Meldrum and Susan E. Eaton, *Resegregation in Norfolk, Virginia: Does Restoring Neighborhood Schools Work?* 56–60 (1994).

77.   See W.A.V. Clark and Eric G. Moore, *Residential Mobility and Public Policy* (1980) (collecting such studies).

78.   Alice Woldt, *Schools and Neighborhoods Research Study: Real Estate Marketing Practices and Residential Segregation*, 14–20 (1978) (report to Seattle School District, City of Seattle, and Joint Advisory Commission on Education).

79.   Matthew A. Crenson, *The Un-politics of Air Pollution: A Study of Non-decisionmaking in the Cities*, vii, 4–5 (1971); Peter Bachrach and Morton S. Baratz, "Two Faces of Power," 56 *Am. Pol. Sci. Rev.* 947, 952 (1962).

80.   See, *e.g.,* Denis E. Gale, *Washington, D.C.: Inner City Revitalization and Minority Suburbanization*, 13–16, 99–107, 154–57 (1987) (discussing demographics of gentrified households in Washington, D.C.).

81.   Ibid., 84–107 (detailing the perceptions and experiences of whites in Washington, D.C., schools). Whites aged 25–29, the prime years for starting a family, moved out of the central cities to the suburbs at greater than a two-to-one margin from March 1993 to March 1994. Kristin A. Hanson, U.S. Department of Commerce, *Geographic Mobility: March 1993 to March 1994*, 84 (1995). Many metropolitan areas show sharp differences in concentrations of the total population of school-age children, in spite of the more affordable housing for young families in central cities. In the Denver metropolitan area, for example, only 8.5% of the city residents were between five and fourteen years of age, while all of the suburban counties had between 11.9% and 20.2% of this group. In Milwaukee,

12.2% were in this age group, compared to 16.0% to 17.3% in the suburbs. In Washington, D.C., the city proportion was 9.7%, compared to 13.3% to 17.8% in all suburbs except Arlington County. U.S. Bureau of the Census, *State and Metropolitan Area Data Book*, 113, 137, 173 (1991).

82.   See Paul A. Jargowsky and Mary Jo Bane, "Ghetto Poverty in the United States, 1970–1980," in *The Urban Underclass*, 252 (Christopher Jencks and Paul E. Peterson, eds., 1991) (stating that approximately 30% of poor blacks in metropolitan areas live in areas of concentrated poverty); see also David R. James, "The Racial Ghetto as a Race-Making Situation: The Effects of Residential Segregation on Racial Inequalities and Racial Identity," 19 *L. & Soc. Inquiry* 407, 409 (1994) (stating that this percentage is increasing); John D. Kasarda, "Inner-City Concentrated Poverty and Neighborhood Distress: 1970 to 1990," 4 *Housing Pol'y Debate* 253, 281–85 (1993) (noting increase of minorities in distressed neighborhoods, especially in major Midwest cities).

83.   Allan C. Ornstein and Daniel U. Levine, *Foundations of Education*, 451 (4th ed., 1989) ("The net result is that city school districts have become increasingly low income and minority in their student composition, with a high proportion of minority students attending predominantly minority, poverty schools").

84.   Orfield, *supra* note 13, at 22.

85.   See Orfield and Monfort, *supra* note 27, at 18–33 (detailing segregation levels for black and Hispanic students).

86.   Gary Orfield and Sean Reardon, "Race, Poverty, and Inequality," in *New Opportunities: Civil Rights at a Crossroads* (Citizens Commission on Civil Rights, ed., 1993).

87.   Gary Orfield, "Federal Agencies and Urban Segregation: Steps toward Coordinated Action," in *Racial Segregation: Two Policy Views* (Gary Orfield and William L. Taylor, eds., 1979).

88.   See *United States v. Yonkers Board of Education*, 624 F. Supp. 1276 (S.D.N.Y. 1985), aff'd, 837 F.2d 1181 (2d Cir. 1987), cert. denied, 486 U.S. 1055 (1988) (holding that the city of Yonkers' racially segregative subsidized housing practices contributed to school segregation).

89.   There were extensive discussions with the Phoenix city government and various community groups about a plan for voluntary housing desegregation to deal with the issues being raised by the Justice Department investigation. The author visited the city during 1980 to consult with city planners, civil rights officials, and the city council about these issues. The planning process ended after the 1980 election removed the Carter administration from power. The issue of interdistrict school and housing segregation was not litigated.

90.   The HUD Title VIII regulation was published, but was rescinded by the Reagan administration before it took effect. The Reagan administration promised to resubmit a regulation, but never did so. See Citizens Commission on Civil Rights, *A Decent Home: A Report on the Continuing Failure of the Federal Government to Provide Equal Housing Opportunities*, 55–56 (1983).

91. Ibid.

92. See generally Cummings, *supra* note 72 (surveying such research).

93. Marshall Kaplan, "Green Valley Ranch: Promise, Hope, and Initial Fulfillment" (paper presented at the National Conference on School Desegregation Research, University of Chicago, 1986, on file with author).

94. Christine H. Rossell, *The Carrot or the Stick for School Desegregation Policy: Magnet Schools or Forced Busing* (1990). See generally Welch and Light, *supra* note 27 (detailing the study prepared for and funded by the U.S. Commission on Civil Rights).

95. James S. Coleman et al., *Trends in School Segregation, 1968–73*, 76–80 (Urban Inst. Paper No. 722-03-01, 1975).

96. U.S. Department of Health, Education, and Welfare, Office of Education, *Equality of Educational Opportunity* (1966).

97. See Gary Orfield, "Research, Politics, and the Anti-Busing Debate," 42 *Law & Contemp. Probs.* 141, 143–49 (Autumn 1978) (detailing Coleman's 1966 report and his 1975 paper as well as the controversy surrounding them).

98. James S. Coleman and Sara D. Kelly, "Education," in *Urban Predicament* (William Gorham and Nathan Glazer, eds., 1976) (arguing that the desegregation of white schools was worsening the problem).

99. See Rossell, *supra* note 94; Welch and Light, *supra* note 27 (arguing that desegregation plans actually increased segregation in many metropolitan areas).

100. See Riddick v. School Board, 784 F.2d 521, 526 (4th Cir.), cert denied, 479 U.S. 938 (1986) (noting Armor's conclusion that "mandatory busing had led to significant white flight").

101. Meldrum and Eaton, *supra* note 76.

102. See Orfield and Monfort, *supra* note 27, at 7 (documenting decline in white enrollment from 1967 to 1986).

103. Ibid., 33 (noting the unlikelihood of meaningful integration occurring where percentage of white students has declined).

104. Welch and Light, *supra* note 27, at 6. County-wide districts have low enrollment loss "because they are concentrated in the Sunbelt and encompass cities and suburbs alike." Id. "Large urban districts are at the other extreme, with large losses in white enrollment and relatively small improvements in segregation levels." Id.

105. Gary Orfield, *Toward a Strategy for Urban Integration* (1981).

106. See generally Kentucky Commission on Human Rights, *School and Housing Desegregation Are Working Together in Louisville and Jefferson County*, 83–85 (1983) (discussing the improvement in the education gap when blacks and whites live in suburban communities as part of housing and education desegregation plans).

107. Peter Schmidt, "Palm Beach Shifts Integration Focus to Housing," *Education Week*, Feb. 26, 1992, at 1, 9.

108. Meyer Weinberg, "Integrating Neighborhoods: An Examination of Housing and School Desegregation," 37 *J. Housing* 630, 636 (1980).

109. Ibid.

110. See generally Robert L. Green et al., *Metropolitan School Desegregation in New Castle County, Delaware* (1980) (report to the Rockefeller Foundation reaching a similar conclusion).

111. See James E. Rosenbaum et al., "White Suburban Schools' Responses to Low-Income Black Children: Sources of Successes and Problems," 20 *Urban Rev.* 28, 38–40 (1988) (noting successes and difficulties of integrating low-income black children into suburban schools).

112. *Cunningham v. Grayson*, 541 F.2d 538 (6th Cir. 1976) (affirming the desegregation plan imposed by the district court for Louisville and Jefferson County); *Buchanan v. Evans*, 423 U.S. 963 (1975) (affirming the Wilmington metropolitan plan). The federal district court followed the Supreme Court's affirmation of the Wilmington metropolitan plan with implementation. *Evans v. Buchanan*, 582 F.2d 750, 756–58 (3d Cir. 1978), cert. denied, 446 U.S. 923 (1980). The initial plan merged 11 independent school districts into a single metropolitan district containing most of Delaware's school children. *Evans v. Buchanan*, 447 F. Supp. 982, 1039 (D. Del. 1978). After desegregation was achieved, the state government divided the large district into four pie-shaped districts—Red Clay, Christiana, Brandywine, and Colonial—combining parts of the city and the suburbs. See *Evans v. Buchanan*, 512 F. Supp. 839, 841 (D. Del. 1981). The district court declared the systems unitary in August 1995. *Coalition to Save Our Children v. State Board of Education*, 901 F. Supp. 784, 824 (D. Del. 1995).

113. See *United States v. Board of School Commissioners*, 506 F. Supp. 657, 663–69 (S.D. Ind. 1979) (ordering one-way busing as one of a number of remedies), aff'd, 637 F.2d 1101, 1103–05 (7th Cir. 1980), cert. denied, 449 U.S. 838 (1980).

114. *United States v. Missouri*, 363 F. Supp. 739 (E.D. Mo. 1973), aff'd in part, 515 F.2d 1365 (8th Cir. 1975) (en banc), cert. denied sub nom., *Ferguson Reorganized School District R2 v. United States*, 423 U.S. 951 (1975); *Hoots v. Commonwealth of Pennsylvania.*, 672 F.2d 1107, 1120 (3d Cir. 1982) (affirming district court order redistricting school system).

115. The community of Englewood Cliffs, New Jersey, sued in state court in 1985 for permission to withdraw from a 20-year-old sending relationship with the Englewood School District, thus increasing the segregation of an Englewood High School. In 1988, the state commissioner of education ruled against the community, as did the state board of education in 1990 and the appellate division of the superior court in 1992. *Board of Education of Englewood Cliffs v. Board of Education of Englewood*, 608 A.2d 914 (N.J. Sup. Ct. App. Div. 1992) aff'd 625 A.2d 483

(N.J. 1993). The court required a study of regionalization, combined the areas, and ruled that home rule and local control must yield to the fulfillment of the educational and racial policies in the state statutes and constitution. Id. at 949, 952. In 1993, the New Jersey Supreme Court upheld the decision, and regionalization plans were submitted in 1995. Robert Hanley, "Island in a Sea of White Resistance: Englewood's Neighbors Oppose All Regional School Plans," *New York Times*, Dec. 21, 1995, at B1.

116. *Liddell v. Missouri*, 731 F.2d 1294, 1300–01 (8th Cir. 1984) (en banc) (detailing St. Louis agreement and rejecting state's appeal of interdistrict transfer order), cert. denied, 469 U.S. 816 (1984), cert. denied sub nom., *Legett v. Liddell*, 469 U.S. 816 (1984).

117. *Armstrong v. Board of School Directors*, 616 F.2d 305, 310–12 (7th Cir. 1980) (detailing Milwaukee agreement).

118. Voluntary Interdistrict Coordinating Council of St. Louis, *Report to the Community*, 7 (1991).

119. The Metropolitan Council for Educational Opportunity (METCO) school integration plan provides financial assistance from Massachusetts to any regional school district that files a school integration plan that seeks to reduce racial imbalance in the public schools. *Massachusetts Annotated Laws*, Ch. 76, § 12A (Law. Co-op., 1984). The financial assistance includes the cost per pupil of educating each nonresident child, the cost of transportation of each child, and the cost of special education services provided to each child. Id.

120. *Sheff v. O'Neill*, 678 A.2d 1267 (Conn. 1996).

121. Minnesota Statute, § 124D.892 (1998) (detailing Minnesota's desegregation plan).

122. *School Board of Richmond v. State Board of Education*, 412 U.S. 92 (1973) (per curiam).

Chapter 6

The Current State of School Desegregation Law: Why Isn't Anybody Laughing?

Drew S. Days III

Then does segregation offend against equality? Equality, like all general concepts, has marginal areas where philosophic difficulties are encountered. But if a
whole race of people finds itself confined within a system set up and continued
for the very purpose of keeping it in an inferior station, and if the question is then
solemnly propounded whether such a race is being treated "equally," I think we
ought to exercise one of the sovereign prerogatives of philosophers—that of laughter. The only question remaining (after we get our laughter under control) is whether
the segregation system answers to this description. Here I must confess to a
tendency to start laughing all over again.

—Charles L. Black Jr.

Few could have anticipated at the time of the *Brown v. Board of Education*[1] decision that school desegregation would still be a national practice
over forty years later. Yet the reality of segregated schools continues largely
unabated. We continue to ponder questions that go to the very heart of
the desegregation process: Does desegregation have any educational justification? Is busing an acceptable desegregation technique under any
circumstances? Are the social and economic costs associated with desegregation so great as to justify abandoning the enterprise altogether?

This state of affairs prompts one to ask whether the current debate
would have been different had school desegregation remained largely a
southern phenomenon devoted to eradicating the state-imposed systems
of racial separation in public education pervasive throughout that region.
Opposition to desegregation did not gain national support until the process
began moving north. It was only then that Congress became interested in

the subject, in some instances enacting legislation designed to curtail both judicial and administrative responses to public school segregation. Presidents Nixon and Ford saw fit to place desegregation on their agendas, particularly the issue of busing. Civil rights coalitions that had fought so successfully in the courts and Congress to promote desegregation in the South began to unravel as their members increasingly found themselves on opposing sides over desegregation at home in the North and West.

I believe that there were many northerners who had genuine difficulty understanding how school boards in their communities, where racial segregation had never been required by law, could be found in violation of *Brown*. They saw segregated schools in the North and West as largely the unavoidable consequence of segregated residential patterns. School boards could not be faulted, they felt, for adhering, on respectable educational grounds, to neighborhood student assignment plans—even where doing so produced a segregated school system that reflected residential segregation.

Subsequent litigation should have shattered the myth that school boards outside of the South have consistently applied racially neutral criteria in administering their districts. Many people nevertheless continue to cling to the view that intensely segregated school attendance patterns cannot be laid entirely at the feet of school officials and that comprehensive desegregation plans requiring busing and the abandonment of neighborhood schools are unwarranted and unfair. These misgivings have, in turn, made northerners and westerners far more sympathetic to claims that current segregation in the Deep South is similarly the result of demographics and segregative forces beyond the control of school boards. Perhaps there *is* something—they say to themselves—to southerners' contention that they have been unfairly punished by the courts for assigning children to neighborhood schools, despite the fact that state-imposed segregation ended years ago. They find themselves echoing many of the concerns previously heard only in the southern and border states. What about these court-ordered remedies? Even granting that a school board acted unconstitutionally, does that conduct justify a system-wide busing plan? How can we be certain that the cure will not be worse than the disease, leaving the schools even more segregated after the court order? Hence, we see the conversion of what initially was seen as a regional issue into a matter of national importance. All those involved in the debate over school desegregation understand that its outcome will profoundly affect the future of the entire country.

The division between the North and South makes less sense when one looks at the anatomy of a northern school desegregation case. Although many are now willing to concede that northern school boards engaged in segregative activity, few truly understand the variety and pervasive nature of such practices. Northern school boards have made racial assignments not only of students, but also of faculty and staff. They have gerrymandered attendance zones, sited and closed old schools, changed grade structures, and controlled school building capacities, all to further segregation. To satisfy the court-heightened requirement of showing that a school district was responsible for segregated schools outside of the South, attorneys challenging northern schools have expended exceptional efforts to describe such events in detail.

Even for those who already know the basic story of segregation in the North, the story revealed by a closer examination of the evidence gives the familiar a power and poignancy that court opinions are unlikely ever to communicate. One watches federal judges, initially skeptical of plaintiffs' claims, slowly but firmly understand that constitutional wrongs have been made. Take, for example, the case in which one lawyer, representing a group of intervening white neighborhood associations opposed to desegregation in Detroit, was so struck by the force of the plaintiffs' case that he persuaded his clients to switch sides, in effect, and to press for full desegregation.

But the story about segregation in the North is not just about school boards. It is also very much about residential segregation and about government culpability in creating it. Consider the story of *Hills v. Gautreaux*,[2] the Chicago public housing discrimination case. *Gautreaux* illustrates initial judicial hostility to the plaintiffs' claim and the eventual full recognition by the courts that the law had been violated. The charge, upheld by both lower courts and, ultimately, the Supreme Court, was that the intense segregation of public housing was not purely the result of voluntary choice and economic imperatives. Quite the contrary, plaintiffs alleged that the Chicago Housing Authority (CHA) actively engaged in segregative conduct over a number of years and that the Department of Housing and Urban Development (HUD) took no steps to prevent or correct such conduct. *Gautreaux* provides a compelling rebuttal to those who claim that residential segregation is the result of purely chance events and, consequently, is not a proper subject for constitutional adjudication.

This chapter argues that segregated schools result from several actions of constitutional significance: (1) school boards take intentional action, such as racial assignment of students, faculty, and staff, and other techniques already mentioned, to maintain a significant degree of racial separation in neighborhood schools; (2) the school boards' actions help create segregated neighborhoods, as families move toward the schools that their children attend; and (3) governmental institutions (local, state, and federal), other than school boards, promote further segregated residential areas through a wide variety of discriminatory practices.

School Board Culpability for Segregation

The Supreme Court has concluded that these first two sources of segregated schools violate the Constitution and that such violation justifies ordering school boards to undertake remedial desegregation programs. Given the fact that, at the time of *Brown*, positive law in southern and border states required or condoned segregated schools, the Supreme Court had little difficulty over the following fifteen years attributing the existence of virtually one-race schools to unconstitutional, local school board action. School boards were charged with an affirmative responsibility to eradicate these dual systems "root and branch."[3]

The debate over school board responsibility for segregated schools arose in the North in districts that either had never been subject to laws promoting segregation or had repealed them almost seventy-five years before *Brown* was decided. As a matter of history, it is noteworthy that school board responsibility was not clearly raised as an issue in many desegregation cases filed during the early 1960s in northern communities, including one early northern desegregation case in Cincinnati.[4] Rather, the plaintiffs' central claim in such cases was that racial segregation (often referred to as "racial imbalance") violated *Brown* irrespective of school board culpability for the condition. What they argued, in essence, was that this form of segregation, while not so pernicious as that addressed directly by *Brown*, was, nevertheless, sufficiently harmful to the self-esteem, education, and life chances of black children to justify imposing upon school boards an affirmative duty to take corrective action. Lower federal courts generally dismissed these arguments. In fact, they flatly excluded evidence in school cases related to the impact of residential segregation upon segregated schools on the grounds that the condition was created by parties not before the court and not subject to school board control.

During this period, the Supreme Court avoided confronting these issues by denying review. In the early 1970s, however, it considered the Denver, Colorado, case of *Keyes v. School District No. 1*.[5] In this case, the lower courts held that even though Colorado and Denver had never required or condoned segregated schools by law, the Denver school board nevertheless had engaged in intentionally segregative acts that violated the Fourteenth Amendment rights of black and Hispanic children. Where, as in Denver, the school board had been engaged in a "systematic program of segregation affecting a substantial portion of the students, schools, teachers and facilities," the board could be held to be administering a dual system in violation of *Brown*. After the Denver decision, it was no longer legally accurate or helpful to distinguish between southern and northern school segregation. Judges in northern desegregation cases would, thereafter, have to focus explicitly upon the extent to which school board action intentionally produced racial separation, free of any presumption to the contrary.

Ironically, the Supreme Court's first recognition of the second source of segregated schools, namely, segregated residential areas that had developed partly as a result of segregative actions by school boards, occurred in a southern rather than a northern case. Prior to *Keyes*, the Court considered, in *Swann v. Charlotte-Mecklenburg Board of Education*,[6] claims by the Charlotte-Mecklenburg, North Carolina, school district that, although state law had required segregated schools at the time of *Brown*, the board had for some years operated its schools on a nondiscriminatory basis. To the extent that its system was still largely segregated, the board claimed that the situation was not of its making. Instead, the board contended, forces over which it had no control had created residential segregation that necessarily resulted in segregated neighborhood schools. The Supreme Court's response, affirming lower court findings, was, first, that the *Charlotte* board had never discharged its affirmative duty imposed by *Brown* to dismantle its prior state-imposed dual system and instead had engaged, post-*Brown*, in a series of intentionally segregative acts. Second, its answer to the board's denial of responsibility for residential segregation, reflected in segregated neighborhood schools, was that there was a reciprocal segregative effect for which the board must be held partially responsible. According to the Court, not only are schools placed where people move, but people move to where schools are placed. Consequently, the board's practices of opening and abandoning schools and of changing grade structures and attendance boundaries of schools to maintain segregation played a part in people's decisions as to where they would live.

The *Swann* decision was a crucial development in school desegregation law, for it broke a logjam in the lower federal courts with respect to the nature and scope of the remedial duty delaying meaningful relief in southern communities for years. Moreover, it provided building blocks for the assault in *Keyes* upon northern school segregation. Although the

Supreme Court's rejection of the *Charlotte* board's claim was not surprising in view of the district history of state-imposed racial separation, one would have thought that the Denver board, acting in a state and city with no such history, would have had more success asserting similar claims. Nonetheless, the Supreme Court found *Swann* controlling.

In retrospect, the Court's failure in *Swann* to address candidly the relationship between school and residential segregation may be significantly responsible, however unintended at the time, for the lack of realism that characterizes today's debate over both liability and remedy in school cases. The truth, which the Court refused to acknowledge except in passing, was that forces beyond the school board's control had produced segregative effects in the case of *Charlotte*. Schools that had been white in 1954 were black in 1971, as white families moved out of adjacent neighborhoods and black families moved in. Economics had allowed many whites, but few blacks, to move into areas on the fringes of the city or in its suburbs, away from black neighborhoods. The Court's failure was not that it held the board responsible, in part, for the residential segregation that its neighborhood schools served. It was clearly correct to do so. Rather, the Court failed by refusing to assess the nature and impact of other forces upon residential segregation and segregated schools.

The Court's omission of this connection, obscured by a unanimous opinion in *Swann*, was subjected to stinging criticism in the Denver case from two justices usually at opposite ends of the spectrum on racial discrimination questions.[7] Both Justice Powell and Justice Douglas pointed out that school boards alone could not be held responsible for the continued existence of segregated schools, either in the North or the South. Rather, they argued that a variety of other forces contributed to the creation and maintenance of segregated neighborhood schools. As to the nature of such other forces, however, Powell and Douglas differed markedly, the former arguing that private choice and economic conditions caused residential segregation, the latter seeing the source of the problem as a web of segregative governmental actions working in tandem with demographic factors. Not surprisingly, in view of their quite different visions of the sources of residential segregation, Justice Powell concluded that a school board could discharge its constitutional duty in a highly segregated residential community merely by adhering to a strict neighborhood school assignment policy. Justice Douglas, in contrast, took the position that one state agency, the school board, should be held responsible for remedying the condition of school segregation caused by other governmental institutions. For Justice Douglas, state responsibility could not be so fragmented as to leave the victims of governmentally fostered segregated schools with no remedy whatsoever. Justice Douglas's opinion in *Keyes* is as close as the Supreme Court has ever come to recognizing residential segregation as the source of segregated schools.

Governmental Institutions and Segregation

Instead of grappling directly with the complexity of residential segregation as it bears on segregated schools, the Court has placed an impressive array of procedural hurdles in the path of school boards seeking to avoid liability for continued racial segregation. The first of these hurdles is the affirmative responsibility of school boards in systems that formerly had been segregated by state statute to eradicate "root and branch" the existence of white schools and black schools. This duty played an important role in the Court's resolution of *Charlotte-Mecklenburg*. It was originally articulated, however, three years before *Swann* in a masterpiece of test case litigation: *Green v. County School Board*.[8]

For ten years after *Brown*, school boards fought any, even token, integration tooth and nail. Civil rights lawyers ultimately defeated a series of these efforts to maintain the status quo ante. In the mid-1960s, however, in hopes of delaying desegregation further, many school boards began instituting so-called "freedom of choice" plans. Under these plans, black and white children formerly assigned to segregated schools by law could choose to attend schools in which their race was not in the majority. Given the inertia produced by generations of segregation and threats directed against those considering transfers, it is not surprising that few students sought reassignment. However, some lower federal courts viewed such plans as eminently fair and non-coercive. Others found them consistent with what they understood as the responsibility imposed upon school boards by *Brown*: to desegregate, not to integrate.[9] In other words, courts believed that the school boards' duty was only to end racial assignment of students, not to correct for continued segregation flowing from earlier state-imposed racial assignment practices.

In order to present an effective challenge to freedom of choice plans, plaintiffs' lawyers needed a case that starkly presented the continued existence of segregation and the unlikelihood of its being remedied without affirmative school board action. *Green*,[10] the New Kent County school case, provided such an opportunity. New Kent had one white school and one black school at the time of *Brown*, a situation that had improved little in the subsequent decade, despite a board-initiated freedom of choice plan permitting students to transfer to the school from which they previously had been excluded by law. During the three years this program was in effect, not a single white child chose to attend the school historically designated for blacks, and only a small percentage of blacks enrolled in the traditionally all-white facility. From a demographic standpoint, not much had changed in rural New Kent County during the intervening years. In addition, there was no significant residential segregation, either at the time of *Brown* or ten years later.

In view of this factual pattern, it was clear to the Court that the creation and continued existence of the segregated schools was the result of board action, unaffected by other forces, governmental or otherwise. The Court also recognized that the remedy for this continued segregation lay within the power of the board.

Swann, however, presented a far more complex picture of school board liability for continuing segregation than did *Green.* In *Swann,* there was evidence of residential segregation both before and after *Brown,* caused by forces of which segregative school board action was only one. Moreover, the presence of these other forces raised questions not evident in *Green* about the board's ability to devise an effective desegregation remedy. Despite these significant differences, the Court applied the *Green* precedent to the facts of *Swann.* The Court's only concession to the reality of intervening segregative causes was to permit the school board, in devising a comprehensive remedy, to demonstrate that remaining one-race schools were not solely the vestiges of the former dual system, but the result of other forces as well.

The second procedural hurdle for school boards was formulated in *Keyes,* the Denver case. Lower courts found intentional segregative school board action with respect to only some schools within the district. Yet throughout the system, a high degree of segregation of blacks and Hispanics from whites existed. How could a system-wide remedy be justified under these circumstances? The Court had two answers. First, it held that where intentional segregative action was found to have been present in a significant part of the system, unconstitutional intent would be presumed at work throughout the system as a whole.[11] Second, where segregative effects of intentional board action could be found in a significant part of the system, similar effects would be presumed as to the entire system.[12] The board was free, however, to rebut either of these presumptions through the introduction of competent evidence.[13] Stated differently, faced with uncertainty as to the impact of forces other than actions of the school board upon racial separation, the Court placed upon the board, rather than upon the plaintiffs, the burden of sorting out the nature, scope and effect of such forces.

The third procedural hurdle was set up by the Supreme Court in the *Columbus* and *Dayton* decisions.[14] In the late 1880s, Ohio repealed laws requiring racial segregation in public schools. Until the early part of this century, the Ohio school districts of Columbus and Dayton assigned children, for the most part, on a non-racial basis. Thereafter, however, both districts began a systematic practice of racial assignment of faculty, staff, and students, which, in the case of faculty and staff, continued almost to the time desegregation suits were filed in the early 1970s. In addition, both districts employed many classic segregative techniques.

The Court accepted a doctrine that, even more clearly than the *Keyes* presumptions, placed the burden on school boards either to prove the effects of intervening segregative forces or submit to the imposition of system-wide remedies. Specifically, the Court applied the full force of the affirmative duty to desegregate articulated in *Green*, a southern case, to systems that had not been required by law to segregate children for ninety years. According to the Court, the records in *Columbus* and *Dayton* reflected that both school districts at the time of *Brown* were operating dual school systems, albeit by board action rather than pursuant to positive law. Consequently, from that date on, both boards had an affirmative constitutional duty to eradicate their dual system "root and branch."

The lower level of proof required to justify system-wide remedies became the feature of this new doctrine most favorable to plaintiffs' lawyers in northern school cases. Under *Keyes*, plaintiffs had the initial burden of establishing that the school board acted with segregative intent. The *Columbus* and *Dayton* decisions, however, required plaintiffs to prove only that a dual system existed in 1954 and that the school board actions had had segregative effect. Board conduct that in another context might be viewed as neutral, such as strict assignment of students to neighborhood schools, would fail under that test. Such acts would simply be further proof of the board's failure to discharge its affirmative responsibility to desegregate.

The Court's adoption of these three procedural hurdles undoubtedly was driven in part by a desire to avoid the difficult problems of multiple causality in school segregation cases. In fairness, however, the Court also relied upon important public policy considerations, as well as upon well-established legal doctrine outside the desegregation area. In *Swann*, the board's own delay in complying with *Brown* had allowed intervening segregative forces to work their effects. If the Court had entertained the board's claims seriously, it would have provided further excuses for *Charlotte* and other districts in the southern and border states to delay, rendering the implementation of any meaningful remedy even more difficult.

In contrast, the Court's setting of 1954 as the bright line for the imposition of an affirmative desegregative responsibility upon school districts outside of, as well as in, the South was nothing less than a tour de force. School boards in the South, to which *Brown* was specifically addressed, did not learn from the Supreme Court until at least 1968 that such an affirmative responsibility existed. Moreover, it was not until 1971 that southern systems were given clear guidance from the Court as to how that affirmative responsibility was to be discharged. Finally, the Court did not seem to regard Ohio's pre-1887 history of state-imposed segregation as a dispositive factor in its decision to link *Columbus* and *Dayton* with *Green* and *Charlotte-Mecklenburg*.

However much one seeks to explain these decisions, from *Green* to *Columbus* and *Dayton*, in precedential terms, below the surface they appear to reflect the frustration of the Court in the face of several realities. First, the justices could not ignore the fact that twenty to twenty-five years after *Brown*, many school districts had not even begun meaningful desegregation efforts. Further passage of time would make the development of meaningful desegregation remedies exceedingly difficult, if not impossible. Second, it was no longer possible to pretend that the continued existence of unconstitutionally segregated schools was only a southern, rather than a national, problem. The Court would have to devise doctrines that responded accordingly.

Plaintiffs also faced procedural hurdles during this period, however, as the cases in Detroit and Wilmington reveal.[15] In Detroit, the plaintiffs were able to establish that the local school board and the state of Michigan had acted in tandem to create and maintain segregated schools within the city of Detroit. Additionally, the record reflected a pattern of school construction that had been approved and funded by the state, both within the Detroit district and in neighboring suburban districts, contributing to the segregated character of all schools in the area. Schools in Detroit were overwhelmingly majority black and Hispanic; those in the suburbs were almost completely majority white.

The lower courts concluded that this history of segregative activity by both the Detroit school board and the state of Michigan necessitated a remedy that went beyond the limits of Detroit to encompass many of the surrounding districts. Like Justice Douglas in *Keyes*, those courts viewed the state as the principal governmental entity reached by the Fourteenth Amendment: where the state was shown to have violated the Constitution, courts could order remedies to the full extent of the state's power to implement them. The fact that the state of Michigan had decided to delegate some responsibilities for public education to numerous local districts should not disable federal courts from providing effective remedies for the state's segregative acts. Whether the suburban districts themselves had engaged in segregative acts was, under this theory, irrelevant.

The Supreme Court disagreed. In *Milliken v. Bradley*, it rejected the proposed metropolitan remedy, announcing the principle that interdistrict desegregation would be constitutionally justified only where a "constitutional violation within one district produces a significant segregative effect in another district."[16] Failing that, federal courts must respect the "deeply rooted" tradition in American public education, honored in Michigan, of local control over the operation of schools. The Court found no significant segregative effects with respect to the fifty-three districts surrounding Detroit.

In *Evans v. Buchanan*,[17] the Wilmington desegregation case, the plaintiffs' lawyers were able to meet the strictures imposed by *Milliken*. However, their success was facilitated by two distinctive features. First, Delaware had been before the Supreme Court urging the constitutionality of its "separate but equal" public school attendance laws as a party to one of the cases decided with *Brown*.[18] Second, the state had, at that time and for many years thereafter, engaged directly in the creation and maintenance of segregation throughout the state, ignoring local district lines to accomplish that end. Unlike Michigan, therefore, Delaware had committed segregative acts that resulted in a virtually all-black city school system (Wilmington), as well as substantially all-white schools in the suburban areas surrounding that city (New Castle County). The lesson of *Evans* was that whatever hope *Milliken* afforded, regarding plaintiffs obtaining metropolitan desegregation remedies, would be found in Deep South or border communities where states engaged in pervasive segregative actions cutting across district lines. Although there may be successful interdistrict lawsuits of this type, the restricted vision of government responsibility remains the principal legacy of *Milliken*. The state may act through various entities to create and promote segregated schools. Only where it can be proven that the state acts through particular school boards or directly upon school systems, however, will desegregation remedies be justified on either an interdistrict or intradistrict basis.

The Supreme Court's Stance on Segregation

Why has the Court not addressed directly the role of governmental institutions other than school boards in fostering the residential segregation that is reflected in segregated schools and school districts, North and South? The explanation cannot lie in the Court's ignorance of such segregative forces in American life. Through its own decisions, the Court has documented the pervasive nature of housing discrimination imposed or condoned by the government, "a relic of slavery."[19] Government actions have ranged from ordinances that forbade any black person to establish a home in a white community and vice-versa,[20] to restrictive covenants enforced by state and federal courts,[21] to the use of referenda to frustrate state and local efforts to achieve housing integration.[22]

The centerpiece of this story is the *Gautreaux* case.[23] It is a textbook example of how the Chicago Housing Authority (CHA) was able to maintain, well into the 1970s, a starkly segregated pattern of public housing with the approval of federal housing authorities. The Court concluded that the segregative acts of CHA, along with the Federal Department of Housing and Urban Development (HUD), resulted not only in keeping black and white housing apart within the city of Chicago, but also in ensuring that public housing outside of the city remained largely white. For, as the Court found, HUD had consciously refused to construct public housing outside of Chicago, which it had the power to do, joining instead with the CHA in keeping blacks in segregated public housing within the city limits. Based upon these findings, the Court approved lower court orders requiring housing remedies in *Gautreaux* that crossed city-suburb boundaries.

Moreover, in a number of school cases the Supreme Court has been presented with records containing substantial evidence and lower court findings of government policies and practices, apart from school board action, that contributed significantly to both housing segregation and segregated schools.[24] The plaintiffs' lawyers in the *Swann* case introduced evidence on how local, state, and federal agencies had promoted and helped to maintain segregated residential patterns through private home-mortgaging practices, location of public housing, urban renewal projects, and construction of highways. Both the trial and appellate courts found this evidence persuasive. Yet the Supreme Court's reaction to such evidence and findings was essentially to ignore it, stating, "One vehicle can carry only a limited amount of baggage."[25]

In the Detroit *Milliken* trial, the attorneys successfully "educated" the trial judge on this issue. They presented proof, for example, that the Michigan Supreme Court enforced racially restrictive covenants in real estate contracts right through to the day in 1948 that the United States Supreme Court ruled such practices unconstitutional in *Shelley v. Kraemer* (St. Louis) and its companion case from Detroit, *McGhee v. Sipes*.[26] They established, moreover, that in 1947 racially restrictive covenants blanketed those areas of Detroit that were still all-white in 1971, and that such restrictive covenants were also prevalent in all of the city's suburbs that had been platted by 1950. Such covenants continued to appear in all subsequent deeds, abstracts, and title insurance policies of Detroit's largest title company until 1969.

The attorneys also offered probative evidence of direct governmental involvement in creating and maintaining residential segregation. The Federal Housing Administration (FHA), for example, had promoted racial restrictions and "whites-only" private housing in Detroit. Racially dual public housing was constructed with black projects in designated black tracts and white projects in neighborhoods reserved for whites. Michigan governmental agencies with responsibility for the licensing of real estate brokers encouraged their licensees to engage in practices that reinforced residential segregation, including discriminatory treatment of black realtors. And law enforcement officials consistently failed in their duty to protect blacks seeking homes in traditionally white areas of Detroit from mob violence that successfully drove them from their intended new homes.

The plaintiffs' expert witnesses gave unrebutted testimony that the racial exclusion of blacks from all-white areas did not stop at the Detroit city limits but extended throughout the neighboring white suburbs. They also testified that racial discrimination, not free choice or economics, appeared to be a primary cause of residential segregation in Detroit. Altogether, the evidence strongly suggested that blacks lacked the option many defenders of neighborhood schools claimed: They could not readily move to provide their children with a desegregated education.

In addition to this Detroit-specific evidence, the plaintiffs' lawyers introduced expert testimony with respect to federal government support for residential segregation nationally. They testified that FHA had long endorsed racial segregation and supported all-white developments, requiring, for example, in a late 1930s underwriters' manual (still in use in the 1950s), that whites-only housing be served by whites-only public schools. Additionally, the plaintiffs' experts testified that the Veterans

Administration, the Federal Public Housing Agency, the Home Loan Bank Board, the Comptroller of the Currency, the Federal Reserve Board, and the Federal Deposit Insurance Corporation all supported residential segregation historically. Even after their active support ended, such governmental organizations were indifferent to the continuing segregative effects of their past practices. All told, these federal agencies had been involved with approximately 80 percent of the housing built in the United States since the mid-1930s.

The trial judge in Detroit found, based upon this evidence, that "[g]overnmental actions and inaction at all levels, federal, state and local, have combined, with those of private organizations, such as loaning institutions and real estate associations and brokerage firms, to establish and to maintain the pattern of residential segregation throughout the Detroit metropolitan area."[27] However, when the court of appeals upheld the lower court's interdistrict remedy, it refused to consider the housing segregation evidence, except as it directly pertained to the school board's policies with respect to the siting of facilities. And the Supreme Court, speaking through the chief justice, held that "the case [did] not present any question concerning possible state housing violations,"[28] even though the plaintiffs strenuously urged such grounds in support of the lower court orders.

Similar evidence of governmental responsibility for residential segregation was presented in the *Columbus* and *Wilmington* cases, with similar judicial responses. In *Columbus*, the trial judge found that housing segregation was pervasive and long-standing and that housing choices were "constrained because in reality there is a dual housing market; one for blacks and another for whites."[29] This system of "choices" was created and maintained by the racially discriminatory practices of federal agencies, local housing authorities, financing institutions, developers, landlords, and real estate brokers, and by the use of restrictive covenants, zoning, and annexation. In *Evans*, the Wilmington case, a three-judge federal court found that, "since *Brown,* governmental authorities have contributed to the racial isolation of city from suburbs" and that these authorities "are responsible to a significant degree for the increasing disparity in residential and school populations between Wilmington and its suburbs in the two decades [after *Brown*]."[30]

The evidence in these specific cases concerning the responsibility of government agencies for residential segregation was amply documented by federal court rulings in other cases, as well as by a large body of social science literature available to the Court. And to make sure the Court could not overlook this enormous body of data, the plaintiffs' lawyers in

Columbus used a procedurally unorthodox technique and appended a "social science statement" to their brief before the Supreme Court. Signed by thirty-seven prominent scholars, it summarized repeated findings of governmental support, including actions by school boards, with regard to residential segregation and segregated schools. Despite the findings by the lower courts and the experts' statements in this case, the Supreme Court upheld the lower courts' findings of unconstitutional segregation in *Columbus* and its ordering of a system-wide remedy—without addressing the responsibility of other governmental agencies for residential segregation.

It should be pointed out that a variety of procedural obstacles influence the degree to which lower court cases progress to the Supreme Court. They might explain, to some extent, why the Court has not explicitly addressed the question of government responsibility, apart from school board action, for segregated schools. The procedural obstacles stem largely from the fact that only school boards have been before the lower courts as defendants.

Although plaintiffs in several cases have been allowed to present evidence as to the culpability of government agencies other than the school boards for segregated systems, those agencies generally have not been formally before the courts and thus have not had an opportunity to defend against such charges. Since any court determination of liability with respect to these absent parties would have violated due process, it is not surprising that the courts usually have made only generalized findings in this connection, avoiding any formal determination of violation. This was the case, for example, in both the *Swann* and *Columbus* cases.[31] Furthermore, efforts by school boards to bring in federal agencies by way of third-party complaints for the most part have been rejected by lower courts. In doing so, those courts have relied upon the fact that Federal Rule of Civil Procedure 14(a) "normally requires that an impleaded party be legally liable to the main defendant," a condition that school boards are unlikely to satisfy in the school desegregation context.

The usual absence of government agencies other than school boards as defendants in desegregation cases, however, cannot be attributed solely to judicial resistance to their inclusion. Often plaintiffs' lawyers have made a strategic decision not to include them. In most instances, as the long history of school desegregation litigation attests, school boards have been formidable opponents. Plaintiffs' lawyers understandably have felt that adding more defendants would make for even greater difficulties in establishing liability and achieving a desegregation remedy.

What is more, the theory that plaintiffs' lawyers were strongly pressing in these cases did not necessitate the joinder of other governmental agencies. Plaintiffs contended that if the state, acting through housing, redevelopment, licensing, and other agencies, was substantially responsible for the creation and maintenance of segregated neighborhoods, then school boards, also creatures of the state, could be held constitutionally responsible for intentionally establishing and adhering to neighborhood assignment patterns that built upon that segregation. School boards could then be ordered to desegregate their systems, even in the absence of other segregative acts. To quote one attorney's favorite metaphor, school boards should not be permitted to ignore evidence of state segregative activity in their communities by simply walking through a "magic door" into their administrative offices and selecting neighborhood assignment plans irrespective of their segregative consequences.[32]

An additional obstacle to courts addressing the responsibility of all government agencies for segregation stems from the fact that, though the pattern has been uneven, the federal government has often played an important role in pressing for school desegregation. Where this assistance has been forthcoming, private plaintiffs have been reluctant to add other federal agencies, HUD for example, as defendants. To do so could alienate at least part of an otherwise sympathetic administration and complicate the role to be played by the Department of Justice as plaintiff in the same litigation. A more promising alternative, it was thought, involved attempting to achieve voluntary assistance, facilitated by the good offices of the Department of Justice.

Plaintiffs' lawyers themselves were reluctant to rely heavily upon theories concerning governmental agency responsibility for school segregation. As good litigators committed to protecting their clients' interests, they saw winning as their primary objective. In the Supreme Court, one does so by making arguments that seem familiar to the justices rather than by suggesting that a favorable outcome requires the creation of new doctrine.

But one must reject these procedural and strategic obstacles as explanations for the Court's refusal, in all of the major school desegregation cases of the 1970s, to address directly claims of pervasive governmental responsibility for residential segregation and segregated schools. A far more reasonable explanation is that at least four justices during that period (Powell, Rehnquist, Burger, and Stewart) had explicitly rejected such a theory of responsibility. Other justices may have felt tentative about either the merits of the issue or the institutional competence of the judiciary to devise remedies for such compound violations. Such may have contributed to personal decisions against depriving the Court of a working majority in any of the previously discussed school desegregation cases.

Justice Powell made his views on this issue clear as early as *Keyes*, where he observed that "geographical separation of the races . . . resulted from purely natural and neutral non-state causes."[33] Chief Justice Burger and Justice Rehnquist shared this vision sufficiently to join in Powell's 1976 separate opinion on remand in the Austin, Texas, desegregation case, where he stated, "Economic pressures and voluntary preferences are the primary determinants of residential patterns."[34] Justice Stewart, in *Milliken*, explicitly ignored the extensive evidence of governmentally fostered residential segregation, both within and outside Detroit. Based upon that selective reading of the record, he concluded that the predominantly black schools in Detroit were "caused by unknown and perhaps unknowable factors such as in-migration, birth rates, economic changes or cumulative acts of private racial fears."[35] Justice Rehnquist made explicit in the *Columbus-Dayton* opinion his view, implicit in the Austin concurrence, that residential segregation was a "melange of past happenings prompted by economic considerations, private discrimination, discriminatory school assignments, or a desire to reside near people of one's own race or ethnic background."[36]

The Restrictiveness of the Supreme Court's Stance on Desegregation

One might ask why the Supreme Court's limited view on this issue should be of any concern to plaintiffs' lawyers, apart from the *Milliken* problem, given the bar's notable success in arguing for expanded school board liability for segregated schools, North and South. Let me suggest a few concerns in this area, the first of which relates to liability. The Supreme Court's silence on whether evidence of governmental discrimination in housing is probative or even relevant in school desegregation cases unduly restricts the way that plaintiffs' lawyers present their cases, that trial courts evaluate evidence, and that appellate courts review lower court findings. In the *Dayton* case, for example, the trial court refused to hear any such evidence. To the extent that it considered the impact of residential segregation upon the school system, the court's conclusion was that the board was free of any constitutional responsibility for separate schools that might have resulted from such segregation.

To be sure, appellate courts in Dayton ultimately found sufficient school board culpability to justify system-wide relief. But the Dayton experience suggests that in other lawsuits applying a similar view of housing discrimination evidence, courts may find that highly segregated school systems do not result from school board action, or at least not in ways sufficient to trigger *Keyes* or *Columbus* and *Dayton* presumptions. In such cases, plaintiffs will be found entitled to only a limited remedy, if any at all. And, given the limits the Supreme Court has imposed in recent years upon appellate court review of factual findings by trial courts in racial discrimination cases, such trial court determinations that school boards are not liable may be effectively insulated from reversal. What this approach invites, in other words, is a determination that the uniform and consistent adherence to a neighborhood assignment plan by one state institution, the school board, will deprive school desegregation plaintiffs of any remedy. This will be the result, even where the school assignment plan builds upon residential segregation fostered by other state entities, as well as by federal agencies.

In addition, one cannot overlook the extent to which liability rules announced by the Supreme Court in *Swann*, *Keyes*, and *Columbus/Dayton* contribute to the impression that school boards are being made scapegoats while other governmental agencies are entirely non-culpable for the school segregation to which they contributed. This may produce a situation where trial courts will be reluctant to find the requisite facts to trigger the *Swann-Keyes-Columbus-Dayton* presumptions, particularly where the incumbent board has shown some contemporaneous willingness to address the problem of continued segregation. Under such circumstances, courts might understandably view it as unjust to saddle school boards with the entire desegregative burden, controlling precedent notwithstanding.

The second set of concerns involves remedial considerations. Even where school boards have been found liable for system-wide school segregation and have been required to develop a comprehensive remedy, experience has taught that meaningful, long-term solutions are often beyond the ability of even the most cooperative urban school board. Unless other governmental agencies, either as formal parties or as voluntarily supportive forces, help devise and implement a remedy, prevailing patterns of residential segregation will tend to undermine the ultimate success of a school desegregation plan. One of the most unfortunate outgrowths of the Supreme Court's school desegregation jurisprudence has been that a host of local, state, and, most notably, federal agencies have been able to avoid almost all legal responsibility for sharing the financial, as well as additional, burdens necessary for achieving desegregation. Were the Supreme Court to establish that other agencies bear liability for segregated schools, more financial and human resources would be directed toward achieving desegregation in the affected community. It would also expand the focus of the national public debate over desegregation to include questions about the roles not only of school boards but of all implicated government agencies in remedying residential segregation and the segregated schools that result.

Under Supreme Court doctrine, however, only school boards have a constitutional responsibility for remedying segregation, and then only to the extent that they eliminate narrowly defined dual systems.[37] Consequently, even when courts find that system-wide segregation exists and then order a comprehensive remedy, other governmental agencies may act in ways that thwart the school board's implementation of the plan. And even when there are no current actions undermining school boards' plans, the continuing effects of other agencies' earlier practices in promoting and maintaining residential segregation may have a similar result. Yet the Supreme Court directs lower courts to look only at whether the school board has discharged its responsibility. If the board has, and the schools remain largely segregated, plaintiffs have no further recourse. This scenario has already taken place in several communities and is now being played out in a number of proceedings in which school boards deny any further duty to desegregate.[38]

Finally, the Supreme Court's school desegregation jurisprudence has produced unnecessary confusion as to the status of voluntary desegregation efforts. In *Swann* and its companion cases, the Supreme Court suggested that the Constitution allows school boards to adopt "racial balance" student assignment plans for educational reasons.[39] Later, in the *Seattle* case,[40] the Court upheld a voluntary plan in the face of a state law prohibiting such action. The Court found that the state prohibition was an unconstitutional racial classification that, in addition, impermissibly infringed upon the important principle, extolled in *Milliken*, of local control of public schools. Yet the Court appeared to go out of its way to reserve the question of whether school boards could, consistent with the Fourteenth Amendment, utilize racial criteria in student assignment in the absence of a proven constitutional violation. The record in *Seattle* was silent on this point. Were the Court to take the broader view of governmental responsibility for school desegregation being urged here, school boards would not be precluded from voluntarily remedying the segregative effects of other proven government agency action, irrespective of any liability on their part.

The Court's restricted view of the sources of school segregation also was responsible for the unfortunate result in *Crawford v. Los Angeles Board of Education*.[41] In that case, California courts had ordered the desegregation of a Los Angeles school based upon the California Supreme Court's determination that California's state constitution required such steps, irrespective of whether the school board was responsible for the segregation. Subsequently, California voters ratified a proposition limiting court authority to order desegregation only to situations involving Fourteenth Amendment requirements. As a result, the court-ordered desegregation of Los Angeles was halted, because the record reflected only a "passive maintenance by the Board of a neighborhood school system in the face of widespread residential racial imbalance."[42] "A school board," said the California appellate court, "has no duty under the Fourteenth Amendment to meet and overcome the effect of population movements."[43]

The Supreme Court viewed the restricting proposition not as an impermissible racial classification like that in *Seattle*, but rather as a decision by the California electorate against continuing to do more than the United States Constitution requires. The *Crawford* decision further reinforces the concept of a state as a fragmented, rather than a unitary, institution. Again, the state remains free to avoid responsibility for segregated schools. Courts are directed to focus solely upon the school board's actions, while ignoring the many ways in which other state and federal agencies have promoted and maintained the conditions that allow such segregation to persist.

Conclusion

The Supreme Court will no doubt have many more opportunities to address the issue of segregated schools and segregated communities. I would hope the Court recognizes that black and Hispanic children locked in segregated schools throughout the nation deserve a better answer than the following: No claim against segregated schools can be made whenever school boards simply incorporate into their student assignment plans our country's equally segregated residential patterns. *Brown* deserves a better legacy than what Dimond calls "our contemporary, albeit substantially sanitized, form of apartheid."[44]

Is there a philosopher in the house?

Notes

The opening quotation is from Charles L. Black, "The Lawfulness of the Segregation Decisions," 69 *Yale L.J.* 421, 424 (1960).

1. *Brown v. Board of Education*, 347 U.S. 483 (1954).

2. 425 U.S. 284 (1976).

3. *Green v. County School Board*, 391 U.S. 430, 438 (1968).

4. *Deal v. Cincinnati Board of Education*, 369 F.2d 55 (6th Cir. 1966), cert. denied, 389 U.S. 847 (1967), reaffirmed after remand to district court, 419 F.2d 1387 (6th Cir. 1969).

5. 413 U.S. 189 (1973), reh'g denied, 414 U.S. 883 (1973), aff'd in part, rev'd in part after remand to district court, 521 F.2d 465 (10th Cir. 1975), cert. denied, 423 U.S. 1066 (1976), remanded, 576 F. Supp. 1503 (D. Colo. 1983).

6. 402 U.S. 1 (1971).

7. See *Keyes*, 413 U.S. at 214 (opinion of Douglas, J.); 413 U.S. at 217 (opinion of Powell, J., concurring in part and dissenting in part).

8. 391 U.S. 430 (1968).

9. This formulation is usually attributed to a three-judge court decision in *Briggs v. Elliott*, 132 F. Supp. 776, 777 (E.D.S.C. 1955) ("The Constitution, in other words, does not require integration. It merely forbids discrimination."). In contrast, the Court of Appeals for the Fifth Circuit held in the mid-1960's that affirmative steps were required. See *United States v. Jefferson County Board of Education*, 372 F.2d 836 (5th Cir. 1966), aff'd en banc, 380 F.2d 385, cert. denied, 389 U.S. 840 (1967).

10. 391 U.S. 430 (1968). The two companion cases decided with *Green*, *Raney v. Board of Education*, 391 U.S. 443 (1968), and *Monroe v. Board of Commissioners*, 391 U.S. 450 (1968), similarly did not involve large urban or metropolitan areas.

11. *Keyes*, 413 U.S. 189, 203 (1973).

12. Ibid., 201–3.

13. Ibid., 211. The Court invited the school board, in the event it could not disprove the claim of segregative intent, to show, for example, "that its past segregative acts did not create or contribute to the current segregated condition" of schools outside the geographic area where its illegal conduct had occurred. *Id.* at 211.

14. *Columbus Board of Education v. Penick*, 443 U.S. 449 (1979); *Dayton Board of Education v. Brinkman*, 443 U.S. 526 (1979) (*Dayton II*).

15. *Milliken v. Bradley*, 418 U.S. 717 (1974); *Evans v. Buchanan*, 447 F. Supp. 982 (D. Del. 1978), aff'd, 582 F.2d 750 (3d Cir. 1978), cert. denied, 446 U.S. 923 (1980), reh'g denied, 447 U.S. 916 (1980).

16. 418 U.S. at 745.

17. 447 F. Supp. 982 (D. Del.), aff'd, 582 F.2d 750 (3d Cir. 1978), cert. denied, 446 U.S. 923 (1980).

18. *Gebhart v. Belton*, 347 U.S. 483 (1954).

19. *Jones v. Alfred H. Mayer Co.*, 392 U.S. 409, 443 (1968).

20. *Buchanan v. Warley*, 245 U.S. 60 (1917).

21. *Shelley v. Kraemer*, 334 U.S. 1 (1948).

22. *Reitman v. Mulkey*, 387 U.S. 369 (1967); *Hunter v. Erickson*, 393 U.S. 385 (1969).

23. *Hills v. Gautreaux*, 425 U.S. 284 (1976).

24. *United States v. Board of School Commissioners*, 456 F. Supp. 183, 189 (S.D. Ind. 1978), aff'd in part and vacated in part, 637 F.2d 1101, 1110–11 (7th Cir.), cert. denied, 449 U.S. 838 (1980) (violations by Housing Authority of the City of Indianapolis partial basis for ordering limited interdistrict remedy); *Evans v. Buchanan*, 393 F. Supp. 428, 435 (D. Del.) (three-judge court), aff'd per curiam, 423 U.S. 963 (1975) (court found violations by Wilmington Housing Authority and ordered interdistrict remedy).

25. *Swann*, 402 U.S. at 22. This phrase could be read as simply an indication that the Court wished to leave this issue for another day, because it had ample basis for requiring the Charlotte-Mecklenburg Board to implement a system-wide desegregation plan. But I think that the phrase is properly read in view of the Court's subsequent actions as a "door-closer" to consideration of such issues in school cases.

26. 334 U.S. 1 (1948).

27. *Milliken*, 338 F.Supp. 582, 587 (E.D. Mich. 1971).

28. *Milliken*, 418 U.S. at 728 n.7.

29. *Penick v. Columbus*, 429 F. Supp. 229, 258 (S.D. Ohio 1977).

30. *Evans*, 393 F. Supp. at 438.

31. Supplemental memorandum dated March 21, 1970, *Swann v. Charlotte-Mecklenburg Board of Education*, 402 U.S. 1, app. at 1228a–29a (1971); *Penick*, 429 F. Supp. at 258–59 (S.D. Ohio 1977).

32. P. Dimond, *Beyond Busing: Inside the Challenge to Urban Segregation*, 239, 251. Ann Arbor: University of Michigan Press, 1985.

33. 413 U.S. 189, 217 (1973) (Powell, J., concurring in part and dissenting in part).

34. *Austin Independent School District v. United States*, 429 U.S. 990, 994 (1976).

35. *Milliken v. Bradley*, 418 U.S. 717, 756 n.2 (1974) (Stewart, J., concurring). It is worth noting, however, that Justice Stewart did leave open the possibility that proof of state housing violations of an interdistrict nature bearing on school segregation might warrant an interdistrict desegregation remedy. Id. at 755. His suggestion was in fact adopted by courts in both Wilmington, *Evans v. Buchanan*, 393 F. Supp. 428, 438 (D. Del.) (three-judge court), aff'd per curiam, 423 U.S. 963 (1975), and Indianapolis, *United States v. Board of School Commissioners*, 456 F. Supp. 183, 189 (S.D. Ind. 1978), aff'd in part and vacated in part, 637 F.2d 1101, 1110–11 (7th Cir.), cert. denied, 449 U.S. 838 (1980).

36. *Columbus Board of Education v. Penick*, 443 U.S. 449, 512 (1979) (Rehnquist, J., dissenting).

37. *Swann*, 402 U.S. at 31–32; *Pasadena City Board of Education v. Spangler*, 427 U.S. 424 (1976).

38. See, e.g., *Ross v. Houston Independent School District*, 699 F.2d 218 (5th Cir. 1983) (district unitary); *Keyes v. School District No. 1*, 609 F. Supp. 1491 (D. Colo. 1985) (district nonunitary); *Riddick v. School Board of City of Norfolk*, No. 84-1815, slip. op. (4th Cir. 1986) (district unitary). A United States Department of Justice press release reports that 117 school districts have been declared "fully desegregated" and 47 have obtained court orders relieving them of any further duty to desegregate. Department of Justice, *Press Release*, Feb. 18, 1986.

39. *Swann*, 402 U.S. at 16.

40. *Washington v. Seattle School District No. 1*, 458 U.S. 457 (1982).

41. 458 U.S. 527 (1982).

42. *Crawford v. Board of Education*, 113 Cal. App. 3d 633, 645 (Cal. Ct. App. 1981).

43. Ibid., 646.

44. P. Dimond, *supra* note 32, at 402.

Chapter 7

Segregation Misunderstood:
The *Milliken* Decision Revisited

Charles R. Lawrence III

In 1974 in *Milliken v. Bradley*,[1] the Supreme Court reversed an affirmative school desegregation order for the first time since the 1954 decision of *Brown v. Board of Education*.[2] By a five to four margin, the Court held that the district court was in error when it ordered fifty-three suburban school districts to participate in the desegregation of the predominantly black Detroit school district. The political implications of the decision were immediately apparent. The Court had sentenced northern school desegregation to the death penalty before the baby had taken its first full breath. Metropolitan-wide relief was the last hope for the meaningful integration of schools in a nation whose urban-suburban demography was becoming increasingly segregated.[3] The *Milliken* decision assured middle-class whites that their mass exodus to the suburbs to seek refuge from blacks had not been made in vain since the Supreme Court also made clear that they would not use school desegregation to invade the suburban fortress of housing for whites only.

The *Milliken* decision stands as a disturbing reflection of the changing political and social mood of the American public. In dissent, Justice Marshall, who had argued *Brown* before the Supreme Court twenty years earlier, closed his opinion with a ringing indictment of his colleagues in the majority: "Today's holding, I fear, is more a reflection of a perceived mood that we have gone far enough in enforcing the Constitution's guarantee of equal justice than it is the product of neutral principles of law. In the short run, it may seem to be the easier course to allow our great metropolitan areas to be divided up each into two cities—one white, the other black—but it is a course, I predict, our people will ultimately regret."[4]

One is tempted to simply say "amen" to Justice Marshall's insightful analysis of the majority opinion as a myopic political accommodation to public mood. The immediate reaction of many critics of the Burger Court, including this author, was to write the opinion off as a not-so-facile rationalization of a politically expedient decision. But the opinion merits closer examination now that time has changed its status from news to well-established precedent. It deserves a closer look, not because Justice Marshall's fears of political motivation were unfounded, nor because people take Supreme Court opinions more seriously once they have been cited in subsequent cases, but because a closer look at the chief justice's opinion will reveal a reflection of perceived public mood that is even more disturbing than a momentary capitulation to modern-day anti-busing forces.

The central inadequacy of the *Milliken* opinion was the Court's refusal to recognize the true nature of segregation as an institution in this country. The purpose of this chapter is (1) to explore just what the Supreme Court has "misunderstood"[5] or chosen to articulate about the reality of segregation; (2) to demonstrate that the Court's misunderstanding results not from lack of evidence clarifying segregation's real meaning and import, but rather from a conscious decision to ignore the obvious meaning of that evidence; and (3) to demonstrate that once segregation is properly understood, the Court's differing treatment of northern (de facto) and southern (de jure) school segregation is unsound and bears reexamination.

Part 1 of the chapter begins with a brief recapitulation of the *Milliken* opinion itself. It notes that the majority opinion's emphasis on the limitations on the equitable powers of federal courts diverts our attention from the initial and necessarily precedent inquiry concerning the nature, source, and scope of the injury to plaintiffs. It argues that the *Milliken* decision reflected the Court's misunderstanding of how segregation injures black children and that this misunderstanding resulted in the Court's failure to recognize the full scope of the constitutional violation involved in the case.

Part 2 of the chapter discusses three characteristics of the institution of racial segregation, characteristics that must be recognized before one can understand the nature and scope of the injury segregated schools inflict on black children: (1) racial segregation injures blacks by labeling them as inferior; (2) the existence of a system of racial segregation, not particular segregating acts, operates to injure black individuals; and (3) once the state has successfully established and institutionalized racial segregation, the institution is self-perpetuating and need not be actively maintained. Considering these three fundamental characteristics of segregation, the chapter maintains that because governmental involvement in the establishment of a racially segregated society was not significantly different in the North and the South, the affirmative duty to disestablish segregation should apply uniformly throughout the country.

In part 3, the chapter traces the development of the Supreme Court's approach to segregation from *Plessy v. Ferguson*[6] through *Brown v. Board of Education,*[7] in order to demonstrate that, far from being an aberration, the *Milliken* Court's misunderstanding is well-established in precedent and has its roots in *Brown*. In part 4, the *Milliken* decision is reconsidered in light of the analytical framework proposed in part 2. Part 5 analyzes three other Supreme Court decisions that rely on *Milliken* to curtail intradistrict relief and suggests that these cases do an injustice to blacks, not so much because they limit the scope of relief but because they refuse to acknowledge that blacks have been injured.[8] The chapter concludes that the Supreme Court's failure to accurately identify and articulate the nature of the injury inflicted by segregation is more than an indication of its failure to understand; it is a reflection of the nation's lack of commitment to achieving true equality for blacks.

The *Milliken* Decision

In 1970, the Detroit branch of the NAACP (National Association for the Advancement of Colored People), joined by individual parents and students, initiated a class action suit against various state and local school district officials seeking relief from alleged illegal racial segregation in the Detroit public school system. The trial court, having found that the Detroit public school system was segregated on the basis of race as the result of official conduct, and having further found that a solely intradistrict remedy would result in increased rather than decreased segregation of the Detroit schools, subsequently deemed that the desegregation proposals were inadequate. The court thus established a desegregation panel and ordered the panel to prepare a remedial plan that consolidated the Detroit school system and fifty-three surrounding suburban school districts. The Court of Appeals for the Sixth Circuit affirmed the district court's order on the grounds that, in view of the racial composition of the Detroit school system, the only feasible remedy required the crossing of boundary lines between the Detroit school district and adjacent or nearby school districts. On appeal, the Supreme Court reversed.

Although the Supreme Court opinion discussed at some length what it saw as practical problems that would be encountered in the consolidation of numerous school districts by judicial decree, its decision to reject the metropolitan desegregation order of the trial court actually turned on what it considered to be fundamental limitations on the remedial powers of the federal courts. The Court said, "A federal remedial power may be exercised 'only on the basis of a constitutional violation' and, as with any equity case, the nature of the violation determines the scope of the remedy."[9] As applied to the instant case, the Court held that, "Before the boundaries of separate and autonomous school districts may be set aside by consolidating the separate units for remedial purposes or by imposing a cross-district remedy, it must first be shown that there has been a constitutional violation within one district that produces a significant segregative effect in another district. Specifically, it must be shown that racially discriminatory acts of the state or local school districts, or of a single school district have been a substantial cause of inter district segregation."[10]

By focusing attention on the limits of the remedial powers of the federal courts, Chief Justice Burger's majority opinion would lead one to believe that this decision turns on neutral principles of law. In fact, the issue of the scope of the Court's equitable power is a straw man. It is incontrovertible that the equitable power of the federal courts is limited to the correction of constitutional violations. The significant question, however, and what was really before the Court, was the definition of "constitutional violation." By holding that the Detroit district court's choice of an interdistrict remedy was in error, and that only an intradistrict remedy was warranted by the facts, the Supreme Court necessarily found that there was no "constitutional violation" existing outside of the boundaries of the Detroit school system. In so finding, the Court declined to find an overall pattern of state involvement and impliedly defined and limited the meaning of "constitutional violation" to be evidenced in the record of specific statutory provisions or purposeful acts by the state or local school district directed at the creation or maintenance of segregated schools.

It is the inadequacy of this definition that lies at the heart of the *Milliken* decision's deficiencies. The definition is derived from the distinction between de jure and de facto segregation, a distinction that was first fully articulated by the Supreme Court in *Keyes v. School District No. 1.*[11] In *Keyes*, the Court held that only de jure segregation violated the Equal Protection Clause of the Fourteenth Amendment. De jure segregation was defined as "a current condition of segregation resulting from intentional state action directed specifically to the [segregated] schools."[12] The Court emphasized that "the differentiating factor between *de jure* segregation and so called *de facto* segregation . . . is purpose or intent to segregate,"[13] and went on to give a detailed list of the kind of evidence that must be produced for the record in order to establish segregative purpose or intent.

Thus, Justice Brennan's opinion in *Keyes* achieved results that were applauded by proponents of school desegregation because it eased the plaintiffs' burden of proving segregative intent in northern districts. The requirement of evidentiary demonstration of segregative purpose or intent as a prerequisite to the Court's finding a constitutional violation, even though less burdensome, nonetheless reinforced the distinction between northern and southern cases; it thereby created an obstacle in *Milliken* and lies at the root of the Court's failure to redress injuries suffered by black children in the Detroit schools.

Besides imposing evidentiary limitations upon proving constitutional violations, the Supreme Court's use of the de jure and de facto labels has circumscribed its analysis and understanding of the constitutional rights subject to violation by segregation and subject to redress by courts' remedial powers. The Court has attempted to draw a distinction between segregation mandated by law or resulting from purposeful or intentional state action and segregation that results randomly or without purposeful or intentional action by the state or government. While the Court does not deny that de facto segregation may injure the black child, it holds that such segregation is not an injury attributable to the state and that, therefore, the injured child has no protected right under the Equal Protection Clause of the Fourteenth Amendment. Because no right has been violated, the Court is without power to effect a remedy or ameliorate the injury to the child. Thus, because the *Milliken* Court misunderstood the nature of the injury inflicted upon Detroit school children, it failed to find the requisite state involvement in the interdistrict infliction of that injury and thereby fashion an interdistrict remedy.

Understanding the Institution of Segregation

In order to recognize the full scope of the constitutional injury inflicted by a segregated school system, one must understand how the institution of segregation functions. Three underlying characteristics of segregation crucial to this understanding are (1) segregation labels black children as inferior; (2) the existence of the institution as a whole, rather than particular acts, constitutes the injury; and (3) the institution is self-perpetuating.

Segregation's Only Purpose Is to Label Blacks as Inferior
What right is ensured to black school children by the imperative that they not be denied equal protection of the law? It is important to remember

that the basic right protected by the Equal Protection Clause is the right not to be classified or labeled in a way that results in one being treated differently or unequally for no legitimate reason.

In general, the Equal Protection Clause requires that when the state classifies or labels persons for purposes of treating them differently, the classification must be rationally related to a legitimate state purpose. Further, if persons are classified or labeled according to race, the state must demonstrate a compelling justification for its disparate treatment of racial groups.

In *Brown v. Board of Education,* the holding that racially segregated schools are inherently unequal makes most sense if it is understood as a recognition of the fact that racial segregation by definition is an invidious labeling device and therefore must violate the Equal Protection Clause. In abandoning the "separate but equal" doctrine of *Plessy v. Ferguson*, it should have been clear to the Court that the injury to black children did not result solely from unequal resource allocation, nor from the fact that they were refused the opportunity to sit next to white children in school. Rather, the injury was due to the fact that attendance at a separate school was part of the system that labeled blacks as inferior and whites as superior.

The institution of segregation and the injury it inflicts on blacks are necessarily misunderstood until one recognizes that its chief purpose is to define, not to separate. This fact is best demonstrated by a brief examination of the development of segregation in the South. Southern whites had no aversion to commingling with blacks so long as the institution of slavery made their status clear. It was only with the demise of slavery that segregation became necessary. C. Vann Woodward notes the virtual absence of segregation in the South during slavery in his authoritative work on the history of segregation:

> In most aspects of slavery as practiced in the antebellum South, however, segregation would have been an inconvenience and an obstruction to the functioning of the system. The very nature of the institution made separation of the races for the most part impracticable. The mere policing of slaves required that they be kept under more or less constant scrutiny, and so did the exaction of involuntary labor. The supervision, maintenance of order, and physical and medical care of slaves necessitated many contacts and encouraged a degree of intimacy between the races unequaled, and often held distasteful, in other parts of the country. The system imposed its own type of inter-racial contact, unwelcome as it might be on both sides.[14]

Although historians differ in their views of when segregation became firmly established as an institution, there is virtual unanimity concerning its purpose and method. Segregation was an instrument of subordination that used a strict and rigid caste system to clearly define and limit the social, political, and economic mobility of blacks. The segregation statutes and "Jim Crow" laws were the "public symbols and constant reminders" of the inferior position of blacks.[15] It is the symbolism of segregation that operates to violate the Fourteenth Amendment. Unless *Brown* is understood in this light, it must fail in its purpose of ensuring black children equal educational opportunity.

In response to contemporaneous attacks on the soundness of the *Brown* decision, Charles Black wrote an article that is brilliant both in its simplicity and its clarity.[16] Professor Black pointed out that while attention is usually focused on the inequalities of the separate facilities themselves, the most significant evidence of the inherent inequality of segregation can be found by examining what it means to the people who impose it and to the people who are subjected to it:

> It is actionable defamation in the south to call a white man a Negro. A small portion of Negro "blood" puts one in the inferior race for segregation purposes. Placing of a white person in a Negro railroad car is an actionable humiliation. It would be the most unneutral of principles . . . to require that a court faced with the present problem refuse to note a plain fact about the society of the United States—the fact that the social meaning of segregation is the putting of the Negro in a position of walled-off inferiority.[17]

The *Brown* Court, unfortunately, was not nearly so articulate in support of its decision. While the Court's unanimous decision found that "separate educational facilities are inherently unequal,"[18] instead of resting that finding on the common knowledge that segregation's purpose and function was to designate the black race as inferior or less than equal, the Court resorted to what it referred to as "intangible considerations." The Court said that "to separate [Negro children] from others of similar age and qualifications solely because of their race generates a feeling of inferiority as to their status in the community that may affect their hearts and minds in a way unlikely ever to be undone."[19] The Court then went on to quote the federal district court in Kansas; it had found that "[a] sense of inferiority [engendered by segregated schools] . . . has a tendency to [retard] the educational and mental development of Negro children."[20]

It is not the Supreme Court's emphasis and reliance on the psychosociological evidence rather than the common sense approach that should be faulted, but the Court's failure to spell out the conditional precedent for black children's feelings of inferiority. That is, the fact that they and everyone else knew that the system of segregation defined them as inferior. It was the *Brown* Court's failure to confront this simple reality about segregation that allowed Chief Justice Burger and the *Milliken* majority to conclude that there was no evidence of state involvement in the violation of the Detroit plaintiffs' constitutional rights requiring an interdistrict remedy.

If it is the act of separating that violates the Equal Protection Clause, then the Detroit children's only right is to be free of specific acts of separation by the state; the scope of the remedy thus turns on whether there is sufficient evidence of such specific acts of separation. If, however, the Equal Protection Clause protects the right not to be labeled or classified on the basis of race, we must look beyond whether the state was involved in specific separating acts. In addition, whether the state was involved in the creation of the sociopolitical system of segregation that labels segregated black children as inferior must be examined. It is this principle that must be understood before a proper approach to desegregation cases can be developed.

The *Milliken* court, having defined the plaintiffs' rights under the Equal Protection Clause as the right not to be separated, looked only for evidence of state involvement in intentional acts of separation of schoolchildren by race. Because this misunderstanding of the nature of segregation caused the Court to misconstrue the scope of those rights and thus to ignore pertinent evidence, the Court found no evidence of state involvement in the violation of the Detroit plaintiffs' constitutional rights.

Black Children Are Injured by the Existence of the System of Segregation, Not by Particular Segregating Acts

A second aspect of the Court's misunderstanding of segregation is related to the Court's adoption of the requirement that evidence of particular segregative acts by a school district must exist before a federal judge may order relief against that district. *Milliken* adopted this requirement from *Keyes v. School District No. 1*,[21] wherein the Court found that there must be evidence that the racial imbalance in the schools was brought about by discriminatory actions of state authorities.

The *Keyes* and *Milliken* requirement of evidence of particular segregative acts by a school district before a federal court may order relief against that district demonstrates a second and related aspect of the Court's misunderstanding of segregation. Because segregation's purpose and function is to define or classify blacks as inferior, the injury that it inflicts is systemic rather than particular. Black schoolchildren are not injured by the fact that a school board has placed them in a school different than that in which it has placed white schoolchildren so much as by the fact that the school exists within a system that defines it as the inferior school and its pupils as inferior persons.

Many black schools that existed within the segregated school systems of the South were in fact superior to their white counterparts. It is ironic that most of these schools achieved their excellence as a direct result of the discrimination inherent in a segregated society, in that the best black professionals were forced into teaching by their virtual exclusion from other fields. The existence of such schools violated the constitutional rights of children attending them—not because a school board or state legislature had taken steps to see that white children did not attend them, and certainly not because of the relative quality of education they provided—but because they were pieces of a larger puzzle that, when fit together, plainly spelled out the words "if you're black, get back."

Once it is understood that segregation functions as a systemic labeling device, it should be clear that any state action that results in the maintenance of the segregated system is a direct and proximate cause of the injuries suffered by black children in segregated schools and is in violation of the Equal Protection Clause of the Fourteenth Amendment. Evidence of such action would, of course, not be limited to acts directly resulting in one-race schools. Segregated housing and zoning practices are equally effective means of labeling blacks as inferior. If the state discriminates by continuing to participate in labeling blacks "not fit to live with," it is surely beside the point that it is not an active participant in particular acts labeling blacks "not fit to go to school with."

Chief Justice Burger and his colleagues in the *Milliken* majority, in what can only be described as selective perception, have blinded themselves to this seemingly obvious reality. The following quote exemplifies this myopia: "Disparate treatment of white and Negro students occurred within the Detroit school system, and not elsewhere . . . The constitutional right of the Negro respondents residing in Detroit is to attend a unitary school system in that district. Unless petitioners drew the district lines in a discriminatory fashion, or arranged for white students residing in the Detroit District to attend schools in Oakland and Macomb Counties, they were under no constitutional duty to make provisions for Negro students to do [so]."[22] And further, "There is no claim and there is no evidence hinting that petitioner outlying school districts and their predecessors, or the 30-odd other school districts in the tri-county area

. . . have ever maintained or operated anything but unitary school systems."[23]

Because Justice Burger limits the right of black children to freedom from acts by the state aimed at segregating the schools, such specific acts are the only kind of evidence considered in determining there has been no violation for which interdistrict relief would be appropriate.

Once the true nature of segregation is understood, it should become equally apparent that because segregation injures by label or classification rather than by separation itself, the scope of that injury cannot be defined by school district lines. State sanction of the purposeful segregation of schools in Detroit operates to stigmatize black children throughout the state. They do not escape that stigma merely by virtue of the fact that the defamation against them occurred in another district; its publication extends throughout the state.

The Fallacy of the North-South,
De Jure-De Facto Distinction

The Court's misunderstanding of the nature of segregation is perhaps best demonstrated by its failure to apply a consistent constitutional standard to southern (de jure) and northern (so-called de facto) varieties of segregation. Since de jure, as compared to de facto, segregation is found to arise by virtue of intentional acts of the state, this distinction is at bottom a state-action question. Although all segregation may result in injury to black children, the factual question that must be resolved by the Court is whether the state can be held responsible. In states that had laws or express policies mandating segregation at the time of *Brown*, the answer was clear: this was de jure segregation and clearly unconstitutional under *Brown*.

In 1973, the Court found that de jure segregation might also exist in the northern and western states where school segregation was not mandated by law in 1954. There is, however, an important difference, relating to the evidentiary burdens, between the Court's approach to establishing the presence of de jure segregation in the North and its approach to the same problem in the South. In the North, the burden is on the plaintiff to demonstrate the state's direct and causal involvement in the segregation of schools. In the South, the Court has held that the burden is on the defendant school district to demonstrate that it has acted affirmatively and successfully to dismantle a previously existing segregated school system. Proof of the absence of laws mandating segregation or continuing purposeful segregating acts by the state is not enough.

In *Green v. County School Board*,[24] the defendant, Virginia School District, asserted the constitutionality of its "freedom-of-choice" plan by arguing that it was no longer directly involved in maintaining or perpetuating a segregated school system. The Court unequivocally rejected that argument and held that the school district had an affirmative duty to convert to a unitary system: "In the context of the state-imposed segregated pattern of long standing, the fact that in 1965 the Board opened the doors of the former 'white' school to Negro children and of the 'Negro' school to white children merely begins, not ends, our inquiry whether the Board has taken steps adequate to abolish its dual, segregated system."[25]

Although the rejection of freedom of choice in *Green* appears to have been brought on by the Supreme Court's loss of patience with various southern schemes designed to resist school desegregation, the Court indicated that the affirmative duty requirement grew directly out of the second *Brown* decision, *Brown II*.[26] In the *Green* case, the Supreme Court set forth broad desegregation guidelines for the implementation of *Brown I*:

> *Brown II* was a call for the dismantling of well-entrenched dual systems tempered by an awareness that complex and multifaceted problems would arise that would require time and flexibility for a successful resolution. School boards such as the respondent then operating state-compelled dual systems were nevertheless clearly charged with the affirmative duty to take whatever steps might be necessary to convert to a unitary system in which racial discrimination would be eliminated root and branch.[27]

> The burden on a school board today is to come forward with a plan that promises realistically to work, and promises realistically to work now.[28]

Thus, according to the Court's language in *Green*, the affirmative duty requirement is limited to those school systems that were segregated by operation of law in 1954 when *Brown* was decided.

It is not clear, however, why the affirmative duty to desegregate should only be made applicable to school boards that were operating state-compelled dual systems at the time of *Brown*. Dual systems in northern school districts have proven to be more firmly entrenched than those in the South. The argument that in the North there is no evidence of recent governmental participation in acts directly resulting in the segregation of schools was the very argument advanced by the New Kent School Board in *Green* and rejected by the Court.

It could be argued that the northern and southern cases are distinguishable on the basis of state action; in the South, state action is present because state laws required the operation of dual school systems, while in the North, state action is absent because segregated schools occurred as the result of segregated housing patterns. This distinction, however, neglects the entire history of segregation in America.

Segregation is northern, not southern, in origin and reached considerable maturity in the North before moving south in full force. Leon F. Litwack's *North of Slavery*, an authoritative account of the treatment of blacks above the Mason-Dixon Line, should be instructive to those who have been led to believe that segregation was a uniquely southern legal institution. In describing conditions in the North circa 1860, Professor Litwack noted:

> In virtually every phase of existence, Negroes found themselves systematically separated from whites. They were either excluded from railway cars, omnibuses, stagecoaches, and steamboats or assigned to special "Jim Crow" sections; they sat, when permitted, in secluded and remote corners of theaters and lecture halls; they could not enter most hotels, restaurants, and resorts, except as servants; they prayed in "Negro pews" in the white churches, and if partaking of the sacrament of the Lord's Supper, they waited until the whites had been served the bread and wine. Moreover, they were often educated in segregated schools, punished in segregated prisons, nursed in segregated hospitals, and buried in segregated cemeteries.[29]

Based on historical fact, it cannot be refuted that the official actions of northern, midwestern, and western states played a predominant role in the entrenchment of segregation within their borders. Given that there was substantial state activity in the promulgation of segregation throughout the nation, the fact that the northern states ceased official enforcement of a segregated school system prior to 1954, while the southern states continued to do so officially, does not appear to be an adequate rationale for exempting northern states from the mandate of *Brown*, as further elucidated by *Green*. Thus, the Supreme Court's distinction between northern and southern cases of desegregation is not really a matter of state action at all and is simply a matter of timing.

Although the Supreme Court holdings dictate a chronological distinction between pre- and post-1954 legislation, the Court's reasoning in *Green* would appear to counsel that the cases be treated on the basis of their facts and not be categorized by region or date. *Green* stands for the proposition that where a system of segregation remains firmly entrenched, the state must do more than cease and desist from further official support of the system; it must act affirmatively to disestablish that system. Once it is understood that segregation achieves its purpose by labeling blacks as inferior, it becomes clear that segregation is firmly entrenched when the label of inferiority is reflected in societal attitudes. Moreover, once the label is firmly affixed, it will not be removed or alleviated by a mere discontinuance of official name-calling. This understanding applies to all instances of segregation and knows no geographic distinctions.

The state has acted to establish a self-perpetuating institution. Because there has been no affirmative action by the state to disestablish the institution, it remains intact. The segregated systems of the North and West are not de facto. They have not occurred in the absence of official action. Rather, they are creatures of the state and the affirmative duty to destroy them that was imposed on the New Kent School District in *Green* should be universally applicable.[30]

Without doubt, it will be argued that the causal link between constitutional violations existing in northern states in the distant past and presently segregated schools is too tenuous to support the application of the *Green* standard to those districts. At the root of this argument lies the belief that racial segregation in the North, as we know it today, is the result of the ingrained racial prejudice of individuals in the absence of state assistance, encouragement, or compulsion. This is simply not the case. Governmental participation in and support of the system of segregation in the northern and western states was not a relic of the past at the time of the *Brown* decision. Three notable examples of modern-day governmental segregation, contemporaneous with *Brown*, that labeled blacks as inferior in the North as well as the South were the continued segregation of the United States Armed Forces until 1948, the Federal Housing Administration's active encouragement of segregated housing until 1950, and the statutory segregation by Congress of Washington, D.C.'s, school system until 1954. State and local officials have played an equally active, although not as well documented, part in the maintenance of the system of segregation in the North. Highways and freeways were built as barriers between black and white communities;[31] building officials did their utmost to hamper construction intended for blacks in white neighborhoods;[32] local police and fire departments excluded blacks by discriminatory hiring practices;[33] and, until 1948, local courts consistently enforced restrictive covenants.[34]

Once the state has effectively institutionalized racial segregation as a labeling device, only minimal maintenance is required to keep it in working order. After the system is established, any attempt to distinguish active governmental involvement in racial segregation from passive or neutral tolerance of private segregation is illusory. Present passivity is merely a continuation of past action. The individual facing well-entrenched segregated housing patterns does not make a wholly private choice when deciding to move into a neighborhood with persons of a like race. That choice is substantially influenced by societal or institutional pressures to conform to the prevailing norm. Job security and opportunity for advancement, availability of financing, and the personal comfort of one's family may all depend upon such conformity. These institutionalized attitudes or norms are directly traceable to a time when the state was actively involved in their establishment. There has not been an intervening period in which these attitudes were not present so that it could truly be said they were private in origin. They remain because the state has never met the *Green* requirement of affirmative disestablishment.

The Heart of the *Plessy* Doctrine Is Alive and Well

While the *Milliken* case is used herein as a point of departure and reference, the Burger Court does not stand alone in history in its misunderstanding of segregation. There is ample precedent for the Court's failure to face up to the realities of Jim Crow. Furthermore, it is evident that the Court's failure has been more intentional than not.

The first and most transparent example of the Supreme Court's choosing not to call it like they must have seen it is *Plessy v. Ferguson*, the source of the infamous doctrine of "separate but equal."[35] In *Plessy*, the Court upheld a Louisiana statute requiring separate facilities for white and black passengers on trains as not violative of the Fourteenth Amendment prohibition of unequal protection of the laws. The Court said the object of the Fourteenth Amendment "was undoubtedly to enforce the absolute equality of the two races before the law, but in the nature of things it could not have been intended to abolish distinctions based upon color, or to enforce social, as distinguished from political equality, or a commingling of the two races upon terms unsatisfactory to either."[36] Yet it was obvious to any adult living in the United States in 1896 that the social and political inequalities of blacks were inextricably interwoven. It is clear that the justices who joined the *Plessy* majority must have understood the nature of segregation, if only because their colleague, Justice Harlan, explained it to them so clearly in his dissent: "What can more certainly arouse race hate, what more certainly create and perpetuate a feeling of distrust between these races, than state enactments, that, in fact, proceed on the ground that colored citizens are so inferior and degraded that they cannot be allowed to sit in public coaches occupied by white citizens? That, as all will admit, is the real meaning of such legislation as was enacted in Louisiana."[37]

Whether the *Plessy* majority feigned blindness to the real and obvious meaning of segregation on railways because they themselves were committed to white superiority or because they realized that the nation's commitment to the same would have made enforcement of a contrary decision impossible and therefore judicially unsound, is open to debate. There is, however, no questioning the fact that the *Plessy* Court's articulation of an incorrect understanding of the nature of segregation was the result of a conscious decision.

The Supreme Court may have been subtler but was no less astute in avoiding any discussion of the real meaning of segregation in the graduate and professional school cases that paved the way for *Brown*. In *Missouri ex. rel. Gaines v. Canada*,[38] *Sipuel v. Board of Regents*,[39] *Sweatt v. Painter*,[40] and *McLaurin v. Oklahoma State Regents for Higher Education*,[41] the Court, in considering the constitutionality of segregated graduate study programs at public universities, found it unnecessary to reexamine the "separate but equal" doctrine in order to grant desegregation relief to the plaintiffs.

In *Sweatt*, by finding that a segregated law school for blacks could not provide them equal educational opportunities, the Court relied on "those qualities which are incapable of objective measurement but which make for greatness in a law school."[42] In *McLaurin*, the Court required that a black admitted to a white graduate school should not be segregated within the classroom and cafeteria and should be treated like all other students. Again, the Court based its decision on the intangible considerations of "his ability to study, to engage in discussions and exchange views with other students, and, in general, to learn his profession."[43] In neither opinion was there mention of the obvious fact that in each case the state had relegated black students to a separate school or separate seats within the classroom for the specific purpose of designating them inferior.

This chapter has already touched upon the Warren Court's failure in *Brown v. Board of Education* to support the holding that segregation is inherently unequal with what was the obvious, simplest, and most clearly unassailable rationale. Instead of taking judicial cognizance of the fact that the manifest purpose of segregation was to designate blacks as inferior and noting that such a purpose was constitutionally impermissible, the Court chose to focus upon the effect of school segregation.

In *Brown*, Chief Justice Warren, speaking for a unanimous Court, began the crucial portion of his opinion by describing the importance of education in achieving political equality. He then proceeded to cite evidence presented to the Court by social scientists indicating that the effect of school segregation on black children was to generate "a feeling of inferiority" that in turn affects the motivation and ability of these children to learn.[44] In short, segregation violated the Equal Protection Clause because of its empirically demonstrated discriminatory effect on the educational-political opportunity afforded blacks. While the evidence and reasoning were sound, the Court's choice of rationale avoided any direct refutation of the *Plessy* dictum that the Fourteenth Amendment was not "intended to abolish distinctions based on color, or to enforce social, as distinguished from political equality."[45] More importantly, by focusing on effect, the Court avoided any recognition of the fact that the purpose of the social inequalities of the system of segregation is the maintenance of political inequality.

Again, there is every indication that the *Brown* Court's choice of a rationale that avoided any explicit mention of the true nature of segregation was not without design. The simplicity of holding segregation unconstitutional because of its impermissible purpose must have been apparent to the Court. Moreover, among the arguments made by counsel for plaintiffs in brief and in oral argument was the argument that the express purpose of the Fourteenth Amendment was to deprive the states of the authority to enforce existing "black codes" or in the future set up additional black codes, and that segregation laws, like the black codes, were designed to establish a caste system. The *Brown* plaintiffs also relied heavily, in both brief and oral argument, upon *Strauder v. West Virginia*,[46] a case that discussed the purposes of the Fourteenth Amendment at some length with the benefit of historical proximity to its adoption. *Strauder*, in holding the total exclusion of blacks from juries unconstitutional, spoke of the Fourteenth Amendment as follows: "The words of the Amendment, it is true, are prohibitory, but they contain a necessary implication of a positive immunity, or right, most valuable to the colored race, the right to exemption from unfriendly legislation against them distinctively as colored, exemption from legal discriminations, implying inferiority in civil society, lessening the security of their enjoyment of the rights which others enjoy, and discriminations which are steps towards reducing them to the condition of a subject race. "[47]

In the period of over twenty years since *Brown*, the Supreme Court has considered numerous school desegregation cases without expanding upon or more fully articulating its rationale. In all of these cases, *Brown* has been cited for its holding that continued school segregation is inherently incompatible with the Equal Protection Clause without significant further comment upon or reconsideration of why.

Milliken **Reconsidered**

Thus far three major points providing an analytical framework for reconsidering the *Milliken* case have been discussed. First, the injury inflicted upon black children by segregation is one of pejorative classification. This injury occurs by virtue of the existence of the system or institution of segregation rather than particular segregating acts. Second, the Equal Protection Clause of the Fourteenth Amendment is violated by significant state involvement in the creation or maintenance of the sociopolitical system of segregation, and the constitutional rights of black children are violated whenever the state acts to perpetuate that system. This is true without regard to whether the purpose or direct result of the act is the segregation of schools themselves, and such a constitutional violation may not be limited in scope by the boundaries of a school district or other subdivision of the state. Third, the affirmative duty to disestablish segregation, as set forth in *Green v. County School Board*,[48] must apply to all states that have played a predominant role in its establishment, regardless of their geographic location or the date upon which statutes mandating segregation were removed from their books.

If the *Milliken* case is reconsidered in light of this analysis, it becomes apparent that affirmation of the district court opinion ordering an interdistrict remedy is compelled on several grounds. First, the state had recently participated in the segregation of Detroit schools; the record contained clear uncontroverted evidence of state involvement in the segregation of Detroit schools.[49] This activity by the state labeled or classified as inferior not just Detroit black children but all black children upon whom the state could exert its power or from whom it could require obedience. Because the injury of the labeling of black children as inferior reached beyond the boundaries of the Detroit school district, the constitutional right to be free of that injury also extended beyond the district. By redefining the nature of the constitutional infringement, the remedy must be likewise altered. According to the *Milliken* majority's own reasoning, "the scope of the remedy is determined by the nature and extent of the constitutional violation."[50] Thus, an interdistrict remedy is clearly appropriate.

Second, in all likelihood, the state had participated in the maintenance of segregated housing in the suburbs. Although Justice Stewart, concurring, found no evidence on the record of racially discriminatory use of housing or zoning laws,[51] it is unlikely that the ubiquitous presence of exclusively white housing in the Detroit suburbs occurred entirely without state participation or accommodation. Such discrimination did as much to classify black children as inferior as sending them to separate schools; it constituted another constitutional violation that was multidistrict in scope and therefore properly subject to an interdistrict remedy.

Third, the state had never disestablished the segregated school system it played a significant role in creating. The *Milliken* majority indicated there was no evidence hinting that outlying school districts had historically maintained any type of school system other than unitary. However, a more careful review of the history of the Michigan legislature reveals that in 1845 the legislature approved the incorporation of a school for Negroes only after the adoption of an amendment expressly prohibiting the admission of whites.[52] It might well be argued that an 1867 Michigan act requiring that school districts provide education without discrimination as to race and a 1963 amendment to the Michigan Constitution providing for nondiscriminatory educational opportunity have operated to repeal the previous discriminatory laws.[53] But mere repeal of segregation statutes and the passage of time are not sufficient to satisfy the command of *Green*. In the face of evidence of a still well-entrenched dual system, Michigan had clearly not met the burden of coming forward with a plan in which racial discrimination was eliminated "root and branch," a plan that "promised realistically to work now."[54]

The Fruit of *Milliken*: The Court Curtails Intradistrict Relief

In three subsequent Supreme Court decisions, the Court reaffirmed its refusal to recognize the true nature of the injury inflicted by the institution of segregation. In vacating federal district and circuit court desegregation orders in *Pasadena City Board of Education v. Spangler*,[55] *Austin Independent School District v. United States*,[56] and *Dayton Board of Education v. Brinkman*,[57] the Court followed the pattern set in *Milliken* and purported to question only the scope of the remedy ordered by the lower courts. A closer look at the three opinions, however, reveals that the remedies ordered are inappropriate only because the Supreme Court has once again ignored the rather obvious truths about segregation set forth above.

In *Pasadena*, the Supreme Court found the district court in error when, in 1974, it refused to modify its 1970 desegregation order to eliminate the requirement that there be "no school in the [district] with a majority of any minority students."[58] The Court noted that the defendant board had been in literal compliance with this provision of the order in the initial year of its operation. While five schools were ostensibly in violation of the district court's "no majority of any minority" requirement at the time of the hearing on the motion to modify, there was no showing that the post-1971 changes in racial mix of those schools were caused by segregative acts chargeable to defendants. The Court found that compliance with the pupil assignment requirement in 1970 "established a racially neutral system" in the school district and that "neither school authorities nor district courts are constitutionally required to make year-by-year adjustments of the racial composition of student bodies once the affirmative duty to desegregate has been accomplished and racial discrimination through official action is eliminated from the system."[59]

But, had the school board met its affirmative duty to eliminate state-created discrimination from the system? Had it established a racially neutral system? The answer is clearly "no." In its original order, the district court had found the existence of a segregated or dual system by virtue of the district's policies with regard to the hiring, promotion, and assignment of teachers and professional staff members; the construction and location of facilities; and the assignment of students.[60] All of the practices served separately and cumulatively to stigmatize blacks and the schools they attended and at which they taught.

The Supreme Court refused to understand, however, that once the stigma is affixed by the existence of a dual school system, the injury remains, at the very least, until the state has ceased all official name-calling, by way of hiring, promotion of teachers, construction and location of schools, and student assignment. The Court perceived the assignment of students as a distinct and separable constitutional violation that could be independently corrected, and held that once the school board had met this requirement of the order, it could not be held responsible for any further violation. The Court ignored the probability that much of the white flight that had caused the desegregation between 1971 and 1974 had occurred because schools continued to be identified as black schools and because teacher assignment practices continued to label blacks as inferior.

In *Austin Independent School District v. United States*, the Supreme Court issued a per curiam opinion, vacating a Fifth Circuit desegregation order requiring extensive busing within the school district.[61] In a concurring opinion echoing the *Milliken* holding that the remedy must be co-extensive with the proven wrong, Justice Powell noted that "large-scale busing is permissible only where the evidence supports a finding that the extent of the integration sought to be achieved by busing would have existed had the school authorities fulfilled their constitutional obligations in the past."[62]

While *Milliken* is cited in *Austin* for the proposition that the remedy should not exceed the scope of the violation, Justice Powell has gone even further in curtailing plaintiffs' chances for gaining relief, establishing a presumption of innocence in favor of the defendant school district. This shifting of the burden of proof is unprecedented; plaintiffs must now prove that each instance of segregation within a district would not have occurred but for the intentional acts of the school board. This represents a radical retreat from *Keyes v. School District No. 1*,[63] which established the rule that once plaintiffs establish an intent to segregate that affects a substantial portion of the school district, it will be presumed that all remaining segregation in the district resulted from intentional state action. The Supreme Court has once again ignored the fact that when the school board intentionally segregates one school, not only has it stigmatized the black children in that school, but it has done so to all of the black children in the district.

Likewise, in *Dayton Board of Education v. Brinkman*,[64] the Supreme Court vacated a federal district court order requiring that all schools be brought within 15 percent of Dayton's 48 percent to 52 percent black-white population ratio. The Supreme Court found that a constitutional violation affecting only high schools, whereby optional attendance zones could be used to allow white students to avoid attending predominantly black schools, would not justify an order requiring that all schools be integrated.

Relying on *Austin*, Justice Rehnquist, writing for the majority, reiterated Justice Powell's new twist on the *Milliken* rule that the scope of the remedy not exceed the scope of the violation. In particular, he found that the district court "must determine how much incremental segregative effect these violations had on the racial distribution of the Dayton school population as presently constituted, when that distribution is compared to what it would have been in the absence of such constitutional violations."[65]

But the Court has done more than simply apply the *Milliken* test. Insult has been added to injury in citing *Keyes v. School District No. 1* as precedent for this novel placement of the evidentiary burden. The rule established in *Keyes* would clearly have required that, a prima facie case of intentional segregation having been made, the burden would shift to the school district to prove that existing segregation in the district was not the result of its acts. The *Dayton* Court, thus, misinterpreted *Keyes* when it placed the full burden of proving constitutional violation or injury on the plaintiffs without applying the *Keyes* presumption.

Only by ignoring the nature of the institution of segregation can the Supreme Court hold that a school board may declare black high school students unfit to go to school with white students and fail to recognize that black elementary school children in the same school district are equally injured by that declaration. When black high school students are labeled inferior by segregation, their younger brothers and sisters in elementary school do not escape that label. Thus, the constitutional violation pervades the entire school system, if not the entire community of Dayton.

Notes

1. 418 U.S. 717 (1974).

2. 347 U.S. 483 (1954).

3. New York, 66%; Los Angeles, 56%; Chicago, 71%; Philadelphia, 66%; and Detroit, 72%. In the next five largest districts (Houston, Baltimore, Dallas, Cleveland, and the District of Columbia), the minority school population averages 68%. Over 1.5 million minority children reside in these 10 districts. U.S. Department of Health, Education, and Welfare, Office for Civil Rights, *Fall 1972 and Fall 1973 Elementary and Secondary School Survey Press Release Format Reports for 95 of the 100 Largest School Districts* (1973).

4. *Milliken*, 418 U.S. at 814–15 (Marshall, J., dissenting).

5. The word "misunderstood" will be used euphemistically throughout this article to refer to the Court's refusal to recognize and articulate the true nature of racial segregation. The author believes that this refusal was more the product of an intentional and knowledgeable decision than the result of any inability to comprehend. However, "misunderstood" offers a useful shorthand and takes into account the possibility that the oppressor is never fully able to comprehend the true nature of his oppression.

6. 163 U.S. 537 (1896).

7. 347 U.S. 483 (1954).

8. *Dayton Board of Education v. Brinkman*, 97 S. Ct. 2766 (1977); *Austin Independent School District v. United States*, 429 U.S. 990 (1976); *Pasadena City Board of Education v. Spangler*, 427 U.S. 424 (1976).

9. *Milliken*, 418 U.S. 717, 738 (1974) (quoting *Swann v. Charlotte-Mecklenburg Board of Education*, 402 U.S. 1, 16 [1971]).

10. Ibid., 744–45.

11. 413 U.S. 189 (1973).

12. *Keyes*, 413 U.S. at 205–6.

13. Ibid., 208 (citing *Swann v. Charlotte-Mecklenburg Board of Education*, 402 U.S. 1, 17–18 [1971]).

14. C. Vann Woodward, *The Strange Career of Jim Crow*, 12 (1974). The absence of segregation in the rural slave-holding South was not an indication of racial harmony but rather a manifestation of the fact that "in so far as the . . . status [of blacks] was fixed by enslavement there was little occasion or need for segregation." Id. at 13.

15. Ibid., 7.

16. Charles L. Black Jr., "*The Lawfulness of the Segregation Decisions*," 69 *Yale L.J.* 421 (1960).

17. Ibid., 426–27.

18. *Brown*, 347 U.S. at 495.

19. Ibid., 494.

20. Ibid.

21. 413 U.S. 189 (1973).

22. *Milliken*, 418 U.S. at 746–47.

23. Ibid., 748–49.

24. *Green*, 391 U.S. 430 (1968).

25. Ibid., 437.

26. *Brown II*, 349 U. S. 294 (1955)

27. *Green*, 437–38.

28. Ibid., 439.

29. L. F. Litwack, *North of Slavery: The Negro in the Free States*, 97 (1961).

30. Recent federal court decisions refusing to find de facto discrimination unconstitutional are indicative of the courts' continuing refusal to acknowledge the self-perpetuating nature of the institution of segregation and other institutionalized discriminatory devices. Increasingly, courts are requiring well-proved evidence of specific discriminatory acts upon which to base relief. See *Village of Arlington Heights v. Metropolitan Housing Development Corp.*, 429 U.S. 252 (1977); *Washington v. Davis*, 426 U.S. 229 (1976); *Regents of the University of California v. Bakke*, 438 U.S. 265 (1978).

31. See Davis, "The Effects of a Freeway Displacement on Racial Housing Segregation in a Northern City," 26 *Phlyon* 209, 214 (1965); Neal A. Roberts, "Homes, Road Builders and the Courts: Highway Relocation and Judicial Review of Administrative Action," 46 *So. Cal. L. R.* 51, 55 (1972); and Charles M. Sevilla, "Asphalt through the Model Cities: A Study of Highways and the Urban Poor," 49 *J. Urb. L.* 297 (1971).

32. See *Hills v. Gautreaux*, 425 U.S. 284 (1976); L. Friedman, *Government and Slum Housing: A Century of Frustration*, 123–31 (1968); Norman D. Peel, Garth E. Pickett, Stephen T. Buehl, Note, "Racial Discrimination in Public Housing Site Selection," 23 *Stan. L. Rev.* 63 (1970).

33. See *Bridgeport Guardians, Inc. v. Members of the Bridgeport Civil Service Commission*, 482 F.2d 1333 (2d Cir. 1973); *Castro v. Beecher*, 459 F.2d 725 (1st Cir. 1972); *Carter v. Gallagher*, 452 F.2d 315 (8th Cir.), cert. denied, 406

U.S. 950 (1972); *Chance v. Board of Examiners*, 458 F.2d 1167 (2d Cir. 1972); *Western Addition Community Organization v. Alioto*, 360 F. Supp. 733 (N.D. Cal. 1973).

34.   See *Shelley v. Kraemer*, 334 U.S. 1 (1948).

35.   *Plessy v. Ferguson*, 163 U.S. 537, 544–45 (1896).

36.   Ibid., 544.

37.   Ibid., 560 (Harlan, J., dissenting).

38.   305 U.S. 337 (1938).

39.   332 U.S. 631 (1948).

40.   339 U.S. 629 (1950).

41.   339 U.S. 637 (1950).

42.   *Sweatt*, 339 U.S. at 634.

43.   *McLaurin*, 399 U.S. at 641.

44.   *Brown*, 347 U.S. at 494

45.   *Plessy*, 163 U.S. at 544. Note that while the Court in *Brown v. Board of Education* said that "any language in *Plessy v. Ferguson* contrary to this finding is rejected" (347 U.S. 483, 494–95 [1954]), the *Brown* finding dealt only with segregated education and has never been read as reversing any part of *Plessy*. Although the Supreme Court's opinion in *Brown* dealt only with the inequality inherent in segregated schools, a subsequent series of per curiam decisions declaring the segregation of public facilities unconstitutional made it clear that the *Brown* holding extended to areas that the *Plessy* Court's definition would have considered social. See, e.g., *State Athletic Commission v. Dorsey*, 359 U.S. 533 (1959) (involving athletic contests); *New Orleans City Park Improvement Association v. Detiege*, 358 U.S. 54 (1958) (involving public parks); *Holmes v. City of Atlanta*, 350 U.S. 879 (1955) (involving public golf courses); *Mayor of Baltimore v. Dawson*, 350 U.S. 877 (1955) (involving public beaches). By using per curiam decisions in these cases, the Court again avoided the opportunity to controvert the *Plessy* dicta distinguishing "social" from "political" equality.

46.   *Strauder*, 100 U.S. 303 (1879).

47.   Ibid., 307–8.

48.   391 U.S. 430 (1968).

49.   In the *Milliken* decision the Supreme Court made note of the findings of the district court and the court of appeals in this regard: "The record before us, voluminous as it is, contains evidence of de jure segregated conditions only in the Detroit schools." 418 U.S. at 745.

50. *Milliken*, 418 U.S. at 744 (citing *Swann v. Charlotte-Mecklenburg Board of Education*, 402 U.S. 1, 16 (1971)).

51. Ibid., 753–55 (Stewart, J., concurring).

52. L. F. Litwack, *supra* note 29, at 122–23 (citing *The Liberator*, Apr. 4, 1845).

53. See *People ex rel. Workman v. Board of Education*, 18 Mich. 400 (1869) (citing Act 34, sec. 28 of 1867 Mich. Pub. Acts). The Michigan Constitution provides, in part, that "every school district shall provide for the education of its pupils without discrimination as to religion, creed, race, color or national origin." Michigan Constitution, art. 8, § 2. The Michigan laws provide, in part, that "no separate school or department shall be kept for any person or persons on account of race or color." Michigan Comp. Laws Annotated § 340.355 (1976), and that "all persons, residents of a school district . . . shall have an equal right to attend school therein." Id. at § 340.356. See also Act 318, pt. 11, chs. 2, 9, Michigan Public Acts of 1927.

54. 391 U.S. 430 (1968).

55. 427 U.S. 424 (1976).

56. 429 U.S. 990 (1976).

57. 433 U.S. 406 (1977).

58. *Pasadena*, 427 U.S. at 431.

59. Ibid., 436 (quoting *Swann v. Charlotte-Mecklenburg Board of Education*, 402 U.S. 1, 31–32 [1971]).

60. *Spangler v. Pasadena City Board of Education*, 311 F. Supp. 501, 505 (C.D. Cal. 1970).

61. *Austin*, 429 U.S. 990 (1976).

62. Ibid., 995 (Powell, J., concurring).

63. 413 U.S. 189 (1973).

64. *Dayton*, 43 U.S. 406 (1977).

65. Ibid., 420.

Chapter 8

Discrimination: A Pervasive Concept

Michael H. Sussman

Judicial treatment of racial discrimination claims deserves greater inquiry and study. Do courts perceive racial discrimination as it exists, or do judicial doctrine and evidentiary rules inhibit plaintiffs from demonstrating the full force and effect of such actions, whether private or public? It appears that courts, and many plaintiffs, fail to appreciate the unitary nature of racial discrimination. I argue that new principles are needed to guide judicial consideration of racism, principles more accurately reflecting the pervasive expression of this anti-democratic phenomenon and more effectively allowing for its extirpation.

I speak from firsthand experience as a litigator in many cases where racial discrimination is the central issue, whether courts recognize it or not. One of the most enlightening cases in which addressing race was unavoidable, *United States v. Yonkers Board of Education*,[1] is described in detail below. Two principles can be drawn from it that should guide proponents of racial justice in the future. The "principle of simultaneity" reflects a reality of state and local government: Laws and policies often work together in ways that may not be obvious to those who refuse to look. The result of this interaction demands attention and the principle of simultaneity is one step toward an adequate recognition of it. The principle of simultaneity posits, briefly, that invidious racial discrimination is not separated into neat sociological, political, or pedagogical areas or topics. There is no such thing as a racially discriminatory motive in setting housing policies that is discrete from a racially discriminatory motive in education decision-making. Racism is a *pervasive* concept.

The "resemblance principle" addresses a related, yet distinct, question: What time period or scope of discriminatory actions is relevant in proving that current practices constitute intentional racial discrimination? The resemblance principle asserts that the entire history of interactions, whether directed at the same individual(s) or at others, is relevant to determining whether the particular action at issue resulted from a discriminatory motive. Both of these principles describe a reality advocates need to put into words. If we continue to argue that laws and policies work together in discriminatory ways that are pervasive in our society, courts and policy makers will see this reality.

Discrimination in Yonkers

In November 1985, the Honorable Leonard Sand held the city of Yonkers, New York, liable for racially segregating the Yonkers public schools in violation of the Fourteenth Amendment. Despite an appointed school board's titular control over school affairs, Judge Sand found that, through mayoral appointments to the board of education, municipal control over the board's purse strings, and, most importantly, segregative housing policies, the city government had intentionally contributed to creating and maintaining racially segregated schools. At the same time, Judge Sand ruled that the city of Yonkers had intentionally segregated all forms of assisted housing by placing them in southwest Yonkers, the city's only area of minority concentration.

In holding the city of Yonkers responsible for school segregation, a holding which the Second Circuit affirmed in December 1987, Judge Sand relied upon two subsidiary conclusions. First, local elected officials, while not necessarily venal or bigoted individually, willfully reflected discriminatory public sentiment in their public policy decisions. Second, by so ignoring the dictates of the Fourteenth Amendment, state actors engaged in illegal conduct affecting agencies beyond their own specific spheres of responsibility. Thus, while city council members did not *directly* establish educational policy, their housing-related decisions effectively and intentionally ensured a high degree of racial segregation in the city's schools.[2]

Rather remarkably, given its late timing in the litany of school desegregation litigation, *Yonkers* represents the first and only case in which a district court has held *municipal* officials liable for intentionally segregating local schools and required them to cure school segregation. In all other northern school desegregation cases, courts have fastened liability only upon those school authorities directly responsible for operating the public schools, or those states deemed responsible for permitting such conditions to persist.[3] In addition, while many civil rights advocates have long articulated the rather elemental relationship between segregated living conditions and segregated schools, in very few prior cases have litigants asked courts to impose liability for school segregation on local officials allegedly responsible for creating segregative housing patterns. More commonly, plaintiffs have sought to introduce evidence of segregative housing policies against *state* officials, seeking orders requiring them to contribute to local school desegregation remedies.[4]

In 1992, the late Judge Vincent Broderick, also from the Southern District of New York, ruled in *Allen v. City of Yonkers*[5] that, in 1982, Yonkers had discriminatorily discharged Wilbert Allen, its first black commissioner. Judge Broderick found that the Yonkers officials were not comfortable entrusting Allen with leadership of its Department of Development, since that responsibility encompassed housing-related issues then under scrutiny in *United States v. Yonkers Board of Education*. Having an African American in such a sensitive position during this high-profile litigation was of concern to Yonkers' provincial officials, who felt they could not trust an African American to keep their racially charged confidence. Judge Broderick found that such stereotypical and race-tainted actions violated 42 United States Code Section 1983's prohibition of racial discrimination by governments and awarded Allen a substantial monetary settlement following the long-delayed finding of liability.

Likewise, in the mid-1980s, the NAACP and the New York Civil Liberties Union brought separate suits under the Voting Rights Act against the city of Yonkers challenging the racial gerrymandering of city councilmanic districts. The historic fracturing of intentionally created areas of minority residential concentration in West Yonkers among five or six predominantly white wards diluted black electoral opportunities. The city council declined to defend these actions and ultimately settled the litigation. This 1985 compromise allowed the election of the city's first African American council member, Joseph Burgess.

In a slightly earlier period, acting on the complaint of the local branch of the NAACP, the Department of Justice filed suit challenging the racial exclusivity of the Yonkers Police and Fire Departments. Both departments signed consent decrees committing them to substantial increases in minority representation in their workforces. Additionally, during the same time period, numerous individuals filed claims and lawsuits against the Yonkers Police Department alleging racially based police brutality. Again, many of these claims settled.

What was the common thread of all this litigation? A large, indeed a controlling, proportion of Yonkers' ruling elite condoned racial discrimination as a governing device. Starting in the 1950s, many of the city's white residents vociferously and actively opposed racial desegregation in housing and schooling patterns. Neighborhood civic associations repeatedly championed racially exclusionary policies and maintained a high degree of vigilance in ensuring no assisted housing encroached upon their territory. Not surprisingly, local politicians of both parties succumbed to this racist sentiment and adopted like-minded policies.[6] Careers were built and lost in the crucible of racial politics. As former New York State lieutenant governor Alfred Del Bello, himself a former mayor of Yonkers and a practitioner of such politics, testified at the 1983 school and housing trial, to be successful in politics in Yonkers during this era, one had to reflect and project acceptance of this broadly held sentiment.[7]

The Principle of Simultaneity

In presenting discrimination claims, lawyers often narrowly focus on the facts of the case. When dealing with state actors,[8] however, such a focus is myopic and unwise. Instead of such a narrow focus, an attorney confronted with such a case should strive to develop and present a broader understanding of the social and racial context in which decision makers operate. Attorneys must understand that the view of reality reflected in sociology and in the titles of law school courses (for example, Employment Discrimination Law, Housing Law, and Education Law,) bear little resemblance to the tapestry that constitutes actual municipal decision-making.

Just as Yonkers politicians understood and intended school segregation to flow from segregating public housing, they also knew municipal employment would likely remain under the control of white citizens as long as African Americans and Latinos were kept out of the Yonkers City Council. Thus, electoral gerrymandering was not adopted merely to maintain white hegemony in the city council. It additionally served as a means of ensuring that blacks did not gain access to municipal decision-making of any sort or, of equal importance, a handle on the patronage train of elective office.

I explain the pervasive nature of racial discrimination through what I call the principle of simultaneity. Understanding how racial discrimination functions through this principle has implications for trial lawyering and should inform judicial rulings concerning the admissibility of evidence. Since *Monnell v. Department of Social Services*,[9] municipalities have been subjected to liability under 42 United States Code Section 1983 only upon a showing that they engaged in a pattern, practice, custom, or usage of violating constitutional rights. This standard, while at first blush detrimental to civil rights practitioners, actually opens the door to the introduction of evidence transcending the case specifics by allowing the demonstration of a similar animus and array of related municipal practices. Indeed, requiring plaintiffs to establish a pattern, custom, policy, or usage makes it incumbent on courts to allow plaintiffs extensive leeway in presenting evidence. The *Monnell* formulation actually implies acceptance of the principle of simultaneity: rather than allow municipal liability to be based, generally, on isolated instances, courts have recognized that to be actionable, racial segregation must be reasonably pervasive.

Such standards of proof invite plaintiffs to engage in the kind of extensive discovery and truth telling that characterized the *Yonkers* litigation. In light of the necessity of such broad proof, plaintiffs must be allowed access to a concomitantly broader range of information during discovery. Furthermore, in order to be consistent, courts that intend to abide by the *Monnell* standard of proof must permit plaintiffs' counsel very broad latitude in admitting evidence.

In developing the *Monnell* standard, the Court concluded that "a municipality cannot be held liable under §1983 on a *respondeat superior* theory."[10] The movement away from *respondeat superior* carries other important implications. Rather than serving as a forum to determine whether a particular municipal agent violated the law, the *Monnell* standard transforms each case into a question of whether the municipality had a broad policy, practice, custom, or usage of racial segregation. Findings against municipalities will carry significant weight in subsequent litigation. Although not *res judicata* in most instances, they constitute a significant step in weaving the tapestry of governmental discrimination in subsequent actions.

In addition, given the standards governing summary judgment motions,[11] courts applying the *Monnell* standard of proof should generally deny such motions and give the plaintiff leave to present all evidence of municipal practice, policy, custom, or usage to the fact finder at trial. This follows because the fact finder may infer, from the array of discriminatory acts presented, that a like motive has substantially dictated the challenged adverse actions. As motive necessarily implicates disputed issues of fact, summary judgment will generally be inappropriate.

While *Monnell* seems consistent with the principle of simultaneity and recognizes that, if racism infects municipal decision-making, it is likely to rear its ugly head more frequently, recent cases have further restricted

municipal liability. The more recent focus has been on whether the decisional authority that allegedly acted in a discriminatory manner did so at
the behest or dictate of the municipal body formally entrusted with the
responsibility for that decision.[12] Absent such a delegation, courts have
declined to hold municipalities liable for the discriminatory acts of their
agents, whether the pervasive, customary nature of such conduct could
be established or not.

Such an overly formalistic legal standard defies the dynamics of municipal decision-making, which is often much less compartmentalized than
this legal standard presupposes. In Yonkers, for instance, housing policy
authority was formally vested in the Yonkers City Council, and the council
was responsible for selecting sites for the development of subsidized units.
Before the city council ever formally considered a site, however, the mayor
and his staff *informally* viewed sites with the affected city council member, that is, the council member in whose ward the proposed site was
located. If the affected member vetoed the site, it never reached the floor
of the city council. The city council ultimately had decisional authority to
approve sites never *formally* designated this function to either the strong
city manager, the weak mayor, or other executive officers or individual
council members. However, in practice, different combinations of such
officials acting together actually controlled what sites came before the
council for approval and, therefore, what sites were approved. In short, a
system of local council vetoes operated as a pre-check on presentations
for the further consideration of any housing site.

Likewise, in the early 1970s, the late Dr. Robert Alioto, a young ener-
getic superintendent, took over leadership of the Yonkers school district.
Arriving in Yonkers with designs to replace an aging bureaucracy, Alioto
hired many new and inspired administrators to remake the special education program, expand programmatic choices in the public schools, and
improve vocational education. At the same time, Alioto decided he would
not attempt to reverse the increasingly severe racial segregation in Yonkers' schools, a phenomenon he personally abhorred. As Alioto and his
aides later conceded, he did not wish to imperil his emerging career by
attempting to restructure school attendance lines or recommending any
other measure to combat increasing racial division in the schools.

While the Yonkers Board of Education had the authority to set school
zones and implement other policies to either decrease or increase racial
segregation, Alioto effectively retained decision-making power by never
forwarding for board consideration any proposal related to desegregation. Just as Yonkers' weak mayor and his administrators insulated the

formal decision-making body from votes on controversial housing sites, Alioto sheltered school board members from public consideration of the persistent patterns of racial segregation in the city's schools.

Any analysis of racial discrimination in Yonkers and other communities cannot therefore focus merely on the actions of those decision-makers authorized by state law. The inquiry must instead consider a context that leads to governmental decision-making and concentrate on those administrators charged with recommending and then implementing policies. If, as in both instances discussed above, governmental bodies intentionally delegate the process of developing policies for their consideration to administrative staff, which in turn avoid proposing plans to alter the racial status quo, such actions should be fairly attributable to the decisional authorities themselves. These actions are therefore relevant to a determination of municipal liability for racial segregation or discrimination.

The principle of simultaneity also has implications for judicial application of the rules of evidence. Suppose that in *Yonkers* the plaintiffs had sought to introduce evidence that the City of Yonkers intentionally gerrymandered councilmanic electoral districts and terminated Wilbert Allen, an African American, rather than allow him to lead the Yonkers Department of Development after city housing policies were challenged. In my view, both strands of evidence clearly would be relevant to demonstrating that the city council was bent on adopting and implementing discriminatory housing policies.

This evidence is relevant because racial gerrymandering, like the use of a poll tax, is intended to reduce the efficacy of minority participation in the electoral and, hence, the political process. In Yonkers, where the siting of public housing was an intensely political issue that had dominated municipal elections for several decades, a court could fairly infer that the same animus underlying the restriction of minority housing options would motivate officials to exclude relevant persons from municipal decision-making. Minority access to the political process could erode the substantive outcomes desired by the gerrymandering majority and provide insight into the inner workings of government, making implementation of racist policies much more difficult. It would also equip the newly elected African American with otherwise unavailable information, creating a potential truth teller whose impact could ultimately be far more significant than his or her single vote on public policy issues. In short, the same mentality striving to maintain racially segregated housing conditions would want to exclude African Americans from the functioning of local government.

In *Village of Arlington Heights v. Metropolitan Housing Development Corp.*,[13] the Supreme Court enumerated the types of evidence from which inferences of intentional racial discrimination could reasonably follow. The two critical forms of evidence cited were deviations from the defendant's own substantive decisional rules and alterations in procedures that the defendant usually utilized in the making of relevant public policy under discussion.

Viewed through this prism, racial gerrymandering represents a significant deviation from substantive principles and a clear effort to shape the process in a way that is disadvantageous to racial minorities. Racial gerrymandering is a technique fundamentally intended to shape the substantive outcome of all other issues considered by a governmental body. This technique directly contravenes the most basic substantive principle of our polity—the encouragement of participation by our citizens in the electoral and governance process.

Instead of forwarding this basic substantive principle, racial gerrymandering sends a contrary message: We do not wish your involvement in the political process, either as participants or as decision makers. We shall erect barriers to your election to political office and expect these barriers to create disinterest in governance among your ranks. This alienation will, most assuredly, leave us better able to dominate the political process and to continue to have our own way on issues of import to us, particularly issues with racial content.

Any court trying to understand the deep-seated nature of such policies should examine the persistence of such electoral gerrymandering and its relationship to the broad sentiment of maintaining the racial status quo, specifically in housing. That this constitutional violation involves voting, not housing, should be of no moment to its relevance, as a court assesses whether, in the housing sphere, the same governmental body acted with discriminatory intent.

Likewise, a court should receive evidence that Yonkers terminated Wilbert Allen, an African American, after its housing policies were challenged as racially discriminatory.[14] The knowledge that Allen advocated scattered-site subsidized housing, in direct contravention to forty years of municipal practice concentrating nearly all such housing in predominantly minority areas, and that this advocacy caused white city council members to lobby for his termination,[15] provides important insights into the less formal implementation of racial segregation.

The same council members who pressed the city manager to terminate Allen because black people could not be trusted to implement policies inspired by bias against "their kind," also vetoed potential housing sites in their wards.[16] The consistency in their conduct provides the court with a more complete picture of the nature of discriminatory municipal practice and policy. Again, breaking from a narrow perspective concerning the admissibility of evidence would significantly aid a fact finder without unjustly prejudicing defendants.

Yonkers takes the principle of simultaneity to a broader, more encompassing level. The district court found, and the court of appeals affirmed, that the commonality underlying discriminatory decisions in housing and education was the desire on the part of elected and appointed officials to capitulate to what they perceived to be majority sentiment.[17]

Proving this racist sentiment was essential for the plaintiffs' victory in Yonkers. In summarizing the applicable standard of law, the court of appeals noted that it was well established that "in order to prove a claim of discrimination in violation of the Equal Protection Clause a plaintiff must show not only that the state action complained of had a disproportionate or discriminatory impact but also that the *defendant acted with the intent to discriminate*."[18] The Yonkers plaintiffs conducted extensive interviews with community leaders and reviewed forty years of newspaper accounts, and the minutes and records of the Yonkers Municipal Housing Authority, the City Planning Board, the Yonkers Community Development Agency, the Yonkers Urban Renewal Agency, the Yonkers City Council, and state and federal funding agencies. The NAACP gathered its minutes and pertinent correspondence from the same time period. This allowed its counsel to demonstrate, through contemporaneously prepared documents, that less segregative solutions received short shrift from Yonkers officials and the outrage of the political majority.

After reviewing these documents, the plaintiffs conducted more than 125 depositions, including those of many former and current, elected and appointed school and housing officials. This extensive inquiry allowed the plaintiffs' counsel to present forty years of comprehensive racial and social history to the district court and led to its epic opinion, some 625 pages in length, chronicling, in great and unassailable detail, racist municipal and school district policies. Such an exhaustive historical review allowed the district court to conclude that the common link over decades and across "subject matter" areas in Yonkers was persistent, racist community sentiments. It further permitted the court to conclude that these sentiments were actualized through pressure on elected and appointed officials to adopt policies perpetuating the racial status quo. Based on the voluminous record created by the litigants, the district court recognized that "subsidized housing in Yonkers has been characterized by a common theme: racially influenced opposition to subsidized housing in certain areas of the City, and *acquiescence in that opposition by City officials.*"[19] These officials succumbed to majoritarianism because if they did not, they believed that they would be replaced by others who would. While some white residents of the city opposed racist policies, and while some elected and appointed officials condemned exclusionary and segregative policies, their opinions held little sway. The long historical moment belonged to those who advocated stereotypical views of racial minorities and wished to structure Yonkers' public life to ensure a pervasive residential segregation then extant in the private market.

In litigating *Yonkers*, the plaintiffs were particularly intent on demonstrating the nexus between private decision-making and public policy. Numerous white families settled in East Yonkers immediately after World War II. They created racially restrictive covenants and, after these lost their force and effect, stoned real estate agents who showed racial minorities homes in their neighborhoods. These same families refused to advertise homes for sale in newspapers, for fear this would more easily open their communities to racial minorities.

In this light, why would these same people not attempt to ensure that public policy led to precisely the same result as their private actions? Why would such people allow or even tolerate assisted or subsidized housing in their neighborhoods? Why would they elect a council member who would seriously and fairly consider such placements? Why would they voluntarily open their schools to minority children from West Yonkers?

Predictably, upon review, the public acts of East Yonkers' elected representatives repeatedly mirrored the private market discrimination played out daily in home sales. Just as residents sought to maintain lily-white suburban developments three and four miles from the urban squalor developing in West Yonkers, their representatives at city hall opposed any incursion of the poor into their developing neighborhoods.[20] When residents demanded personal preference and values to overcome the dictates of the Fourteenth Amendment, local government actors ignored the country's founding principles in favor of this pernicious majoritarianism. Public and private discriminatory sentiment combined into a single pervasive system of racism.[21]

Just as evidence that Yonkers' politicians discriminated in other spheres of political and social life should be admissible to prove the racially discriminatory intent behind decisions made in the housing and education spheres, so too should courts faced with issues of racial discrimination pierce any distinction between the private and public spheres. Communities that have intentionally excluded blacks or cabined minorities in particular neighborhoods succeed in this endeavor by simultaneously implementing common racist designs in both the private market and public sphere. The principle of simultaneity should cause us to scrutinize closely both sides of the equation, not cause fixation on one to the exclusion of the other.

The Debate over Unitary Status:
An Application of the Principle of Simultaneity

Southern schools were segregated as a matter of law. Northern schools were segregated as a matter of practice and custom. In both cases, school segregation truly resulted from official capitulation to epochal social norms and mores. In the South, these norms were legislated and formal. In the North and West, these norms were usually expressed through incremental state action, where discriminatory decision-making was masked as episodic and discretionary, as opposed to being dictated immediately by legislation.

Having previously entered often-complex injunctions requiring school districts throughout the country to cure and extirpate racial segregation and discrimination in and from public schools, federal courts in the last ten years have faced challenges to their ongoing supervisory role.[22] Should not courts now declare school districts unitary, release them from ongoing federal court supervision, and allow local communities again to control their own destinies? This would, it is asserted, allow local authorities again to make unfettered decisions concerning new construction, school attendance zones, and other matters pertinent both to school district management and racial mixing.

Initially, courts identified six factors to analyze in determining whether school districts deserved to manage themselves without further court supervision.[23] The so-called "*Green* factors" each represented an allegedly different aspect of school affairs. Courts were directed to assess whether local districts had conducted themselves nondiscriminatorily and exhibited good faith in each of these areas: student assignments, faculty assignments, staff assignments, transportation, extracurricular activities, and school facilities.

In *Freeman v. Pitts*,[24] the Court indicated that federal courts could gradually reduce their supervisory role, in an "area by area" fashion as opposed to an "all or nothing" manner, upon a finding that the school district had complied with court orders in a specific area. This nebulous formulation spawned much interest among educators, who envisioned public-placating motions seeking gradual cessation of court supervision and correspondingly receiving incremental applause from their constituents upon the grant of such motions. Thus, even if a school district had not fully desegregated or complied with existing court orders, it could show the community progress in getting out from under court orders by gaining "partial unitary status."

The premise of Justice Kennedy's opinion for the majority in *Freeman,* that "the ultimate objective" of the school desegregation decree was "to return school districts to the control of local authorities,"[25] and his suggestion that the district courts have a "duty" to do so, are ill-conceived and ahistorical. The objective of the desegregation decree is to remedy racial segregation that violates the Constitution. The Court's conservative majority seems to believe that the return to local control is a value as essential to our Constitution as eliminating racial segregation. It is not: Once a community engages in pervasive racial segregation, the presumption that it merits local control weakens, and judicial emphasis must turn to the eradication of the effects of the illegal conduct. After such a finding, courts should err on the side of the victims of racial discrimination and show less concern for those who violated the Constitution, particularly regarding control of the institutions they used as weapons of discrimination. Furthermore, the presumption that local control is some form of safeguard against racial discrimination lacks historical foundation or moral validity.

It is far more productive to embed the principle of simultaneity in our judicial standards and in doing so encourage courts to determine whether school authorities have been motivated by a desire to comply with school desegregation orders. If, on balance, districts have shown a strong proclivity to comply and have structured the totality of their school affairs in a manner consistent with antidiscrimination principles, the court should make a second-level inquiry. That is, does community sentiment suggest it is likely that, absent court supervision, substantial pressures will descend upon school authorities and cause a retreat from compliance with equality norms? This inquiry will provide the greatest insight into the need for continuing court supervision.

Courts should ask, for example, Are community residential patterns segregative or integrative and, if the former, why? Are African Americans well-represented as decision makers on those governmental bodies affecting, directly and indirectly, school policies? Is municipal employment distributed in a nondiscriminatory manner? Each of these questions offers some insight on whether it is prudent for a court to cease supervision of a desegregation remedy. While the answer to no single such question should be dispositive, each provides some assurance to the district court that broader community sentiment will not again rear up and demand a return to conditions of pervasive segregation within the jurisdiction's schools. These inquiries show realistic judicial acknowledgment that school segregation did not arise in a vacuum and that a condition of existing compliance can easily be compromised.

Despite the limitations of *Pitts*, the Court opened the door to broader inquiry when it recognized that "the potential for discrimination and racial hostility is still present in our country."[26] One might reasonably wonder why the majority chose the term "potential" in light of the plethora of decisions reaching its docket each term that contain findings of pervasive racial discrimination. In any event, the Court's focus on the good faith of school authorities broadens the inquiry from the *Green* factors. By reviewing what school authorities had done, a court could analyze the *Green* factors historically. However, "good faith" is a more elastic concept, inviting the court to inquire into motivation and reasoned speculation as to how school authorities will behave in the future. *Pitts* commands courts, therefore, to make a prediction that *Green* did not contemplate: How will these decision makers handle increased and unsupervised authority? The Court has also prudently instructed district courts to assess the prospects of local compliance with constitutional principles absent judicial supervision. The Court unfortunately provided little guidance on what factors, beyond "the school system's record of compliance,"[27] courts should or must assess before concluding that school officials acted in good faith and that compliance is likely to continue.

Such an unpointed direction from the Supreme Court is an invitation to district judges to apply their own ideology to the issue of continuing judicial supervision. The Court should provide judges clearer direction as to those factors that it believes bear on these related issues—good faith and the prospects for future compliance.

In approaching the issue of good faith, courts should analyze whether school authorities have consistently made choices to foster or retard racial segregation. Apart from determining whether districts have technically complied with court orders, courts should assess the commitment of local administrators and teachers to the spirit of the order. Such an inquiry gauges the breadth of motion and discretion such officials have and, without the necessity of direct inquiry, indicates their perception of community sentiment. Has compliance been begrudging, reflecting an awareness of generally adverse community sentiment, or has it been internalized deeply into the school system's operation, reflecting a firmer acceptance of antidiscrimination in that community's social life? Do the principles underlying school desegregation—a commitment to nondiscrimination and equal opportunity—pervade the operation of the school district or are they merely touted to satisfy judicial directives? In short, a school district demonstrates good faith in how administrators act when no one is looking over their shoulder, when they have some discretion to act, and when they are acting to satisfy constituents other than the federal courts.

Courts may also assess good faith by analyzing whether school district officials have championed implementation of the desegregation order or shied away from its advocacy. In Jacksonville, Florida, for instance, school officials signed a consent decree to comply further with long-standing desegregation orders in July 1990. However, the same leaders who ballyhooed the terms of the agreement at a joint press conference with the NAACP later distanced themselves from its critical terms, communicated to the public in a manner adverse to its intent, and failed to champion its spirit in repeated jousting with community groups. In sum, these leaders demonstrated that if left on their own, they had neither the capacity nor the will to stand up to contrary community pressure in the defense of desegregated schools. In such an instance, unitary status remains a distant dream.

Similarly, in assessing whether school authorities are likely to voluntarily make decisions consistent with the Fourteenth Amendment, plaintiffs should present, and courts should review, evidence of how municipal officials in the same community deal with race-sensitive issues. This is the best barometer both of the kinds of pressures that school authorities will face once relieved of judicial supervision and of how they will likely respond or have to respond. If, for example, a court finds that the community in question is evidencing a high level of racial polarization in selecting sites for assisted housing and exhibits severe patterns of racially segregated housing, it is unlikely that school authorities will be able to administrate schools in a nondiscriminatory manner. Embedded community sentiment, as expressed in the citizenry's manifested desire to maintain existing segregative housing patterns, strongly counsels against releasing school authorities from judicial supervision in such instances.

Some may assert that this kind of inquiry is unfair to school authorities or that school districts are separate juridical entities that can carry only so much baggage. Therefore, courts should not evaluate school authorities on the basis of local authorities' conduct regarding race-related issues. School district management, however, has historically reflected broader community values. A school district that has discriminated against and engaged in segregating racial minorities in the past likely did so either because legislation required this result or because less formal, but equally intense, social pressures mandated it. School officials did not invent or instigate racial segregation. Generally, they conformed the organization of schools to broader social patterns and forces. In determining whether federal court supervision of schools is still necessary, it is fair to examine the state of current community sentiment as reflected in the actions of other juridical bodies and the likelihood that, absent the check provided by the federal judicial presence, segregation and discrimination will reemerge.

Such a broad inquiry admittedly reflects a certain erring on the side of caution. When fundamental principles of American constitutional law with potentially immense impacts on the future of institutions and individuals are implicated, however, such caution is warranted. This is particularly true in light of the internalized force and pernicious effects that racial discrimination continues to hold in our society. The persistence of racism in the American psyche lends plausibility to the notion that, in general, racial polarization will animate public policy absent court supervision. The severity of the effects of discrimination indicates that, as a society, we should attempt to structure our affairs to prevent such sentiments from dominating institutional life before, not after, they are actualized. This is, of course, particularly appropriate where the institution involved so clearly shapes the hearts and minds of our children.

While stricter judicial scrutiny may appear onerous, our national legacy makes it a price worth bearing for at least two reasons. Judicial supervision serves as a check on the more extreme forces among us. Such oversight presents a known and efficacious barrier to those who would try to impose their bigotry upon our civil institutions. In addition, such supervision, when viewed fairly, does not inhibit *lawful* experimentation and management by local institutions. This alleged problem, though widely cited in Supreme Court cases as a basis for relieving federal courts of jurisdiction at the earliest possible moment,[28] is in reality a red herring, and its invocation presents an emotional and false choice. This objection fails because courts do not typically mandate specific means of meeting desegregation and antidiscrimination imperatives.

In *Yonkers*, for instance, Judge Sand repeatedly offered to modify extant remedy orders to allow for fuller expression of the municipality's own methods of curing segregation and discrimination.[29] His rather futile, if oft-repeated, effort was for Yonkers to take greater ownership of the remedial process. More generally, local control is fundamentally compatible with judicial supervision. What is incompatible with such supervision is the expression, through local control, of racist sentiment.

In short, judicial supervision remains warranted if, after an exhaustive and broad review, a court concludes that the withdrawal of such authority is reasonably likely to lead a school district to retreat from its active efforts to desegregate. In addition, courts should continue their supervision if the plaintiffs show that the school district is not complying, in full or in part, with extant desegregation orders. Courts should not desist their supervisory role merely upon a finding that it is unlikely districts will engage anew in unconstitutional conduct or a finding that in some specific area compliance has been achieved, though it is lacking in others.

The issue should be whether entities that have been found liable for intentionally violating the constitutional rights of minority schoolchildren will remain as committed to remedying such violations absent judicial oversight as they would be in its presence. If school districts seeking unitary status cannot convince courts that, left to their own devices, they will carry out remedial policies and comply with court orders, they should not be released from close supervision.

The principle of simultaneity should guide courts in assessing the current community sentiments concerning race before reducing judicial oversight. If other local institutions appear racially polarized, there is every reason to believe that school authorities will again be subjected to similar influences, whether formal or informal, and, as in prior times, capitulate to them. This conclusion entails no pejorative judgment on the character of those administering or running school districts. Instead, it is a historically based commentary on how difficult it is for such actors to resist the influence of pervasive racial bias. Put another way, it recognizes that school organization has followed, not forged, broader social trends. Moreover, as providing equal opportunity and ending discrimination are crucial national imperatives, more important than returning full control over school affairs to local officials, courts must err on the side of retaining jurisdiction, particularly where rampant discriminatory majoritarianism threatens institutional advancement.

Conclusion

Courts have expended too much energy in recent years attempting to narrow and delimit claims of racial segregation and discrimination. Likewise, courts have placed too much focus on ending the role of federal supervision, despite the continued high level of racial segregation in our national life and schools. Recognizing the nature of racism, specifically its simultaneous effect across allegedly divisible areas of social life, will allow courts to better evaluate both individual claims of discrimination and institutional assertions of judicial supervision as being unnecessary. The principle of simultaneity cautions strongly against any retreat from federal jurisdiction over extant school desegregation orders without a showing that community acceptance of such principles is high and the absence of supervision will not prompt a return to racial segregation. Likewise, in adjudicating individual claims, courts should provide plaintiffs broad leave to demonstrate the presence of discrimination in other areas. A more truncated interpretation of the Rules of Evidence both disserves the truth and protects racial discrimination from exposure and elimination.

Notes

1. 624 F. Supp. 1276 (S.D.N.Y. 1985), aff'd., 837 F.2d 1181 (2d Cir. 1987), cert. denied, 486 U.S. 1055 (1988).

2. *United States v. Yonkers Board of Education*, 624 F. Supp. 1276, 1539–43 (S.D.N.Y. 1985).

3. See, e.g., *Brinkman v. Gilligan*, 610 F. Supp. 1288 (S.D. Ohio 1985) (holding local school authorities responsible); *Penick v. Columbus Board of Education*, 519 F. Supp. 925 (S.D. Ohio) (holding state authorities responsible), aff'd, 663 F.2d 24 (6th Cir. 1981), cert. denied, *Ohio State Board of Education v. Reed*, 455 U.S. 1018 (1982); *Reed v. Rhodes*, 500 F. Supp. 404 (N.D. Ohio 1980) (holding state authorities responsible), aff'd, 662 F.2d 1219 (6th Cir. 1981), cert. denied, *Ohio State Board of Education v. Reed*, 455 U.S. 1018 (1982).

4. See, e.g., *Little Rock School District v. Pulaski County Special School District No. 1*, 778 F.2d 404, 426 (8th Cir. 1985) (describing findings of state culpability in creating segregative housing conditions), cert. denied, 476 U.S. 1186 (1986); *United States v. Board of School Commissioners*, 573 F.2d 400, 407–09 (7th Cir. 1978) (describing how plaintiffs in an Indianapolis school desegregation case sought to show that state-supported housing was rejected in suburban municipalities and that this, along with the passage of Uni-Gov, which consolidated much of Marion County's governance but left many autonomous and unconnected school districts, provided a basis for state liability); *Evans v. Buchanan*, 393 F. Supp. 428, 438 (D. Del.) (finding that a variety of conduct by governmental authorities contributed to housing discrimination patterns), aff'd, 423 U.S. 963 (1975).

5. 803 F. Supp. 679 (S.D.N.Y. 1992).

6. See *United States v. Yonkers Board of Education*, 837 F.2d 1181, 1193 (2d Cir. 1987), cert. denied, 456 U.S. 1055 (1988).

7. Ibid., 1191 (describing Del Bello's testimony that council members were strongly influenced by their constituents' opposition to subsidized housing and that "race was definitely a consideration in many of the demonstrations and visible opposition that we had [during the site selection process]").

8. Although there is some utility in applying the principle of simultaneity to private actors, it is most applicable in cases involving state action. The principle attempts not merely to draw out the commonality in motive across subject matter, it attempts to show the nexus between public and private decision-making. In other words, the state actors act out the discriminatory animus rife in the community. This practice may also occur in private companies, but most likely to a lesser degree and less frequently.

9. 436 U.S. 658 (1978).

10. *Monnell*, 436 U.S. at 691.

11. "[S]ummary judgment is proper 'if the pleadings, depositions, answers to inter-rogatories, and admissions on file, together with the affidavits, if any, show that there is no genuine issue as to any material fact and that the moving party is entitled to a judgment as a matter of law.'" *Celotex Corp. v. Catrett*, 477 U.S. 317, 322–23 (1986) (quoting Fed. R. Civ. P. 56[c]); see also *Chambers v. TRM Copy Centers Corp.*, 43 F.3d 29, 36 (2d Cir. 1994).

12. See e.g., *St. Louis v. Praprotnik*, 485 U.S. 112, 123 (1988) (citing *Pembauer* to state that "only those municipal officials who have 'final policymaking authority' may by their actions subject the government to § 1983 liability"); *Pembauer v. Cincinnati*, 475 U.S. 469, 481 (1986) ("Municipal liability attaches only where the decision maker possesses final authority to establish municipal policy with respect to the action ordered").

13. 429 U.S. 252 (1977).

14. *Allen v. City of Yonkers*, 803 F. Supp. 679, 698–700 (S.D.N.Y. 1992). In this wrongful termination action, the district court noted that whatever the council members' separate reasons were for terminating Allen, "the action of these ulti-mate decision makers as a body was decisively influenced by Mr. Allen's race at a time when his ethnicity was unpopular in the context of a locally unpopular na-tional housing policy." Id. at 699.

15. Ibid., 696–700.

16. *United States v. Yonkers Board of Education*, 624 F. Supp. at 1356–63.

17. *United States v. Yonkers Board of Education*, 837 F.2d at 1223. The court of appeals noted: "Even assuming, contrary to the findings and record in the present case, that the actions of the municipal officials are only responsive rather than leading the fight against desegregation, we conclude that the Equal Protection Clause does not permit such actions where racial animus is a significant factor in the community position to which the city is responding." Id. at 1224.

18. *United States v. Yonkers Board of Education*, 837 F.2d at 1216 (emphasis added).

19. *United States v. Yonkers Board of Education*, 624 F.Supp. at 1370 (emphasis added).

20. Ibid., 1314–25. Interestingly, many East Yonkers' neighborhoods adopted post office boxes of the neighboring, more exclusive, white suburbs, like Bronxville, Scarsdale, Tuckahoe, and Eastchester. While these residents lived in Yonkers, mail sent to them bore the name of another, more prestigious community. This caused Sarah Lawrence, a well-known liberal arts college, to print sweatshirts in 1990 which read, "Sarah Lawrence is in Yonkers."

21. Again, this history has clear implications for practicing attorneys. Rather than divide the public from the private at the outset, in public discrimination cases we

should clearly ascertain relevant private market practices that, one can argue persuasively, gain expression through public policy.

22. See *Board of Education v. Dowell*, 498 U.S. 237, 246–50 (1991) (holding that because federal supervision of local schools is a temporary measure to remedy past discrimination, a court should discontinue its supervision when a school system is operated in compliance with the Equal Protection Clause and it is unlikely the school authorities will return to their former ways).

23. *Green v. County School Board*, 391 U.S. 430, 435 (1968).

24. *Pitts*, 503 U.S. 467 (1992).

25. Ibid., 489.

26. Ibid., 490.

27. Ibid., 491.

28. In *Freeman v. Pitts*, 503 U.S. 467, 490 (1992), for example, the Supreme Court stated: "Returning schools to the control of local authorities at the earliest practicable date is essential to restore their true accountability in our governmental system. When the school district and all state entities participating with it in operating the schools make decisions in the absence of judicial supervision, they can be held accountable to the citizenry, to the political process, and to the courts in the ordinary course." See also *Board of Education of Oklahoma City v. Dowell*, 498 U.S. 237, 248 (1991) ("Local control over the education of children allows citizens to participate in decision making, and allows innovation so that school programs can fit local needs").

29. See, e.g., *United States v. City of Yonkers*, 833 F. Supp. 214, 225 (S.D.N.Y. 1993) (holding that the steps taken so far by school and city officials to remedy segregation in the schools "are inadequate to eradicate vestiges of segregation 'root and branch,'" and that school officials should take a leading role in crafting effective reforms); *United States v. Yonkers Board of Education*, 662 F. Supp. 1575, 1576 (S.D.N.Y. 1987) (reminding the parties to the suit that "the constructive participation by the Yonkers City Council . . . and other civic groups in the formulation of a housing remedy is welcomed and is to be encouraged").

Chapter 9

The Boundaries of Race: Political Geography in Legal Analysis

Richard Thompson Ford

During the seventies and eighties a word disappeared from the American vocabulary—the word was "segregation." It is now passé to speak of racial segregation. In an America that is facing the identity crisis of multiculturalism, where racial diversity seems to challenge the norms and values of the nation's most fundamental institutions, to speak of segregation seems almost quaint. The physical segregation of the races would seem to be a relatively simple matter to address; indeed, many believe it has already been addressed. Discrimination in housing, in the workplace, and in schools is illegal. Thus, it is perhaps understandable that we have turned our attention to other problems, on the assumption that any segregation that remains is either vestigial or freely chosen. However, even as racial segregation has fallen from the national agenda, it has persisted. Even as racial segregation is described as a natural expression of racial and cultural solidarity, a chosen and desirable condition for which government is not responsible and one that government should not oppose, segregation continues to play the same role it always has in American race relations—to isolate, disempower, and oppress.

Segregation is oppressive and disempowering rather than desirable or inconsequential because it involves more than simply the relationship of individuals to other individuals; it also involves the relationship of groups of individuals to political influence and economic resources. Residence is more than a personal choice; it is also a primary source of political identity and economic security.[1] Likewise, residential segregation is more than a matter of social distance; it is a matter of political fragmentation and economic stratification along racial lines, enforced by public policy and the rule of law.

Segregated minority communities have been historically impoverished and politically powerless. Today's laws and institutions need not be explicitly racist to ensure that this state of affairs continues; they need only perpetuate historical conditions. In this chapter, I assert that political geography—the position and function of jurisdictional and quasi-jurisdictional boundaries[2]—helps to promote a racially separate and unequal distribution of political influence and economic resources. Moreover, these inequalities fuel the segregative effect of political boundaries in a vicious cycle of causation: each condition contributes to and strengthens the others. Thus, racial segregation persists in the absence of explicit, legally enforceable racial restrictions. Race-neutral policies, set against a historical backdrop of state action in the service of racial segregation and thus against a contemporary backdrop of racially identified space—physical space primarily associated with and occupied by a particular racial group—predictably reproduce and entrench racial segregation and the racial caste system that accompanies it. Thus, the persistence of racial segregation, even in the face of civil rights reform, is not mysterious.

This chapter employs two lines of analysis in its examination of political space. The first demonstrates that racially identified space both creates and perpetuates racial segregation. The second demonstrates that racially identified space results from public policy and legal sanctions—in short, from state action—rather than from the unfortunate but irremediable consequence of purely private or individual choices. This dual analysis has important legal and moral consequences: if racial segregation is a collective social responsibility rather than exclusively the result of private transgressions, then it must either be accepted as official policy or remedied through collective action.

Part 1 argues that public policy and private actors operate together to create and promote racially identified space and thus racial segregation. In support of this assertion, I offer a hypothetical model to demonstrate that even in the absence of individual racial animus and de jure segregation, historical patterns of racial segregation would be perpetuated by facially race-neutral legal rules and institutions. I conclude the discussion in part 1 by arguing that the significance of racially identified political geography escapes the notice of judges, policy makers, and scholars because of two widely held yet contradictory misconceptions: one assumes that political boundaries have no effect on the distribution of persons, political influence, or economic resources, while the other assumes that political boundaries define quasi-natural and prepolitical associations of individuals. As we shall see, these two assumptions lead jurists and policy makers to believe that segregated residential patterns are unimportant to the political influence and economic well-being of communities and that such residential patterns are beyond the proper purview of legal and policy reform. These beliefs are often unstated, but they inform judicial decisions and the political and sociological analyses underlying those decisions.

Part 2 demonstrates how racially identified space interacts with facially race-neutral legal doctrine and public policy to reinforce racial segregation rather than to eliminate it gradually. Legal analysis oscillates between two contradictory conceptions of local political space; they correspond to the two misconceptions of space described in part 1. One conceives of local jurisdictions as geographically defined delegates of centralized power, administrative conveniences without autonomous political significance; the other treats local jurisdictions as autonomous entities that deserve deference because they are manifestations of an unmediated democratic sovereignty. Both accounts avoid examination of the potentially segregated character of local jurisdictions—the first by denying them any legal significance, the second by reference to their democratic origins, or by tacit analogy to private property rights, or both. Thus, legal authorities that subscribe to either of these accounts never confront the problems posed by the many jurisdictions that are segregated or promote racial segregation and inequality.

Two competing normative analyses mirror the doctrinal oscillation between the conception of local governments as agents of state power and the conception of local governments as self-validating political communities. One holds that local governments are powerless creatures of the state and prescribes greater autonomy for local governments; the other, which insists that local governments are powerful, autonomous associations, advocates bringing the "crazy quilt" of parochial localities under centralized control.

Part 2 also returns to our original focus on race relations and suggests that the characteristic oscillation in local government doctrine informed by democratic theory is related to a particularly American conflict between the goals of racial and cultural assimilation, on the one hand, and separatism, on the other. Neither assimilation nor separatism is fully acceptable, and race-relations theorists tend to waver between the two. The reification of political space thus mirrors a reification of race in American thought: race is assumed either to be irrelevant, merely the unfortunate by-product of an ignoble American past and a retrograde mentality, or to be natural and primordial, a genetic or biological identity that simply is unamenable to examination or change.

Finally, part 3 attempts to mediate the characteristic conflicts between local parochialism and centralized bureaucracy, pluralist competition and republican dialogue, and racial assimilation and racial separatism. In part 3 I argue that the location of the politics of difference must be the metropolis, the political space in which the majority of Americans now reside, work, and enjoy recreation, and in which individuals confront racial, cultural, and economic differences. Against the nostalgia of the whole and the one, the "pure" homogeneous community, we should strive for the achievable ideal of the diverse democratic city.

Conceptions and Consequences of Space

The Construction of Racially Identified Space

> Segregation is the missing link in prior attempts to understand the plight of the urban poor. As long as blacks continue to be segregated in American cities, the United States cannot be called a race-blind society.
> —Douglas S. Massey and Nancy A. Denton, *American Apartheid*

This chapter focuses primarily on residential segregation and on the geographic boundaries that define local governments. Although these are not the only examples of racially identified space, they are so intimately linked to issues of political and economic access that they are among the most important. Residence in a municipality or membership in a homeowners association involves more than simply the location of one's domicile; it also involves the right to act as a citizen, to influence the character and direction of a jurisdiction or association through the exercise of the franchise, and to share in public resources. "Housing, after all, is much more than shelter: it provides social status, access to jobs, education and other services."[3] Residential segregation is self-perpetuating, for in segregated neighborhoods "[t]he damaging social consequences that follow from increased poverty are spatially concentrated . . . creating uniquely disadvantaged environments that become progressively isolated—geographically, socially, and economically—from the rest of society."[4] Local boundaries drive this cycle of poverty.

Actors public and private laid the groundwork for the construction of racially identified spaces and, therefore, for racial segregation as well. Explicit governmental policy at the local, state, and federal levels has encouraged and facilitated racial segregation. The role of state and local policies in promoting the use of racially restrictive covenants is well known; less well known is the responsibility of federal policy for the pervasiveness of racially restrictive covenants. The federal government continued to promote the use of such covenants until they were declared unconstitutional in the landmark decision *Shelley v. Kraemer*.[5] Federally subsidized mortgages often *required* that property owners incorporate restrictive covenants into their deeds. The federal government consistently gave black neighborhoods the lowest rating for purposes of distributing federally subsidized mortgages. The Federal Housing Administration, which insured private mortgages, advocated the use of zoning and deed restrictions to bar undesirable people and classified black neighbors as nuisances to be avoided along with "stables" and "pig pens."[6]

Not surprisingly, "[b]uilders . . . adopted the [racially restrictive] covenant so their property would be eligible for [federal] insurance,"[7] and "private banks relied heavily on the [federal] system to make their own loan decisions. . . . [T]hus [the federal government] not only channeled federal funds away from black neighborhoods but was also responsible for a much larger and more significant disinvestment in black areas by private institutions."[8] Although the federal government ended these discriminatory practices after 1950, only much later did it do anything to remedy the damage it had done or to prevent private actors from perpetuating segregation.[9]

Racial segregation was also maintained by private associations of white home-owners who "lobbied city councils for zoning restrictions and for the closing of hotels and rooming houses . . . threatened boycotts of real estate agents who sold homes to blacks . . . [and] withdrew their patronage from white businesses that catered to black clients."[10] These associations shaped the racial and economic landscape and implemented by private fiat what might well be described as public policies. Thus, private associations as well as governments defined political space.

The Perpetuation of Racially Identified Spaces: An Economic-Structural Analysis

The history of public policy and private action in the service of racism reveals the context in which racially identified spaces were created. Much traditional social and legal theory imagines that the elimination of public policies designed to promote segregation will eliminate segregation itself, or will at least eliminate any segregation that can be attributed to public policy and leave only the aggregate effects of individual biases (which are beyond the authority of government to remedy). This view fails, however, to acknowledge that racial segregation is embedded in and perpetuated by the social and political construction of racially identified political space.

Trouble in Paradise: An Economic Model

Imagine a society with only two groups, blacks and whites,[11] differentiated only by morphology (visible physical differences). Blacks, as a result of historical discrimination, tend on average to earn significantly less than whites. Imagine also that this society has recently (during the past twenty or thirty years) come to see the error of its discriminatory ways. It has enacted a program of reform which has totally eliminated legal support for racial discrimination and, through a concentrated program of public education, has also succeeded in eliminating any vestige of racism from its citizenry. In short, the society has become color blind. Such a society may feel itself well on its way to the ideal of racial justice and equality, if not already there.

Imagine also that, in our hypothetical society, small, decentralized, and geographically defined governments exercise significant power to tax citizens, and they use the revenues to provide certain public services (such as police and fire protection), public utilities (such as sewage, water, and garbage collection), infrastructure development, and public education.

Finally, imagine that, before the period of racial reform, our society had in place a policy of fairly strict segregation of the races, such that every municipality consisted of two enclaves, one almost entirely white and one almost entirely black. In some cases, whites even reincorporated their enclaves as separate municipalities to ensure the separation of the races. Thus, the now color-blind society confronts a situation of almost complete segregation of the races—a segregation that also fairly neatly tracks a class segregation, because blacks on average earn far less than whites (in part because of their historical isolation from the resources and job opportunities available in the wealthier and socially privileged white communities).

We can assume that all members of this society are indifferent to the race of their neighbors, co-workers, social acquaintances, and so forth. However, we must also assume that most members of this society care a great deal about their economic well-being and are unlikely to make decisions that will adversely affect their financial situation.

Our hypothetical society might feel that, over time, racial segregation would dissipate in the absence of de jure discrimination and racial prejudice. Yet let us examine the likely outcome under these circumstances. Higher incomes in the white neighborhoods would result in larger homes and more privately financed amenities, although public expenditures would be equally distributed among white and black neighborhoods within a single municipality. However, in those municipalities which incorporated along racial lines, white cities would have substantially superior public services (or lower taxes and the same level of services) than the "mixed" cities, due to a higher average tax base. The all-black cities would, it follows, have substantially inferior public services or higher taxes as compared to the mixed cities. Consequently, the wealthier white citizens of mixed cities would have a real economic incentive to depart, or even secede, from the mixed cities, and whites in unincorporated areas would be spurred to form their own jurisdictions and to resist consolidation with the larger mixed cities or all-black cities. Note that this pattern can be explained without reference to "racism": whites might be color blind yet nevertheless prefer predominantly or all-white neighborhoods on purely economic grounds, as long as the condition of substantial income differentiation obtains.

Of course, simply because municipalities begin as racially segregated enclaves does not mean that they will remain segregated. Presumably, blacks would also prefer the superior public service amenities or lower tax burdens of white neighborhoods, and those with sufficient wealth would move in; remember, in this world there is no racism and there are no cultural differences between the races—people behave as purely rational economic actors. One might imagine that, over time, income levels would even out between the races, and blacks would move into the wealthier neighborhoods, while less fortunate whites would be outbid and would move to the formerly all-black neighborhoods. Hence, racial segregation might eventually be transformed into purely economic segregation.

This conclusion rests, however, on the assumption that residential segregation would not itself affect employment opportunities and economic status. However, because the education system is financed through local taxes, segregated localities would offer significantly different levels of educational opportunity; the poor, black cities would have poorer educational facilities than would the wealthy, white cities. Thus, whites would, on average, be better equipped to obtain high-income employment than would blacks. Moreover, residential segregation would result in a pattern of segregated informal social networks: neighbors would work and play together in community organizations such as schools, PTAs, Little Leagues, Rotary Clubs, neighborhood-watch groups, cultural associations, and religious organizations. These social networks would form the basis of the ties and the communities of trust that open the doors of opportunity in the business world. All other things being equal, employers would hire people they know and like over people of whom they have no personal knowledge, good or bad; they would hire someone who comes with a personal recommendation from a close friend over someone without such a recommendation. Residential segregation would substantially decrease the likelihood that such connections would be formed between members of different races. Finally, economic segregation would mean that the market value of black homes would be significantly lower than would that of white homes; thus, blacks attempting to move into white neighborhoods would on average have less collateral with which to obtain new mortgages, or less equity to convert into cash.[12]

Inequalities in both educational opportunity and the networking dynamic would result in fewer and less remunerative employment opportunities, and hence lower incomes, for blacks. Poorer blacks, unable to move into the more privileged neighborhoods and cities, would remain segregated; and few, if any, whites would forgo the benefits of their white neighborhoods to move into poorer black neighborhoods, which would be burdened by higher taxes or provided with inferior public services. This does not necessarily mean that income polarization and segregation would constantly increase (although at times they would) but, rather, that they would not decrease over time through a process of osmosis. Instead, every successive generation of blacks and whites would find itself in much the same situation as the previous generation, and in the absence of some intervening factor, the cycle would likely perpetuate itself. At some point an equilibrium might be achieved: generally better-connected and better-educated whites would secure the better, higher-income jobs, and disadvantaged blacks would occupy the lower-status and lower-wage jobs.

Even in the absence of racism, then, race-neutral policy could be expected to entrench segregation and socioeconomic stratification in a society with a history of racism. Political space plays a central role in this process. Spatially and racially defined communities perform the "work" of segregation silently. There is no racist actor or racist policy in this model, and yet a racially stratified society is the inevitable result. Although political space seems to be the inert context in which individuals make rational choices, it is in fact a controlling structure in which seemingly innocuous actions lead to racially detrimental consequences.

Strangers in Paradise: A Complicated Model

[Even u]nder the best of circumstances, segregation undermines the ability of blacks to advance their interests because it provides . . . whites with no immediate self interest in their welfare . . . . [Furthermore,] a significant share [of whites] must be assumed to be racially prejudiced and supportive of policies injurious to blacks.
—Douglas S. Massey and Nancy A. Denton, *American Apartheid*

If we now introduce a few real-world complications into our model, we can see just how potent the race-space dynamic is. Suppose that half—only half—of all whites in our society are in some measure racist or harbor some racial fear or concern. These might range from the open-minded liberal who remains somewhat resistant, if only for pragmatic reasons, to mixed-race relations (Spencer Tracy's character in *Guess Who's Coming to Dinner*), to the avowed racial separatist and member of the Ku Klux Klan. Further suppose that the existence of racism produces a degree of racial fear and animosity of blacks, such that half—only half—of blacks fear or distrust whites to some degree. These might range from a pragmatic belief that blacks need to "keep to their own kind," if only to avoid unnecessary confrontation and strife (Sidney Poitier's father in the same film), to strident nationalist separatism. Let us also assume that significant cultural differences generally exist between whites and blacks.

In this model, cultural differences and socialization would further entrench racial segregation. Even assuming that a few blacks would be able to attain the income necessary to move into white neighborhoods, it is less likely that they would wish to do so. Many blacks would fear and distrust whites and would be reluctant to live among them, especially in the absence of a significant number of other blacks. Likewise, many whites would resent the presence of black neighbors and would try to discourage them, in ways both subtle and overt, from entering white neighborhoods. The result would be an effective "tax" on integration. The additional amenities and lower taxes of the white neighborhood would often be outweighed by the intangible but real costs of living as an isolated minority in an alien and sometimes hostile environment. Many blacks would undoubtedly choose to remain in black neighborhoods.

Moreover, this dynamic would produce racially *identified* spaces. Because our hypothetical society is now somewhat racist, segregated neighborhoods would become identified by the race of their inhabitants; race would be seen as intimately related to the economic and social condition of political space. The creation of racially identified political spaces would make possible a number of regulatory activities and private practices that would further entrench the segregation of the races. For example, because some whites would resent the introduction of blacks into their neighborhoods, real estate brokers would be unlikely to show property in white neighborhoods to blacks for fear that disgruntled white home-owners would boycott them.

Even within mixed cities, localities might decline to provide adequate services in black neighborhoods and might divert funds to white neighborhoods in order to encourage whites with higher incomes to enter or remain in the jurisdiction. Thus, although our discussion has focused primarily on racially homogeneous jurisdictions with autonomous taxing power, the existence of such jurisdictions might affect the policy of racially heterogeneous jurisdictions, which would have to compete for wealthier residents with the low-tax and superior-service homogeneous cities. This outcome would be especially likely if the mixed jurisdictions were characterized by governmental structures that were either resistant to participation by grassroots community groups or were otherwise unresponsive to the citizenry as a whole. A dynamic similar to what I have posited for the homogeneous jurisdictions would occur *within* such racially mixed jurisdictions, with neighborhoods taking the place of separate jurisdictions.

Each of these phenomena would exacerbate the others, in a vicious circle of causation. The lack of public services would create a general negative image of poor, black neighborhoods; inadequate police protection would lead to a perception of the neighborhoods as unsafe; uncollected trash would lead to a perception of the neighborhoods as dirty, and so forth. Financial institutions would redline black neighborhoods—refuse to lend to property owners in these areas—because they would be likely to perceive them as financially risky. As a result, both real estate improvement and sale would often become unfeasible.

The Implications for Racial Harmony

Empirical study confirms the existence of racially identified space. The foregoing economic model demonstrates that race and class are inextricably linked in American society, and that both are linked to segregation and to the creation of racially identified political spaces. Even if racism could magically be eliminated, racial segregation would be likely to continue as long as we begin with significant income polarization and segregation of the races. Furthermore, even a relatively slight, residual racism severely complicates any effort to eliminate racial segregation that does not directly address political space and class-based segregation.

One might imagine that racism could be overcome by education and rational persuasion alone: because racism is irrational, it seems to follow that, over time, one can argue or educate it away. The model shows that even if such a project were entirely successful, in the absence of any further interventions, racial segregation would remain indefinitely.

Contemporary society imposes significant economic costs on nonsegregated living arrangements. In the absence of a conscious effort to eliminate it, segregation will persist in this atmosphere (although it may appear to be the product of individual choices). The structure of racially identified space is more than the mere vestigial effect of historical racism: it is a structure that continues to exist today with nearly as much force as when policies of segregation were explicitly backed by the force of law. This structure will not gradually atrophy because it is constantly used and constantly reinforced.

Toward a Legal Conception of Space

> A whole history remains to be written of spaces—which would at the same time be the history of powers (both these terms in the plural)—from the great strategies of geo-politics to the little tactics of the habitat, . . . passing via economic and political installations.
>
> —Michel Foucault, "The Eye of Power"

There is no self-conscious legal conception of political space. Most legal and political theory focuses almost exclusively on the relationship between individuals and the state. Judges, policy makers, and scholars analogize decentralized governments and associations either to individuals, when considered vis-à-vis centralized government, or to the state, when considered vis-à-vis their own members—yet they consider the development, population, and demarcation of space to be irrelevant. Space is *implicitly* understood to be the inert context *in* which, or the deadened material *over* which, legal disputes take place.

Legal boundaries are often ignored because they are imagined to be either the product of aggravated individual choices or the administratively necessary segmentation of centralized governmental power. This representation of boundaries, and, hence, of politically created space, allows us to imagine that spatially defined entities are not autonomous associations that wield power. At the same time, space also serves to ground governmental and associational entities. We imagine that the boundaries defining local governments and private concentrations of real property are a natural and inevitable function of geography and of a commitment to self-government or private property. These two views of political geography justify judicial failures to consider the effect of boundaries and space on racial segregation.

However, the development, population, and demarcation of space—those characteristics which must be considered irrelevant in order for space to be seen as merely the aggregation of individual choices or the organizing medium of centralized power—are precisely the characteristics that distinguish spaces politically and economically. Localities define spaces as industrial, commercial, or residential; home-owners' associations define spaces according to density and type of development; zoning and covenanting prescribe who can occupy certain spaces. This spatial differentiation is what I mean by the political geography of space. Features such as these—features that are not primordial or natural but *are* inherently spatial because they distinguish one space from another—are the product of collective action structured by law.

The Tautology of Community Self-Definition

Space is a salient characteristic of political entities even as it entrenches that segregation. In order to understand why this is so, consider an association that is not spatially defined. Such an association must be defined by particular criteria that can be examined, criticized, and challenged. These criteria also distinguish the association from the mere aggregation of individual member preferences. Even though members are empowered to alter the criteria through a democratic process, the initial selection of membership will affect the outcome of subsequent elections. Thus, although the governance of such an association may be democratic in form, it may well not be democratic ("of the people") in substance if the initial selection of members was highly exclusive. If those excluded from the association claim a right to join, the association cannot justify their exclusion on the basis of democratic rule. Nor can the justification for such an association be that it has a right to self-definition, because the "self" that seeks to define is precisely the subject of dispute.

This tautology of community self-definition is masked when a group can be spatially defined: "We are simply the people who live in area X." Space does the initial work of defining the community or association and imbues the latter with an air of objectivity, indeed, of primordiality. But the tautology is only *masked*, it is not resolved: why should area X be the relevant community when area X plus area Y might provide an equally or more valid definition of community? The answer cannot appeal to the right of community self-determination: if the people in area Y claim to be part of the larger community X plus Y, then should not their opinion be considered as well as that of the people in area X? It is the question of how communities are and should be defined that concerns us here. Close attention to spatial construction will help us to break free of established but untenable definitions of political community and thereby to open new avenues for combating entrenched structures of residential segregation.

I begin by examining the construction of political space and the consequent construction of racially identified space in both public and private law.

The Doctrinal Context of Political Space

Exclusionary Zoning and Local Democracy:
The Racial Politics of Community Self-Definition

Along with historical de jure segregation, racially exclusionary zoning introduces the racial element into local political geography and thereby creates a structure of racially identified space. The zoning power is justified by reference to an internal local political process: hence the polis that votes on local zoning policy is defined and legitimated by an opaque local geography. At the same time, the effect of this political exclusion for the excluded racial group is considered insignificant: the very local geography in question in the challenged zoning policy is rendered transparent.

Exclusionary zoning is a generic term for zoning restrictions that effectively exclude a particular class of persons from a locality by restricting the land uses they are likely to require. Today, exclusionary zoning takes the form both of restrictions on multifamily housing and of minimum acreage requirements for the construction of single-family, large-lot homes. Exclusionary zoning is a mechanism of the social construction of space. Local space is defined by zoning ordinances as suburban, family-oriented, pastoral, or even equestrian. The ordinances are justified in terms of the types of political spaces they seek to create: a community that wishes to define itself as equestrian may enact an ordinance forbidding the construction of a home on any lot too small to accommodate stables and trotting grounds, or may even ban automobiles from the jurisdiction. The desire to maintain an equestrian community is then offered as the justification for the ordinance. Courts have generally deferred to the internal political processes of the locality and upheld such exclusionary ordinances.

Such a construction of space has a broader political impact than the immediate consequence of the ordinance. By excluding non-equestrians from the community, a locality constructs a political space in which it is unlikely that an electoral challenge to the equestrian ordinance will ever succeed.[13] The "democratic process" that produces and legitimates exclusionary zoning is thus very questionable: in many cases, the only significant vote that will be taken on the exclusionary ordinance is the first vote. After it is enacted, exclusionary zoning has a self-perpetuating quaility.[14]

When local policies are challenged as *racially* discriminatory, local boundaries may do the discriminatory work. Because these boundaries are left unexamined, it is impossible for plaintiffs to demonstrate discriminatory intent: the discrimination appears to be the result of aggregated but unconnected individual choices or merely a function of economic inequality, and therefore beyond the power of the courts to remedy. In *Village of Arlington Heights v. Metropolitan Housing Development Corp.*,[15] the Supreme Court upheld a village's prohibition of multifamily housing despite demonstrable racially restrictive effects.[16] The court accepted the locality's professed neutral motivation of a commitment to single-family housing and rejected the contention that this commitment could be inextricably bound up with racial and class prejudices.[17]

Most important for our purposes, the court tacitly accepted the zoning policy as the legitimate product of the local democratic process. It relied on the same conception of space that held sway in *Euclid*, and accepted local boundaries as the demarcation of an autonomous political unit; but the boundaries, combined with the zoning policy, exclude outsiders from the political processes of the locality.[18] Because it may be the homogeneity of the local political process that is responsible for the racially exclusionary policy, the court's deference to the locality's internal political process is unjustified: it is this very political process (as well as the boundaries that shape that process) that is at issue.[19]

Indeed, racial minorities with significant cultural particularities present an especially strong claim for political inclusion in a jurisdiction: if racial minorities are to enjoy equality in an otherwise racially homogeneous jurisdiction, they must have the opportunity to change the character of the political community, and not merely the right to enter on condition of conformity. Furthermore, even if minorities were willing to conform to a homogeneous community's norms, when exclusionary zoning takes on an economic character, the option may simply be unavailable. According to our economic model, the impoverished condition of segregated minorities is, at least in part, a function of their exclusion from the communities that control wealth and employment opportunities.

The Distributive Consequences of Spatial Education: *Milliken* and *Rodriguez*

Racially identified spaces demarcated by local boundaries have distributive as well as political consequences. Our economic model demonstrates that, because localities administer many taxing and spending functions, boundaries that segregate on the basis of wealth or race ensure that taxes are higher and quality of services lower in some jurisdictions than in others. Moreover, because local boundaries are regarded as sacrosanct in the implementation of desegregation remedies, if interlocal rather than intralocal segregation is more prevalent, the remedies will be of little consequence.

In *Milliken v. Bradley*,[20] the Supreme Court held that court-ordered school busing designed to remedy de jure racial segregation in the Detroit schools could not include predominantly white *suburban* school districts. The court found that because there was no evidence that the suburban districts that would be included under the court-ordered plan had themselves engaged in de jure discrimination, they could not be forced to participate in the busing remedy. This rationale is puzzling unless one views cities not as mere agents of state power but as autonomous entities. If cities were mere agents of state power, the state as a whole would be ultimately responsible for their discriminatory actions. Thus, the state as a whole would bear responsibility for remedying the discriminatory practices: an apportionment of blame and responsibility within the state would be arbitrary, and any such apportionment that hindered effective desegregation would be unacceptable.

One may object that because Michigan had allocated power and authority to cities, the court correctly allocated blame and responsibility in the same manner. However, the court failed to examine the motivation for the position of local jurisdictional boundaries; and by conceiving of local political space as opaque—as defining a singular entity—the court failed to consider the facts that Detroit's racial composition had changed and that responsibility for historical segregation could no more be confined within Detroit's city limits than could its white former residents.

By accepting the municipal boundaries as given, the *Milliken* court ironically segregated the scope of the remedy to racial segregation and, thereby, may have allowed the historical segregation to become entrenched rather than remedied. "The plaintiffs were to be trapped within the city's boundaries, without even an opportunity to demand that those boundary lines be justified as either rational or innocently irrational."[21]

A similar pattern and misconception of space prevailed in *San Antonio Independent School District v. Rodriguez*,[22] in which the court held that a school-financing system that was based on local property taxes and produced large disparities in tax-burden-to-expenditure ratios among districts did not violate the Equal Protection Clause. The court reasoned that a commitment to local control obliged it to uphold the Texas school-financing scheme. The court also rejected the argument that the Texas system of local funding was unconstitutionally arbitrary, and it asserted that "any scheme of local taxation—indeed the very existence of identifiable local governmental units—requires the establishment of jurisdictional boundaries that are inevitably arbitrary."[23] The court's argument here is essentially circular. The appellees began by *challenging* as arbitrary the use of local boundaries as a means of determining the distribution of educational funds. The court's response asserts that arbitrariness is inevitable *if* local boundaries are to be respected. This is precisely what was at issue: Are local boundaries to be used to determine school finance levels or not?

The court's circular reasoning reflects another level of incongruence in its logic. While the court based its refusal to overturn the Texas system on respect for local autonomy and local boundaries, at the same time it justified the arbitrariness of Texas's local boundaries on the grounds that local boundaries are irrelevant. If respect for local government were as important as the court claimed, it seems strange that the court would so casually dismiss the fact that the boundaries defining these governments are arbitrary. However, if arbitrariness is inevitable, it seems illogical to accord arbitrarily defined subdivisions such respect.

The court's decision rests on two conflicting conceptions of local government and the political space it occupies. On the one hand, the court conceived of local space as transparent and thus viewed localities as mere subdivisions, the inconsequential and administratively necessary agents of centralized power; on the other, it conceived of local space as opaque and thus viewed localities as deserving of respect as autonomous political entities.

Autonomy and Association

My thesis in this section has been that political space does the work of maintaining racially identified spaces, while reified political boundaries obscure the role of political space, representing it either as the delegation of state power, and therefore inconsequential, or as natural, and therefore inevitable. Doctrine insists that local governments are merely the geographically defined agents of centralized government. Although such delegation is viewed with great suspicion when the delegate is not geographically defined, courts have shown extreme deference to local political processes. For example, local boundaries become a talisman for purposes of voting rights, even when those denied the right to vote are directly affected by the policies of the jurisdiction. Local boundaries are regarded as sacrosanct even when doing so prevents an equitable distribution of public resources for *state* purposes or interferes with the constitutionally mandated desegregation of *state* schools. Thus, the decisions of the court in the foregoing cases rest on a shifting foundation of local sovereignty and local irrelevance.

One caveat is in order. My discussion has posed the issue as one that involves localities excluding outsiders with possible rights to inclusion. However, we must remember that local government law reflects a *conflict* between democratic inclusiveness and the exclusiveness that makes community possible. Indeed, because our focus is on racial minority groups, the related tension between integration and separatism warrants consideration. We must not forget that in order to reject segregation we need not unreservedly accept integration; indeed, especially for racial minorities, some degree of separatism may represent the best or only avenue of empowerment and fulfillment. In the cases I have examined, the reification of political space ensured that the conflict between integration and separatism, inclusion and exclusion, was never even addressed. In some cases, however, there may be good reasons to grant a locality the power to exclude. What are we to make, for example, of cases such as *Belle Terre*,[24] in which one set of associational rights clashes with another, or associational rights clash with rights to political participation?

I have no formula for resolving these issues, but I do submit that we must recognize these conflicts for what they are. If we do so, we may find that often the true conflict is falsely framed in terms of a generic "local sovereignty." As Laurence Tribe notes, the justification of *associational* autonomy is often unpersuasive—many localities are merely spaces where atomistic individuals sleep and occasionally eat.[25] Hence, our desire for local autonomy is often less an impulse to preserve something that is already there than it is a desire to realize an ideal. In realizing this ideal, we must attend to issues of racial segregation and discrimination—in short, to issues of racially identified space—not only because constitutional principles so guide us, but also because the ideal is debased if we do not. As Iris M. Young has written; "The aggregate model . . . reduces the social group to a mere set of attributes attached to individuals. The association model also implicitly conceives the individual as ontologically prior to the collective, as making up, or constituting, groups."[26]

Just as I criticized a *typical* interest group pluralism and republicanism, I have also criticized a liberal *type* of political thought above. There are articulations of liberal political theory, articulations which are potentially more hospitable to racial-group identification and to a recognition of the salience of political geography. Many liberals would argue that racial groups are not inconsistent with but, rather, are assimilable to the general liberal typology that conceives of individuals as ontologically prior to groups. On such a view, liberal pluralists should support racial-group identification because it is a precondition to meaningful individual choice.[27] Similarly, liberal republicans argue that individually based rights to privacy and association *are* important, though primarily as a means of facilitating the group identification that allows individual citizens to develop views relatively independent of the state.[28]

I disagree with the critics who insist that such attempts to combine insights about the necessity of group and cultural membership with pluralist and republican thought are hopelessly self-contradictory.[29] Such a criticism misses the point that *all* political thought deals in tensions that are an unavoidable feature of the political.[30] The best of political thought recognizes such conflicts and attempts to mediate them. I believe that my proposals and the analysis herein are largely consistent with these more sophisticated forms of liberalism, pluralism, and republicanism.

The Political Geography of the Democratic City:
A Provisional Map

Seeing Through but Not Overlooking Space: Statutory and Doctrinal Recognition of the Role of Political Space

Thus far, we have focused on the general tendency in legal analysis both to overlook the consequences of political space in geographically defined entities and to cede talisman significance to politically created boundaries, thereby at once ignoring and reifying political space.

Cultural Desegregation: Toward a Legal Practice of Culturally Plural Political Space

Desegregation versus Integration
My discussion of racially identified spaces has been critical of the political boundaries that define these spaces. I have argued that contemporary society, through the mechanism of law, creates and perpetuates racially identified spaces without doing so explicitly. Thus, no attempt is made to justify the political spaces that are so perpetuated. Many readers may take my critique of racialized space as a call for a planned program of spatial integration, such as the systematic dispersal of inner-city minority populations to the suburbs with mandatory busing to maintain public

school integration. But this type of integration assumes the *existence* of racialized space, space that needs to be integrated. Through the elimination of racially identified space, we may find that some of the classic centralized methods of racial integration are no longer necessary or desirable.

If one accepts the importance of political geography, one might nevertheless object that the reforms proposed in this chapter will disrupt established communities and introduce elements of uncertainty and instability by removing the system that allowed these communities to come into existence. Political spaces create cultural communities; an implicit part of my thesis is that space, at least as much as time, is responsible for racial and/or cultural identity. Even for those members of a racial group who do not live in a racially identified space, the existence of such a space is central to their identity.[31] Hence, to decenter racially identified space is to some extent to decenter racial identity.

The foregoing analysis should make clear that no political system, including the current one, can remain neutral in the face of the social construction of geography; no system can simply reflect or accommodate "individual choice" as to residence and geographic association; no system is without some systematic bias. Because a truly neutral system is impossible, we must rewrite the laws to *favor*, rather than to obstruct, racial and class desegregation.[32]

A system of desegregated spaces would certainly result in fewer homogeneous spaces and more numerous integrated ones, but such a system is different from the classic model of integration in two important respects. First, it does not impose a particular pattern of integration; rather, it removes the impediments to a more fluid movement of persons and groups within and between political spaces. Second, this model does not accept the current manifestation of political space and simply attempt to "shuffle the demographic deck" to produce a statistical integration; rather, it challenges the mechanism by which political spaces are created and maintained, and, by extension, it challenges one of the mechanisms by which racial and cultural hierarchies are maintained.

Thus, cultural desegregation is both more mild and more radical than classic integrationism. It is more mild because it does not mandate integration as an end: group cohesion may exist even in the absence of spatially enforced racial segregation, such that no significant increase in statistical integration will occur. Indeed, I imagine that spatially defined cultural communities that have experienced the exodus of many of their wealthier members (many of whom exit not due to a desire to assimilate but for economic reasons) would experience an increase in group cohesiveness, either because the middle and upper classes would return to culturally defined neighborhoods in the absence of economic and political disincentives, or because, as spatial boundaries become more permeable, geography would become a less important part of community definition. Individuals could be part of a political community that is geographically dispersed, even as many are now a part of dispersed cultural committees. Desegregated space would encourage cultural cohesion by rendering racialized political boundaries more permeable and thus allowing members of culturally distinct communities to act on their cultural connections regardless of where they happen to reside.

In this latter sense, though, cultural desegregation is also more radical than integration. Cultural desegregation insists that cultural associations may be respected and encouraged regardless of the spatial dispersal of their members. It rejects both the assimilationist notion that individuals should aspire to become members of some imperial master culture, and leave their cultural identity behind in order to gain acceptance by "society at large,"[33] and the separatist notion that only through geographic consolidation and cultural anarchy can people of color hope to avoid cultural genocide (or suicide).

Desegregated Cultural Identity

Cultural desegregation aspires to a society in which cultural identity is dynamic in its definition and cultural communities are fluid but not amorphous. These two ideals are linked in a paradox: because cultural identity is established only in the context of a community or association, the position of cultural associations is critical to the formation of cultural identity; there is no individual cultural identity, for culture implies a community. At the same time, though, cultural specificity must imply an interaction with other cultures: a culture has a specific character only in that it is unlike other cultures with which it compares itself through interaction. However, interaction with other cultures will change a cultural community, and in some sense reduce its specificity. This paradox gives rise to fear of assimilation and inspires some to advocate cultural autarchy.

The solution to this paradox lies in understanding culture as a context, a community of meaning, rather than as a static entity or identity. A cultural community exists in a symbiotic relationship both with its members and with outsiders. It can neither totally shape its members nor completely exclude outsiders. Yet this does not mean that the community is nothing more than the aggregation of its individual members; a cultural community has autonomy in that it can exert influence over individual members, construct morality, values, and desires, and provide an episte-mological framework for its members. One may understand culture "to refer to the cultural community, or cultural structure, itself. On this view, the cultural community continues to exist even when its members are free to modify the character of the culture."[34]

If this understanding is correct, then culture is not threatened by inter-nal dissent, outside influences, eventual transformation, nor even by the exit of certain members, just as the character of a democratic government is not threatened by changes in administration. To be sure, some changes are for the better and some for the worse, and some changes may indeed threaten the very structure of the culture, just as McCarthyism and the imperial presidency were thought to threaten the very structure of Ameri-can democracy. However, the process of change itself is not to be feared—in fact, it is to be welcomed, for it is a part of the life of a culture. Although there are certainly distinct cultural communities, the boundaries between them often are a good deal more permeable than most discussions of cultural pluralism and cultural membership would suggest.

Cultural Identity in Desegregated Space

Cultural associations are among the groups that exercise power, both formally and informally, through their control of physical spaces. Although the link between race and culture is not direct or unproblematic (and is beyond the scope of this chapter), we can identity this link in the creation and maintenance of racially identified spaces occupied by racial and cul-tural communities.

As the tautology of community self-definition demonstrates, it is im-possible for any community truly to determine its own identity. Thus, the desegregation of political space cannot provide an atmosphere of unme-diated "free choice" for racial and cultural identity formation. What de-segregation can do is level the hierarchies of racial and cultural identity so that presently disempowered and subordinated communities are no longer systematically deprived of the political and economic resources that would allow them to thrive rather than merely to survive, and so that such com-munities can more readily interact with American society as a whole.

Desegregation will undoubtedly alter the character of all racial commu-nities: white communities are defined in part by their position of privi-lege, while minority communities are defined in part by their subordina-tion and isolation. However, it is unclear exactly what the result of desegregation will be for established racial and cultural groups. Some groups may experience dispersal and disintegration, as ethnic white communities have in many parts of the nation. Some groups may grow stronger and more cohesive as their members gain greater resources and feel less economic pressure to leave racially identified neighborhoods and cities, while those who do leave will be able to experience group solidarity that does not depend on geographic proximity. New but distinct cultural communities may form as permeable political borders allow social, political, artistic, and educational alliances between previously isolated communities to develop. Whatever the result, it will reflect a form of cultural association and pluralism that is more consistent with the best of American democratic ideals.

Conclusion: The Boundaries of Race

This chapter has attempted to bring several distinct discourses to bear on the persistent issue of race relations and racial segregation in the United States. I have employed political economy and political geography, Legal Realist analytics, ideal and nonideal normative political and social theory, Critical Legal Theory and Critical Race Theory, and a light dash of postmodernist social theory as well as urbanist theory. My focus herein has been necessarily sweeping and has, I fear, often sacrificed detail for breadth. Every discourse I have employed has a long academic tradition in which countless scholars have probed many of these issues in much greater depth than this chapter could allow. My goal here is to bring the insights of these various conversations together in order to demonstrate that racial segregation is a consequence of law and policy, that it can be changed by law and policy, and that there is ample precedent in American legal and political thought for the types of changes that would dramatically decrease the degree of segregation in America and the cities.

This chapter is the beginning of what I hope will be an ongoing project. It probably raises more questions than it answers. I would like to have discussed in much greater detail such questions as the role of political space in the social construction of racial identity and the consequences of political space for identity politics and identity communitarianism, the complexities of all the policy proposals I have advanced, and the importance of changes in the economic structure and cultural logic of late twentieth-century America for contemporary racial and spatial relations. However, these questions are for another space.

A note on methodology may now be in order. One objection to the relentlessly structural analysis that I have employed is that it devalues human agency and individual morality—that, by focusing on structures, one downplays the personal responsibility of flesh-and-blood people for social inequity. Some may well object that I let racists off the hook by proposing that political and economic institutions make racism inevitable. It is not my intention to supplant a strictly moral argument against racist practices but, instead, to augment such an argument. I do not know what evil lurks in the hearts of men and women; but I do believe that the existing structure of what I have dubbed "racially identified political space" is likely to encourage even good men and women to perpetuate racial hierarchy. We need moral condemnation of racism, but we also need viable solutions. I do not intend this chapter to in any way stifle the former; I hope it may contribute to identifying the latter.

We need solutions now. The threat of a racially fragmented metropolis and nation looms large on the horizon. The United States is rapidly fulfilling the grim prophesy of the Kerner Commission and becoming *at least* "two societies, one black, one white—separate and unequal."[35] Race relations are at a low ebb, a circumstance that contributes to the declining desirability of life in racially diverse urban areas. At the same time, though, the 1990 census shows for the first time that more than half of all Americans live in megacities—metropolitan areas of more than one million inhabitants. To survive and thrive in the metropolis that is America, we must attend to matters of race and of political space; it is not only space as much as time that hides consequences from us, but it is also location as much as history that defines us. If, as Douglas Massey and Nancy Denton assert, segregation is the missing link in previous attempts to explain the conditions of the underclass, then political geography is the missing element in attempts to reconcile the ideals of majoritarian democracy and private property with those of racial equality and cultural autonomy. The question of political space is not one of narrow concern, the province of cartographers and surveyors; its domain includes the democratic idealist, the activist lawyer, and the scholar of jurisprudence. Most of all it is the domain of every citizen who believes in the experiment of self-government. The study of political space reveals that "we the people" is not a given but, rather, a contested community in a democratic society. The recognition that political spaces are often racially identified reveals that the boundaries of a democracy share territory with the boundaries of race.

Notes

1. "Housing denotes an enormously complicated idea. It refers to . . . a specific location in relation to work and services, neighbors and neighborhood, property rights and privacy provisions, income and investment opportunities." R. Montgomery and D. R. Mandelker, eds., *Housing in America: Problems and Perspectives*, 3 (2d ed., 1979).

2. By "quasi-jurisdictional boundaries" I mean the boundaries that define private entities that perform governmental functions. These entities, which exercise all the relevant power of governments, constitute an important part of political geography.

3. R. G. Bratt, C. Hartman, and A. Meyerson, "Editor's Introduction," in R. G. Bratt, C. Hartman, and A. Meverson, eds., *Critical Perspectives on Housing*, xi, xviii (1986) (quoting E. P. Achtenburg and P. Marcuse, "Towards the Decommodification of Housing: A Political Analysis and a Progressive Program," in C. Hartman, ed., *America's Housing Crisis*, 202, 207 [1983]).

4. D. S. Massey and N. A. Denton, *American Apartheid: Segregation and the Making of the Underclass*, 2 (1993).

5. 334 U.S. I (1948).

6. See Charles Abrams, *Forbidden Neighbors: A Study of Prejudice in Housing*, 231 (1955); see also Massey and Denton, *supra* note 4, at 50–53 (describing the practice of redlining).

7. M. Mahoney, "Note, Law, and Racial Geography: Public Housing and the Economy in New Orleans," 42 *Stan. L. Rev.* 1251,1258 (1990).

8. Massey and Denton, *supra* note 4, at 52.

9. Ibid., 36.

10. Massey and Denton, *supra* note 4.

11. Although this chapter's primary focus is on the position of blacks within a racially segregated political geography, much of the analysis herein will also be applicable to other racial minority groups. Nonetheless, black segregation is far more pronounced than that of any other racial group; see D. Massey and N. Denton, "Trends in Residential Segregation of Blacks, Hispanics, and Asians, 1970–1980," 52 *Am. Soc. Rev.* 802, 823 (1987). Moreover, racial segregation is an especially important factor in contributing to the concentration of poverty among blacks in particular; see D. S. Massey and M. L. Eggers, "The Ecology of Inequality: Minorities and the Concentration of Poverty, 1970–1980," 95 *Am. J. Soc.* 1153, 1185–86 (1990). Therefore my analysis will be of the greatest significance to black segregation.

This chapter will use terms such as "racial minority" or "people of color" when its analysis has broader applicability, and will use more limiting terminology when the empirical or historical context is limited to a particular group. The goal throughout is to limit the object of the analysis whenever necessary and to leave open the possibility of broad applicability whenever possible.

12. See Robert Staples, *The Urban Plantation: Racism and Colonialism in the Post Civil Rights Era*, 204–5 ("[A] house in a predominantly black neighborhood is devalued by thousands of dollars . . . . [B]lacks receive 1.2 percent of their income from property, compared with 7 percent for whites"); S. Minerbrook, "Blacks Locked out of the American Dream," *Bus. and Soc'y. Rev.* 3 (Sept. 22, 1993) ("In 1988, the U.S. Census Bureau concluded that white families had 10 times the wealth of blacks in America. Crucially, 40 percent of that difference was the lack of home equity between black and white families").

13. Moreover, because most state constitutions provide for local home rule, there is frequently no basis upon which to challenge such an ordinance in state courts.

14. This is merely one example of the tautology of community self-definition. One must decide who is a member of the community before one can inquire as to the community's opinion of itself, whether that inquiry takes the form of a judicial determination, an election, or a referendum.

15. 429 U.S. 252 (1977).

16. Ibid., 268–71.

17. Ibid.

18. *Amber Realty Co. v. Village of Euclid*, 297 F. 307, 316 (N.D. Ohio 1924); Laurence H. Tribe, *American Constitutional Law*, § 13-11 to 13, at 1086–91. Mineola, N.Y.: Foundation Press, 1978.

19. It is true that the plaintiffs did not raise the issue of voting rights in *Arlington Heights*. Of course, their failure to do so is no objection to the thesis that a misconception of political space obscured the tension between local autonomy and centralized power. Indeed, it is further proof: the plaintiffs neglected a potentially powerful argument against the zoning restriction because they did not imagine challenging the boundaries that separated them from the political process of Arlington Heights.

20. *Milliken*, 418 U.S. 717 (1974).

21. Tribe, *supra* note 18, §16–18, at 1495.

22. 411 U.S. I(1973). *Rodriguez* does not explicitly involve race, although racial overtones shade its discussion of school districts with vastly disparate tax bases. The *Rodriguez* appellees would have been hard pressed to state a race-based claim without evidence of intentional discrimination. Even if the plaintiff could have shown an overrepresentation of Mexican-Americans in poorer districts, such a showing could be easily dismissed as coincidental unless one were to examine the

interaction of race and the structure of political geography in a comprehensive way. Because this Article does that, *Rodriguez* provides a useful supplement to *Milliken* by demonstrating the distributive consequences of local boundaries: segregated localities with unequal tax bases promote a racially disparate distribution of public funds.

23.   Tribe, supra note 18, §16–19, at 53–54.

24.   *Village of Belle Terre v. Boraas*, 416 U.S. 1 (1974).

25.   Tribe, *supra* note 18, §15–17, at 1406, 1407.

26.   Iris M. Young, *Justice and the Politics of Difference*, 44 (1990). I would add to Young's conception that the "authentic self" stands apart from, and outside of, political space.

27.   See, for example. W. Kymlicka, *Liberalism, Community, and Culture*, 197 (1989) (arguing that group-based rights are consistent with liberal political thought).

28.   See, for example, Frank I. Michelman, "Law's Republic," 97 *Yale L.J.* 1534–36 (1988).

29.   See, for example, C. Kukathas, "Are There Any Cultural Rights?" 20 *Pol. Theory* 105, 115–24 (1992) (criticizing Will Kymlicka's liberal defense of cultural rights); Cynthia V. Ward, "The Limits of 'Liberal Republicanism': Why Group-Based Remedies and Republican Citizenship Don't Mix," 91 *Colum. L. Rev.* 583–84, 589–96, 603–06 (1991) (criticizing Michelman's and Sunstein's republican defenses of group-based rights for oppressed minorities).

30.   See generally B. Honig, *Political Theory and the Displacement of Politics*, 200–211 (1993) (arguing that "the perpetuity of contest" is the essential, and most valuable, quality of democratic politics); D. Kennedy, "The Structure of Blackstone's Commentaries," 28 *Buff. L. Rev.* 205 (1979) (arguing that legal and political analysis is characterized by a "fundamental contradiction" between the need for individual autonomy and the need for affirmation and solidarity in groups).

31.   Anyone who doubts the importance of a geographical base need only look to the immigrant and racially identified communities that reconstruct a "racionational" space within their new home country and that look toward their ancestral homeland long after any tangible connections have disintegrated. Consider the emotional bond of Miami Cubans to a Cuba that is unlikely to accept them within this century and is undoubtedly far less familiar to many of them than southern Florida. See generally, D. Rieff, *The Exile* (1993). Or consider the ties that bind American Jews to Israel despite, in many cases, the lack of any personal familial connection or any plans to relocate there. Consider also the creation of mythical or quasi-mythical homelands where no real-world racial space is available, such as Atzlan for Launos and the mythologized Africa of much "Afrocentric" thought—it bears little resemblance to any part of Africa that exists or has ever existed in history. Racially identified urban spaces are in this sense a microcosm of the nationalist homeland ideology projected onto the geography of the metropolis; see R. T. Ford, "Urban Space and the Color Line: The Consequences, Demarca-

tion, and Disorientation in the Postmodern Metropolis," 9 *Harv. Black Letter J.* 117, 132–33 (1992).

32. The loss of racial-identity elements that are a function of segregation may be a partially positive development. I reject the "culture of poverty" thesis, which often attempts to explain the conditions of the underclass without acknowledging the role of the structural bias and inequity of which residential segregation is the linchpin; see D. P. Moynihan, U. S. Dep't. of Labor, *The Negro Family: The Case for National Action*, 29–30 (1965), in L. Reinwater and W. L. Yancey, eds., *The Moynihan Report and the Politics of Controversy*, 75 (1967). The idea of a harmful and debilitating "culture of segregation," by contrast, has much to recommend it. As Massey and Denton argue, "residential segregation has been instrumental in creating a structural niche within which a deleterious set of attitudes and behaviors . . . has arisen and flourished . . . . [These] attitudes and behaviors . . . are antiethical and often hostile to success in the larger economy"; Massey and Denton, *supra* note 4, at 8. To the extent that racial identity reflects the debilitating and desperate segregative conditions that have been imposed on the urban poor, it is nothing to celebrate. The sort of loss of cultural cohesion that might occur due to desegregation would only be a loss of mutual shackles and chains.

33. I am always troubled by my loss of eloquence when I attempt to describe what I and many others clumsily refer to as the "dominant culture," the "broader society" (as if the culture of most of the world is somehow narrow), or, worst of all, "white culture." I am most certainly referring to something by way of these terms, something I vaguely imagine resides in windowless rooms in oak-paneled estates near New Haven or Cambridge (Massachusetts or England, you decide). Still, I know of few people of any race who truly belong to this dominant culture. It seems to me that this dominant culture is dominant only in that it dominates our collective psyche as a nation—it is a phantasm that haunts American social life; it goes "bump" in the night even as Americans listen to the blues and jazz, mambo and mariachi, eat kimchi and tapas, read Amy Tan and James Baldwin. It is time we exorcise this phantasmal dominant culture once and for all and embrace the multicultural mosaic that has always been America.

34. Kymlicka, *supra* note 27, at 167.

35. U.S. Advisory Commission on Civil Disorders, *Report I* (1968).

Chapter 10

Equality and Educational Excellence: Legal Challenges in the 1990s

Theodore M. Shaw

[Editors' Note: These comments are excerpted from Mr. Shaw's speech at the forum "In Pursuit of a Dream Deferred: Linking Housing and Education," held April 22, 1995. Minneapolis, Minnesota.]

On June 12, 1995, the Supreme Court issued its opinion in the Kansas City desegregation case, *Missouri v. Jenkins*,[1] which Mr. Shaw had argued before the Court. The Court, in a five-four decision, held that the district court had exceeded its remedial authority in crafting orders designed to attract white students to the Kansas City School District and to improve conditions in district schools. Concurring, Justice Thomas stated, "It never ceases to amaze me that the courts are so willing to assume that anything that is predominantly black must be inferior."[2]

On June 29, 1995, the Court handed down its decision in *Miller v. Johnson*,[3] the redistricting case from Georgia. Again split five-four, the Court held that Georgia's legislative redistricting, effected after intervention by the Justice Department under the Voting Rights Act, violated the Equal Protection Clause.[4] Quoting *Shaw v. Reno*, the Court stated that "racial gerrymandering, even for remedial purposes, may balkanize us into competing racial factions; it threatens to carry us further from the goal of a political system in which race no longer matters, a goal that the Fourteenth and Fifteenth Amendments embody, and to which the Nation continues to aspire."[5] Justice Stevens responded in dissent that the Court's refusal to distinguish an enactment that helps a minority group from enactments that cause it harm is especially unfortunate at the intersection of race and voting, given that African Americans and other disadvantaged groups have struggled so long and so hard for inclusion in that most central exercise of our democracy.

A number of important issues face those of us who care about racial justice. Education, housing, and segregation are at the top of this list. I will examine the discussion of race and segregation in our country, but instead of focusing on education and housing per se, I focus on the use of language. In particular, I examine our public discourse, in which the Supreme Court and conservative pundits have appropriated much of the civil rights language for their neo-segregationist agenda. I was in the Supreme Court recently when two of the most important civil rights cases in decades were argued before the Court: *United States v. Hays*,[6] from Louisiana, and *Miller v. Johnson*,[7] out of Georgia. These two cases involve the question of whether a state legislature, pursuant to the Voting Rights Act of 1965,[8] can redraw districts where the majority of voters are members of minority groups. That is, does the Constitution allow the creation of majority black districts in southern states with histories of discrimination, segregation, and racially polarized voting? Racially polarized voting refers to the practice of people voting largely along racial lines. The significance of this practice is that unless blacks represent a majority in a given district, they are not able to elect a candidate to represent them.

There are a number of historical conditions that make this practice even more pernicious. Until the passage of the Voting Rights Act of 1965, blacks were effectively disenfranchised from political participation through a number of mechanisms, including poll taxes, testing, and intimidation. After 1965, whites used new strategies to deny the black vote, including the creation of voting districts so that blacks never constituted a voting majority. This practice, along with polarized voting, meant that blacks could not elect legislators to represent their interests. These practices existed despite the Fifteenth Amendment, which declares that race-based denial of the right to vote is unconstitutional.

Recent voting district cases demonstrate how white voters continue to challenge attempts to correct racially polarized voting. The plaintiffs in *Hays* and *Miller* were white voters who argued that the creation of majority black districts deprived them of the constitutional right to equal protection under the law. In the plaintiffs' opinion, these districts, because they were intentionally created as majority black districts, discriminated against white voters. Ironically, the voting districts discussed in *Hays* and *Miller* are among the most integrated districts in the country. The district under challenge in Louisiana was 55 percent black at the time of the suit; the district in Georgia, 60 percent black. Even the North Carolina district under challenge in *Shaw v. Reno*[9] had 53 percent black residents. Once in a while, perhaps it might be a healthy thing for whites to be a minority in a majority black district. Nevertheless, in *Hays*, *Miller*, and *Shaw*, the electorates are integrated, and the politicians cannot ignore the significance of white voters in those districts.

What is important about these cases? What is their relevance to school and housing segregation? How are these cases relevant to the desegregation battles that are being waged in states like Kansas, Minnesota, California, and Georgia—indeed, all across this country? Certainly the cases are important both because they were wrongly decided and because they set back the movement for racial justice in this country. Equally important, these cases are significant for the discourse the Court uses in frustrating the hope of full citizenship for blacks and other racial minorities.

What we are seeing today is a gross distortion of the realities of race in this country, in which black is white and up is down. Opponents of majority black districts are appropriating the language of the civil rights movement, saying that what they want is a color-blind society.[10]

However, it is clear they are not really interested in color blindness, but instead in what Frankenburg calls "race and power evasiveness." It is difficult to persuade those holding this view, including the Court, to alter this position, in part because of the seemingly underlying agenda to roll back civil rights. As Archbishop Tutu stated, "It is hard to wake a man who is pretending to be asleep." The white plaintiffs and the Court are pretending to be asleep on issues of race and power. This allows facts to be ignored or twisted. For example, in Louisiana alone, no black person has been elected to a state office in this century. No black person has been elected from a majority white district to the state legislature. No black person has been elected from a majority white district to Congress. And, if left to the majority of white voters, David Duke would be the governor today—not twenty years ago, not ten years ago, not five years ago, not yesterday, but right now.

Language is never neutral. What something means is not simply a question of interpretation; it is also a question of struggle, context, and power. The neo-segregationists are turning back the clock and are misappropriating the language of the civil rights movement to do so. Indeed, the neo-segregationists' attempt to endorse a color-blind society through the careful manipulation of language is a strategy to maintain white supremacy and racial hierarchy. This scenario occurred a century ago when the Court in *Plessy v. Ferguson*[11] used the language of equality to justify the racial subordination of blacks.

The plaintiffs in *Hays* and *Miller* also use the language of equality to advance their hostility toward meaningful black participation. In so doing, they ignore the continuing history of racially polarized voting at the expense of black citizens. They suggest that redrawing these district lines discriminates against white people and abandons the kind of color-blind society championed by Justice Harlan in his dissent to *Plessy v. Ferguson.*[12] They also claim this nation has abandoned Dr. Martin Luther King Jr.'s principles, particularly his dream that one day we would live in a society in which his "four little children [would] be judged not by the color of their skin but by the content of their character."[13] According to these neo-segregationists, it is an insistence on race consciousness by African Americans that is keeping racial divisiveness and district balkanization alive. Indeed, in her opinion in *Shaw v. Reno*, which initiated these voting district cases, Justice O'Connor discussed how racially redrawn districts run against the constitutional command to weld together the various ethnic, racial, and religious groups in this country. O'Connor spoke of the tradition of welding together these groups, not as a matter of social policy, but as a matter of constitutional command. According to this view, these districts are balkanizing and divisive. In fact, Justice O'Connor compared them to political apartheid.[14]

The problem here is apparent. Blacks have attempted to empower themselves politically, given a set of ugly realities imposed on them by a race-obsessive white society: Neighborhoods are largely and heavily segregated in this country according to race; whites continue to run from socializing and living with black neighbors; public school segregation continues; and jurisdictional fragmentation is designed to exclude blacks. African Americans who have found themselves within this segregated reality simply want to empower themselves politically. At the very least, they want to elect the representatives of their choice. This aspiration for limited equality in a racially segregated world, however, is castigated as divisive. According to the neo-segregationists, such actions abandon the dream of a color-blind society and go against civil society and civil rights.

Language, again, plays a major role in this problem. We often characterize these dilemmas as "discriminatory." It is discriminatory to redraw a district to produce a black voting majority. It is discriminatory to redraw a district in favor of a white majority. It is discriminatory to draw a district in favor of Democrats, or Republicans. In the narrow sense, this is correct. However, only certain types of *invidious* discrimination, as interpreted against this nation's history, violate our constitutional norms. Arguments for freedom from discrimination are grounded in the Fourteenth Amendment, but the amendment itself does not use the term "discrimination." Rather, our public discourse has lured us into believing that this is the crux of the Fourteenth Amendment. Yet, as recently as 1978, the Court suggested the Fourteenth Amendment was an *anti-subjugation* amendment.[15] If we were to ask whether drawing a black majority district *subjugates* whites, the answer would likely be, "No."

My point, however, is not that if we pick the proper language we may solve these problems. My point is that we must be aware of how language is being used and for what result. Recently, when the Court has adopted the color-blind doctrine, minority rights have been denied.

The NAACP Legal Defense Fund and many other people in the civil rights movement have been fighting for desegregation for decades, and we continue to fight these desegregation struggles. At the same time, we know this fight is not accepted with grace or welcomed by the majority in this country, at least not in practice, regardless of policy or principle. Hypocrisy is apparent. In American society today, blacks are being told *they* are responsible for maintaining a race consciousness that poses a divisive element in the national agenda. Yet the Founding Fathers of this country are responsible for placing race on the national agenda. This country fought a Civil War about race, and race has always been the great American divide. It is ironic, therefore, that African Americans suddenly are responsible for and have the power to maintain the racial divide, while white Americans are running from blacks, from cities, and from desegregation. Despite the continued relatively weak position of blacks in our society, they are credited with maintaining the ugly reality of both race relations and racial inequality. What a strange world when African Americans are criticized for trying to politically empower themselves within segregated realities and, at the same time, can be labeled separatists, segregationists, or balkanizers simply because *they stopped chasing white America* and instead tried to empower themselves.

Discussions exhibiting this kind of hypocrisy are everywhere in our national discourse. In "Good Intentions Are Not Enough,"[16] Katherine Kersten discusses her opposition to a voluntary metropolitan school desegregation plan in Minneapolis, Minnesota. Kersten writes that if the Minnesota Board of Education adopts the desegregation rules it is considering, Minnesota will take a giant step away from the color-blind society envisioned by *Brown v. Board of Education* and Dr. Martin Luther King Jr. Essentially, she argues that if we begin to make these kinds of decisions to assign students, develop plans that allow students to be assigned to schools, or allow students to choose to go to schools with desegregation in mind, then we will promote racial divisiveness. Here, Kersten's logic inverts the truth and makes a remedy to segregation the problem. Such a discussion invariably turns to busing and the argument that busing is bad. Busing, however, is not the issue. The truth is that whites will put their children on buses and send them to West Hell, if at the end of that ride there is an all-white, quality school. In fact, the great majority of public school students in this country are bused to school for the purpose of just getting to school. Only a fraction of that busing is for desegregation. So busing is not the issue. What we are really talking about is whether or not we are committed to having desegregated education. If this country is not committed to desegregation, perhaps that fact should be acknowledged, and a discussion opened about what we *are* willing to do.

Kersten's article led me to ask this question: If good intentions are not enough, then what *is* enough? Before these neo-segregationists can blame blacks for balkanizing society, they must tell us what they have done lately in their daily lives to promote desegregation. What have they done, or what are they doing to promote the principles they say we should hold aloft?

Let me clarify the issue here. What drives school desegregation is not the principle that there is something inherently wrong with all-black institutions. There is *nothing* inherently wrong with an all-black institution. There *is* something inherently wrong with all-black institutions created and maintained by a predominantly white power structure, and that do not have proper resources because whites withdraw those resources when they flee. But can those institutions provide quality education? Absolutely. I believe there is nothing wrong with all-black institutions, and I do not have to live next door to whites to feel good about myself. At the same time, however, I think that in a multicultural society there are some real advantages to all of us being educated in a desegregated environment. Therefore, we are not talking about all-black institutions as inherently inferior because something magical about white children rubs off on black children, allowing them to learn in a better way. That is not the underlying principle. Rather, we are talking about the structural realities that continue to exist within this society and within the schools, that make learning next to impossible. When we see inner city all-black schools, we also see high-poverty schools and schools starved for needed resources.

For example, Kersten discusses the Kansas City case, *Missouri v. Jenkins*,[17] distorting the issues. I know about this particular Kansas City case, because I have spent much of my professional life in recent years working on it. After the Kansas City School District became majority black,[18] although the city and electorate were still majority white, it became impossible for the district to get the support it needed. From the moment the school district became majority black, not one tax levy or one bond issue passed.[19] As a consequence, the district court found, those schools literally crumbled, and the quality of education began to decline.[20] The result was that Kansas City had separate and unequal education.

We fought an interdistrict lawsuit, and the court ruled against us on interdistrict desegregation. The evidence we put before the court was powerful and compelling, and I think the court's decision was wrong. As a consequence of the remedy we *did* receive in Kansas City, we were able to turn around a district with schools that were crumbling. Although some people would have you believe otherwise, *Jenkins* does not involve $2 billion spent on a useless remedy. I went into the schools, and I remember looking at the ceiling of one classroom and seeing the sky. I remember going into bathrooms that were filthy, that were not fit for young children to use. I remember schools that were too hot in the summertime and not adequately heated in the wintertime. Nothing was being done about it because the legislature did not have the will. I am unapologetic about the fact that the state and the Kansas City School District have recently spent $1.3 billion to begin to turn those schools around. Since the Kansas City School District has made significant changes, test scores among younger students have been improving.[21]

The issue that we argued before the Supreme Court in January 1995 was manufactured by the state because it wanted to escape its remedial obligations. The court noted in passing that in order to escape this obligation, the school district had to show that it had remedied the educational harms resulting from segregation, but test scores still showed disparity between black and white students. Because the state could not show that it had done all it could do, it argued that the court was requiring it to equalize test scores between black and white students, yet there is no constitutional command to do so. The subtext was, "the bell curve—can't do it."

The Supreme Court granted *certiorari* because some conservative activist justices on the Court were interested in the Kansas City remedy and thought it had gone too far. However, the issue we argued is not the issue the case actually presents. The real issue is whether test scores can be a measure, among many measures, of the efforts of the Kansas City School District to eliminate the effects of segregation. States utilize test scores often to measure whether students are learning what they should be learning. If students are measured via tests, and schools give weight to those scores, then test scores should also be a measure of educational quality.

School desegregation cases have worked imperfectly. Nothing in life is perfect, however, and the standard that people apply to these school cases is one that is applied to few other fields of human endeavor. It ultimately becomes a question of will. Initially, in a Connecticut state trial court, we lost a case, *Sheff v. O'Neill*, in which we were trying to litigate the question of how race and poverty affect the educational opportunities of children in the Hartford School District, one of the most segregated school districts in the country. We offered evidence before the court that the state constitution mandates equal educational opportunity and minimally adequate education. The district court judge in *Sheff* simply failed as a matter of will, I believe, to rule in our favor. The state supreme court agreed and overturned the district court.[22]

There are opportunities to take different paths, but it requires a conscious exercise of will. Without will, these problems will not go away. They will continue to snowball, they will continue to grow, and as we move further and further away from the point where these problems begin, they will prove harder to address, because the compounding effects of race and poverty only become more intractable as time passes.

There is very little fortuitous segregation in this country. Segregation is a consequence of years, indeed centuries, of social *policy*. Governmental policy on the local, state, and federal levels combined with private actions have worked to produce the patterns of race segregation that exist in this country today. Segregation is a consequence of social engineering. A different kind of social engineering is the aim of civil rights lawyers. I gladly accept the label of "social engineer." The great lawyer Charles Houston, who was the architect of the civil rights legal struggle, has noted that a lawyer is either a social engineer or a parasite on society. If we do not give these problems attention, we cannot wish them away or sweep them under the rug. They will not go away. We have to consciously engineer our way out of them.

In closing, I note my admiration for my colleagues in this anthology. Gary Orfield is one of the biggest optimists I know; john powell is one of the most gentle warriors I know. I tend to be susceptible to anger. I have to fight bitterness, because bitterness is corrosive and destructive. I may not be as optimistic as some about where we are on race in this country. I do know that if we lay down and cease to struggle, these problems will only get worse. We are not going to be able to ignore this problem as we move into the twenty-first century. W. E. B. DuBois said that the problem of the twentieth century would be the problem of the color line,[23] and he was right. The problem of the twenty-first century will be the problem of the color line and the class line, and if we do not address it, the social fabric will tear. We will not sustain ourselves as a country or as a community if the disparities between the rich and poor continue to grow, as they have grown over the last twenty years. It simply will not happen. People will not buy into the social compact. So, while I may be angry and sometimes bitter, I also know that we have to continue the struggle and we must reclaim our language. I am reminded of a wonderful African proverb. It goes like this:

> Life has meaning only in a struggle.
> Victory and defeat are in the hands of the Gods.
> So let us celebrate the struggle.

Notes

1. 515 U.S. 70 (1995).

2. Ibid., 114 (Thomas, J., concurring).

3. 515 U.S. 900 (1995).

4. Ibid., 917–28.

5. Ibid., 912 (quoting *Shaw*, 509 U.S. at 657). In the other redistricting case, *United States v. Hays*, the Court held that the plaintiffs lacked standing. 515 U.S. 737 (1995).

6. 515 U.S. 737 (1995).

7. 515 U.S. 900 (1995).

8. 42 U.S.C. § 1973 (1999).

9. 509 U.S. 630 (1993).

10. See, e.g., *Hays*, 515 U.S. at 750–51 (citing appellees' complaint that Louisiana's redistricting scheme violated voters' right to engage in a color-blind process); *Shaw*, 509 U.S. at 641–42 (pointing to language in appellants' complaint that North Carolina's redistricting scheme deprived voters of the right to participate in a color-blind election process).

11. 163 U.S. 537 (1896).

12. 163 U.S. at 552 (Harlan, J., dissenting).

13. Dr. Martin Luther King Jr., address at the Civil Rights March (Aug. 28, 1963).

14. *Shaw*, 509 U.S. at 647 ("A reapportionment plan that includes in one district individuals who belong to the same race, but who are otherwise widely separated by geographical and political boundaries, and who may have little in common with one another but the color of their skin, bears an uncomfortable resemblance to political apartheid.").

15. *Regents of the University of California v. Bakke*, 438 U.S. 265, 357 (1978) (Brennan, J., concurring in the judgment in part and dissenting in part).

16. Katherine Kersten, Center for the American Experiment, "Good Intentions Are Not Enough: The Peril Posed by Minnesota's New Desegregation Plan," *Star Tribune* (1995) (on file with the Minnesota Law Review).

17. 515 U.S. 70 (1995).

18. School District of Kansas City, Mo. Report, "The Real Facts" (1994) (reporting on the progress of "halting the decline of non-minority enrollment in the [Kansas City School] district").

19.   *Jenkins*, 672 F. Supp. 400,411,412 (W.D. Mo. 1987).

20.   Ibid., 403, 410–11.

21.   School District of Kansas City, Mo. Report, "The Real Facts" (1994).

22.   *Sheff v. O'Neill*, 678 A.2d 1267 (Conn. 1996).

23.   W. E. B. DuBois, *The Souls of Black Folk*, 3 (Library of America ed., 1990).

Conclusion

Drawing a Blueprint for Linking Housing and Education

Vina Kay

The Institute on Race and Poverty's forum "In Pursuit of a Dream Deferred: Linking Housing and Education" was an opportunity for the presenters and other participants to reflect on the shared goal of desegregation that came out of the *Brown v. Board of Education* decision.[1] They came with a greater sense of wisdom, gained in the years since the case was decided, about how to implement the reforms necessary to achieve desegregation. Schools must be linked to housing, they claimed, for the benefits of desegregation could not be maintained unless entire communities were desegregated. Desegregation itself became an insufficient goal—what was really necessary for lasting change was integration, a goal that was broader and more respective of the communities involved.

We have revisited the articles that came out of that forum, along with some additional insights, out of a need to remind ourselves of the hope we carried following that meeting. Now, there is a sense of loss among some as communities seem to move further from desegregation and increasingly resegregate. A study on school resegregation trends has found southern states, in particular, resegregating at a rapid rate, with the rest of the country following that pattern.[2] In spite of these trends, the federal government has failed to address segregation, even within the context of issues on race and civil rights.[3] Shortly after the forum, the Supreme Court handed down its decision in *Missouri v. Jenkins*,[4] further limiting the possibility for interdistrict desegregation of schools. Urban centers continue to become increasingly poor and minority, placing further strain on central cities to provide adequate housing, education, and social services. At the same time, suburban growth is spreading farther from the cities, taking with it growing businesses, quality schools, and transportation resources.[5] The once more broadly shared value of diversity and integration has now been rejected in our two largest states. California and Texas have eliminated state-sponsored affirmative action, cutting off opportunities for many disadvantaged students of color wishing to attend the state colleges and universities.

The Supreme Court has not decided any major housing or school cases since *Missouri v. Jenkins.* The current framework for thinking about interdistrict remedies has been so limited by past Supreme Court rulings that cities are forced to create solutions for populations that are 70, 80, and 90 percent minority and overwhelmingly poor. Indeed, the Clinton administration completely failed to provide leadership in this area. The question for civil rights lawyers, and for those who provide the valuable research support they use, is what strategies should they turn to as they continue to struggle against government-supported segregation in schools and housing. How can they respond constructively to Court withdrawal from the foundation of *Brown* and desegregation?

In many respects this is the wrong place to start the discussion. The promise of the legal system is also a limitation—litigation comes as a response after substantial harm has already been done. Although the result of litigation can be dramatic action and change, its role is limited to those instances where everything lines up: grave harm, wrongful action, substantial evidence, and a court that has the potential for sympathy. In the meantime, policy makers, researchers, and housing and education specialists must continue the forward-looking struggle to remedy the harm that they already recognize.

Currently, a mood exists for reform in schools. The public is appalled at statistics demonstrating how little students know when they leave the school system and how unprepared they are to compete in a competitive world. Test scores paint a dramatic picture of the failures of students, schools, teachers, and the entire education system. But they also tell the story of who is losing the most in the race for education: impoverished students and students of color. That these two groups overlap significantly and that they are the students with the lowest test scores, the lowest graduation rates, and the lowest college attendance rates rarely come as a surprise to anyone. The response has focused on measures such as local control, school choice, higher testing standards, and teacher accountability. School districts have also responded with experiments in private administration of schools and charter schools. These efforts have met with some success. Some districts are reporting increases in their standardized test scores. Some charter schools have provided the kind of individualized education some students needed. Success stories raise the question of how to replicate the success, providing hope that broader change is possible.

Few reform efforts have had dramatic results, however, certainly not as dramatic as the struggles faced by children of color in poverty-ridden urban school districts. Although the importance of continued efforts at improving schools cannot be disputed, how we should go about achieving dramatic change, particularly in urban schools, is a constant question. Certain facts are impossible to ignore. The majority of students in urban schools are increasingly poor and minority. This is becoming true for more and more inner-ring suburbs as well. The correlation between high, concentrated poverty rates and failing schools is difficult to miss. Yet few reforms have addressed this very issue.

School reforms have attempted to address concerns that grow out of low-achieving schools. Failing test scores, low parent involvement, and high dropout rates are all symptoms of schools in heavily poor and minority communities. The reforms that address these issues, however, do not and cannot come close to solving the real problem of segregated and impoverished schools and communities. These schools face not so much low-achieving students or groups of students, but the failure of the entire school—as well as, oftentimes, the entire neighborhood. As an institution, the school structure is unable to meet the needs of its students. This is not to say that reforms that address the symptoms of poor and segregated schools should be abandoned. Rather, they should play supporting roles to a larger initiative that addresses the entire structure in which low-income families of color struggle.

Research has shown that schools with lower poverty rates, whatever the racial makeup of the students, have better results than schools with high poverty. Although it is clear that a black child need not sit next to a white child in order to learn, it is also clear that less burdened structures are better able to serve students than overly burdened structures. Given this, why do we continue to focus reform efforts on in-place changes in urban schools? How can we better alleviate the burden these schools face and make it possible for them to educate all of their students well? Our system of public education has become a two-tiered one, in which those who can afford it receive a better education in predominantly white, middle- and upper-middle-class schools, while those who cannot afford it languish in overly burdened and failing schools made up of predominantly low-income students of color. If we believe in the value of public education, of access to education for all, then we cannot allow public schools to travel further down this path.

Affordable housing reform has seen a similarly mixed bag of results amidst a growing urgency to provide safe and affordable housing for people living in poverty. In Minneapolis, where a 1995 lawsuit settlement promised increased low-income housing in middle-class communities and the demolition of dilapidated housing projects, project residents later demanded that the projects remain. Although the fight was in response to fear that new units were not being built quickly enough for displaced families, there is also a mood rejecting the notion that poor families need to "deconcentrate" for their situations to improve. Why not create the opportunities for business growth and revitalization in poor neighborhoods, the argument goes. However, what much of the research in this volume has shown is that access to the structures of opportunity is vital for people in poverty to improve their situations. Yet despite studies showing the success of the voluntary movement of low-income families from a depressed housing project in Chicago's inner city to middle-class communities, the Chicago Housing Authority is now talking about dismantling the *Gautreaux*[6] program. An end to scattered-site housing in Chicago would be devastating to the years of experience and research *Gautreaux* has provided, and a serious threat to similar programs across the country.

Gautreaux has taught us that lasting opportunity structures are not created out of thin air, but rather are the result of government and market forces supporting growth and development. Put simply, this means that we need people with resources (i.e., the middle class) to support the opportunity structures in order for them to thrive. When low-income people live in an environment where such opportunity structures are supported, they benefit by having access to the same opportunities. The result is better schools, decent housing, good transportation systems, and job opportunities. Although it seems that these opportunities should be available wherever people live, the reality that any look at urban and suburban growth patterns will show is that they are not. Abandoning urban centers should not be an option, but further burdening them has an equally negative result.

Missing in all the efforts at change is a coordinated system where schools and affordable housing can work together for lasting change. This was the point of the "Linking Housing and Education" forum in 1995. Then we were told of the necessity of such a coordinated effort, the urgency faced by children of color in poverty, and, to some extent, how to achieve change. But the "how" element requires further work, particularly in light of the continually changing political landscape.

An opportunity exists in the current attention to urban and suburban sprawl. Often seen as a concern primarily of environmentalists and land-use planners, the issue of sprawl is very much a civil rights concern as well. At the same time sprawl has detrimental effects on the availability of open spaces and the environment, it also takes an extreme toll on the infrastructure of our communities. When middle-class and upper-middle-class people move farther and farther from urban centers, they take with them resources that are vital for a community. Meanwhile, suburban communities continue to rely on urban centers for infrastructure support and identity. As the concentration of wealth moves away, businesses, transportation dollars, teachers, and other important resources are quick to follow. Although growth is inevitable and positive for a thriving community, the danger comes when we create concentrations of wealth and concentrations of poverty. Growth that will benefit an entire community must be balanced and available to a broad range of people. What we cannot continue is a throwaway philosophy of urban planning that simply abandons inner cities as opportunities move farther away.

Communities of color must invest themselves in issues of metropolitan growth and regionalism now as metropolitan areas across the country become more concerned with the issue. Those who have long been concerned with school desegregation and affordable housing have the chance to help frame the debate around regionalism in a way that reflects these concerns. The sprawl question presents a unique opportunity to truly coordinate efforts rather than continue working on the interrelated issues independently. The Institute on Race and Poverty has begun the Racial Justice and Regional Equity Project that will work to reframe the regionalism dialogue to emphasize the impact sprawl has on communities of color living primarily in central cities and declining-inner ring suburbs. Strategies to engage communities of color in regional policy making must also be sensitive to community concerns about political control and cultural cohesion. The goal of the project is to respect and address these concerns while building a stronger, more inclusive framework for regional reform.

Critics of regionally based efforts will argue that we must preserve the choice of people to live where they want, that those who have the resources should not have to live next door to poverty, and that some degree of poverty is inevitable and must exist somewhere. Such critics fail to see that it is not poverty itself that takes such a toll on our communities, but rather the concentrated poverty that presents little opportunity for creating a better life. Although society will likely always have some degree of poverty, it is not inevitable, nor should it be acceptable, that entire communities live in extreme and concentrated poverty. Nor should it be inevitable that poverty is a given for generation after generation. It is one thing for poverty to be a situation stemming from current misfortune; it is quite another for children to assume that poverty is a given and never to expect more.

In many respects, linking housing and education seems like an obvious solution to what is anything but a simple problem. But the chapters in this volume demonstrate just how pervasive and ingrained the problem of segregation is in the United States, now nearly fifty years after the *Brown v. Board of Education* decision. The work of these lawyers, sociologists, and housing and education experts also demonstrates how very complicated linking housing and education as a policy strategy can be. Lack of political will aside, formulating strategies that are both feasible and have lasting impact remains a difficult task. Adding the problem of political will to the mix makes the work ahead seem daunting.

These passionate voices have made clear, however, that our goal must be large and that our steps must be bold in tackling the persistent segregation in our country. We must not let the difficulty of the task keep us from moving forward. The half-hearted steps toward desegregating schools following the *Brown* decision clearly have not been sufficient. Nor have the scattered, though at times transforming, housing reforms been enough to have a broad and lasting effect on the lives of impoverished people. There have been some dramatic victories. There have been some troubling defeats. The Yonkers, New York, case was an example of a court looking at the issue of segregation broadly and blaming the acts of an entire municipal government, including its housing policy, rather than focusing on a school district alone. The landmark *Gautreaux* case gave residents of a Chicago housing project the opportunity to move out of an impoverished community and into middle-class suburban neighborhoods.[7] Studies of the *Gautreaux* project indicate that the families involved have benefited greatly from this move.[8] As so many contributors here have noted, the Supreme Court's decision in *Milliken v. Bradley*[9] was a major blow to efforts at creating interdistrict remedies to school segregation. Since then, as expected, urban school districts have become more and more segregated by both race and poverty.[10] The court's 1995 decision in *Missouri v. Jenkins* made even voluntary interdistrict remedies difficult.

The question then is what do we do with this disparate history, this mixed bag of policy and political will? The authors here have given us a place to start—all of them taking up Kenneth Clark's call for new energy and leadership. John powell writes of the need for integrated communities, not just schools. By integration he means something broader than simply desegregated according to a numerical balance. Integration, in his view, refers to a level of racial and economic balance, coupled with respect and support of the racial and cultural differences that make up the community. Meredith Lee Bryant presents this concept as well in arguing for a set of positive rights to racial equality, rather than the traditionally articulated negative rights. Richard Thompson Ford makes clear the oppression—economic, social, and political—that results from geographic segregation, calling for a focus on the entire metropolis in striving for a truly diverse democracy.

Nancy Denton and Gary Orfield, in their thorough and compelling pieces, paint a stark picture of political and social reality in America. Denton's research shows us how deep attitudes about race and poverty run in our society. Her questioning of the myths and explanations of segregation enables us to examine this issue much more directly and accurately. Her work also makes clear how necessary it is for us to move forward with a solution to this problem of persistent segregation if we are ever to construct a multiethnic society where opportunity is truly equal. Orfield recalls the frustrating reality of government policies that create and maintain segregation, such as the small, local school districts of the segregated North. At the same time, he demonstrates how broad initiatives that involve entire metropolitan areas have been successful and hold the promise for achieving real integration.

Several authors remind us of both the harms and the responsibility we must take for the limits of recent school desegregation cases. Drew Days points to the culpability of not only school boards, but also larger government entities—municipalities and states—in causing and maintaining segregation. Courts must also recognize the very real harm, to black children more than others, of racial segregation, argues Charles Lawrence in his critique of the aftereffects of the *Milliken v. Bradley* decision. The harm was what *Brown* was all about, Kenneth Clark's historical perspective tells us, and, sadly, the harm of segregation still affects children every day.

The practicing lawyers in this volume give insight into a legal system that at times seems more random than fair. Despite the many false starts and backwards steps in the areas of school desegregation and affordable housing, these lawyers continue the struggle. The victories can be sweet and enlightening, as Michael Sussman demonstrates, but the defeats do not slow the struggle, as both he and Theodore Shaw show us. Shaw's dedication and fight against the bitterness that could so easily drown a person's hope give us inspiration to find a solution and make it work.

So now, almost fifty years after *Brown*, these pieces give us an idea of what we have accomplished. Not much, skeptics might say. Yet every one of these authors speak in terms of progress and hope, in spite of defeat. We have lessons to learn and places to go with these experiences. The pursuit of desegregated schools and decent, affordable housing cannot remain separate, distinct goals. Rather, these struggles must be linked together to achieve lasting results in both arenas. Moreover, limiting our efforts to desegregation will yield only limited results. We must strive for true integration in both the housing and education arenas. Despite Supreme Court reluctance to view integration broadly, there are opportunities for shaping new legal approaches for integrating schools and communities. However, the legal fight cannot progress without the support of further research and policy initiatives. The process as well as the result must be integrated. This is why the work of the contributors here, as well as others pursuing change in this area, must continue and must be collaborative.

Where do we go from here? Diagnosing the problem has not been so difficult as formulating a solution for the combined effects of failing education and concentrated poverty. Research, analysis, and common sense tell us who is bearing the burden of the poorest urban schools and neighborhoods: children living in poverty, predominantly children of color. We may even know that the most successful solution would be to move these children and their families out of conditions of extreme and concentrated poverty and into neighborhoods where they are not surrounded by the ill effects of these conditions.[11] Yet, instead of formulating and moving ahead with what is likely to be the most successful strategy, we fumble about with reforms that, while meaningful and well-intentioned, could never begin to solve the problem on a large scale. Head Start, one of the federal government's largest and most revered programs for low-income preschool children, while beneficial in the early years, has not resulted in a sustained benefit as those children continue through the public school system.[12] Head Start and other programs, such as Title I, which provides additional funding to impoverished schools, cannot alone do anything about the impoverished environments children live in every day.

The reason for these limited strategies is clear: the most successful strategy will likely be the most difficult. Moving people around is not a popular solution on many levels. Obviously, suburban, middle-class communities do not want subsidized housing in their neighborhoods. They have seen what has happened to urban neighborhoods and inner-ring suburbs that have become increasingly poor. Their feelings are based in simple economics, they argue. And they are right, to some extent. But another element is the racism that runs very deep in our society and that we can largely avoid discussing by focusing on the myth of choice. Nancy Denton points out that white attitudes about segregation in theory differ substantially from white attitudes in practice. At the same time that whites believe that blacks should be able to purchase homes wherever they can, most whites do not want to live in an integrated setting. Moreover, her research indicates that whites believe that blacks should prefer to live in segregated black communities.[13]

At the same time, people of color living in poor neighborhoods are not necessarily eager to embrace the concept of moving out of their communities. Predominantly white and middle-class neighborhoods do not seem very neighborly and may, in fact, not be. However, one must question, as Denton does in her chapter, whether a choice to self-segregate based on fears of racism is actually a choice.[14] Communities of color may also be concerned about losing their political power by dispersing, and about losing their cultural identity by assimilating into middle-class culture.[15] These are valid concerns that comprehensive research and analysis have yet to address.

The question for the next round of research seems clear: How do we paint a realistic picture of our communities that links housing and education? The goal is to equalize access to opportunity structures in a way that builds communities, but how do we move beyond ideas and toward achieving the goal? The next steps must include a blueprint for reform. A blueprint, although still a piece of paper, is intended to be used. It tells us how a structure will look and it gives us a clearer idea of how the parts will actually work. Part of the work of convincing communities of the necessity of changing the way cities work for people is showing the *possibility*. Seeing that something *can* work is the first step toward making it happen. Without this insight, the danger grows of losing sight of the problem and the goal.

A continuing necessity is to search our metropolitan areas for examples of efforts that have worked or show signs of working, whether in housing, education, transportation, or employment. Researchers should examine what has been successful on a small scale and whether similar reforms could work on a larger scale. Further research on the long-term effects of metropolitan-wide desegregation plans is necessary. Of the cities that have attempted large-scale desegregation in schools, housing, or both, which ones are still implementing such plans? What are the results in terms of academic achievement, college attendance, and student attitudes about race? If they have abandoned metropolitan-wide plans, why and to what detriment to desegregation efforts? Gary Orfield has pointed to a number of long-term metropolitan school desegregation plans, primarily in rapidly growing Sunbelt areas, that may give us some insight into how region-wide desegregation can work.[16] Beyond chronicling the attempts, problems, and successes of reforms, researchers need to weave these examples together. Although no one solution could work for every metropolitan area, the opportunity exists to learn from other experiences and possibly apply one community's lessons to another situation.

A more difficult task is to examine more closely our political will. As schools resegregate and cities become more heavily burdened with poverty and we move further from rather than toward positive change, it is becoming critical for us as individuals and communities to face up to the hard problems of racism, fear, and lack of political will. Some scholars are questioning whether integration, though once viewed as desirable, may even be possible in our nation. In their book examining race and integration, Leonard Steinhorn and Barbara Diggs-Brown come to the conclusion that real integration was never close to happening and likely will never happen. Despite the desire for this ideal, the reality is that most Americans are not willing to make the sacrifices necessary for true integration: "social engineering, constant vigilance, government authority, official attention to racial behavior, and a willingness by citizens to relinquish at least some personal choice for the greater good."[17] Steinhorn and Diggs-Brown's argument presents a daunting challenge. In addition to examining, and perhaps confessing to, a lack of political will, we must conceive of ways to change it. Capitulating to a current mood or set of beliefs as inevitable may be the weakest and most destructive path to take.

Part of changing political will is making an issue a shared one. If the middle class sees failing schools and poor neighborhoods as a problem only for those suffering in them, there will never be a sufficient reason for actively changing that situation. Moreover, changing the balance of opportunity and wealth may even be a threat to those who already have both. How can we frame the discussion around segregated schools and housing so that the middle class and whites see these as concerns for them as well? What aside from moral or emotional claims will draw middle-class communities into the debate about the future of our schools and cities?

Abandoning cities is not an option if entire regions are to thrive. A thriving region requires the infrastructure of a thriving city, not one that is limited by the needs of impoverished neighborhoods and schools. What happens to the economic and political infrastructure of a city that is abandoned in favor of growing, middle-class suburbs? Metropolitan areas like Cleveland and Detroit are only now beginning to recover from such a decline.[18] What can we learn from these experiences?

How do we teach children to get along with and work with others, avoid stereotyping, and develop compassion in our increasingly diverse world? It is not possible to rely on a homogenous community to teach these skills to our children. We must cultivate something more.

The Institute on Race and Poverty has begun some work to address some of the issues raised here. It has recently completed a series of interviews with high school students across the country about their opinions on schools and integration. *Student Voices Across the Spectrum: The Educational Integration Initiatives Project* (EIIP) reaffirms the value of integration in schools for promoting academic achievement across races as well as for creating a more inclusive and supportive learning environment.[19] At the same time, *Student Voices* found that schools highly segregated by race and poverty faced the greatest obstacles to achieving integration. The institute's project on regionalism and racial justice will help communities of color reframe the regionalism dialogue to include issues of poverty and access to opportunity structures. These projects will contribute to the ongoing work of linking race and poverty with housing and education so that future research and policy reflect these intersections.

A blueprint for reform requires collaborative work on many levels so that all the parts are in sync. The work must be collaborative from the beginning for the final product to be as complete and useful as possible. An initial step is for researchers and policy makers to identify further questions. A few issues have been identified here, but other voices are necessary to give a complete picture of the problems metropolitan areas face.

The Institute on Race and Poverty is doing some work, but what are other researchers and organizations doing that relate to this issue? To help answer this question, the institute is initiating a collaborative, interdisciplinary research effort to address housing and education issues as they affect impoverished communities of color as well as entire metropolitan areas. This effort will bring together social scientists, lawyers, and policy makers to identify issues for further research. Together they will frame the debate and enable themselves and others to conduct research in their individual fields with the collaborative framework as a guide. When these experts come together again, their contributions will be richer for having had the larger perspective as a backdrop to their individual work. The result will be a blueprint that takes into account the different elements necessary for a sound and functional structure.

Collaboration was what *In Pursuit of a Dream Deferred: Linking Housing and Education* was about when the forum and this volume were first conceived. A collaborative effort continues to be necessary as the contributors here and others in the field prepare to refocus their effort on the segregated schools and housing that continue to rob people of access to opportunities. The discussion around urban and suburban sprawl provides one opportunity for these researchers to frame the debate to include the realities of concentrated poverty and urban decay. We must take this opportunity and create others if we are to succeed in the pursuit of the dream.

Notes

1. *Brown v. Board of Education*, 347 U.S. 483 (1954).

2. Gary Orfield and John T. Yun, *Resegregation in American Schools*, 12, 14 (1999).

3. Ibid., 32.

4. *Missouri v. Jenkins*, 515 U.S. 70 (1995).

5. Myron Orfield, *Metropolitics: A Regional Agenda for Community and Stability* (1997); john a. powell, *Race*, "Poverty, and Urban Sprawl: Access to Opportunities through Regional Strategies," 28 *Forum for Social Economics* 1 (1999).

6. *Gautreaux v. Chicago Housing Authority*, 503 F.2d 930 (7th Cir. 1974), aff'd *Hills v. Gautreaux*, 425 U.S. 284 (1976).

7. Ibid.

8. James E. Rosenbaum et al., "Can the Kerner Commission's Housing Strategy Improve Employment, Education, and Social Integration for Low-Income Blacks," 71 *N.C. L. Rev.* 1519 (1993).

9. *Milliken v. Bradley*, 418 U.S. 717 (1974).

10. See Charles R. Lawrence III, "Segregation Misunderstood: The *Milliken* Decision Revisited," chapter 7 in this volume, for a discussion of *Milliken* and its implications.

11. James Traub, "Schools Are Not the Answer," *New York Times Magazine*, Jan. 16, 2000, 90.

12. Valerie E. Lee and Susanna Loeb, *Where Do Head Start Attendees End Up? One Reason Why Preschool Effects Fade Out* (1995); Traub, *supra* note 9.

13. See Nancy Denton, Chapter 4 in this volume, page 95.

14. See Nancy Denton, Chapter 4 in this volume, page 97.

15. See, e.g., Jerry Frug, "The Geography of Community," 48 *Stan. L. Rev.* 1047, 1101–1103 (1996); John O. Calmore, "Random Notes of an Integration Warrior," 81 *Minn. L. Rev.* 1441 (1997); John O. Calmore, "Spatial Equality and the Kerner Commission Report: A Back-to-the-Future Essay," 71 *N.C. L. Rev.* 1487 (1993).

16. Gary Orfield, Chapter 5 in this volume, page 126.

17. Leonard Steinhorn and Barbara Diggs-Brown, *By the Color of Our Skin: The Illusion of Integration and the Reality of Race* (1999), 222–23.

18.   powell, *supra* note 5.

19.   Institute on Race and Poverty, Student Voices Across the Spectrum: The Educational Integration Initiatives Project (May 2000).

Contributors

Gavin Kearney
Director of Research, Institute on Race and Poverty

Kenneth B. Clark
President, Kenneth B. Clark Associates, Inc.; Distinguished Professor of Psychology, Emeritus, City University of New York. "Beyond *Brown v. Board of Education*: Housing and Education in the Year 2000," reprinted by permission of the author and the *University of Minnesota Law Review*.

john a. powell
Professor of Law, Marvin J. Sonosky Chair of Law and Public Policy University of Minnesota Law School; Executive Director, Institute on Race and Poverty; National Legal Director, American Civil Liberties Union, 1987–1993. "Living and Learning: Linking Housing and Education," reprinted by permission of the author and the *University of Minnesota Law Review*.

Meredith Lee Bryant
Morgan, Lewis and Bockus, Princeton, New Jersey. "Combating School Resegregation Through Housing: A Need for a Reconceptualization of American Democracy and the Rights It Protects," reprinted by permission of the author and the President and Fellows of Harvard College from *Harvard Black Letter Law Journal*, Vol. 13, page 127.

Nancy A. Denton
Professor of Sociology, State University of New York, Albany. "The Persistence of Segregation: Links Between Residential Segregation and School Segregation" reprinted by permission of the author and the *University of Minnesota Law Review*.

Gary Orfield

Professor of Education and Social Policy, Harvard University. "Metropolitan School Desegregation: Impacts on Metropolitan Society," reprinted by permission of the author and the *University of Minnesota Law Review*.

Drew S. Days III

Professor of Law, Yale Law School. Prior to joining the Yale faculty, Mr. Days was Assistant Attorney General for Civil Rights in the Carter administration from 1977 to 1980. In that capacity, he directed the government's school desegregation litigation, including arguing the *Columbus/Dayton* cases before the Supreme Court and initiating the *Yonkers* lawsuit described in some detail in this anthology. "The Current State of School Desegregation Law: Why Isn't Anybody Laughing?" reprinted by permission of the author and The Yale Law Journal Company and Fred B. Rothman & Company from *The Yale Law Journal*, Vol. 95, pages 1737–1768.

Charles R. Lawrence III

Associate Professor of Law, University of San Francisco School of Law. "Segregation Misunderstood: The *Milliken* Decision Revisited," reprinted by permission of the author and the *University of San Francisco Law Review*.

Michael H. Sussman

Attorney, Yonkers and Orange County, New York. Mr. Sussman has been lead counsel for the NAACP in the Yonkers, New York housing and school segregation cases since June 1981, and in the Jacksonville, Florida school desegregation case since February 1985. Prior to establishing his own law firm, Mr. Sussman worked with the U.S. Department of Justice, Civil Rights Division, and for five years as Assistant General Counsel for the NAACP. "Discrimination: A Pervasive Concept," reprinted by permission of the author and the *University of Minnesota Law Review*.

Richard Thompson Ford

Professor of Law, Stanford Law School. The edited version of "The Boundaries of Race: Political Geography in Legal Analysis" is reprinted by permission of the author and the editors of *Critical Race Theory: The Key Writings That Formed the Movement* (Kimberle Crenshaw, Neil Gotanda, Gary Peller, Kendall Thomas, eds., New York: The New Press 1995).

Theodore M. Shaw

Deputy Director, NAACP Legal Defense and Education Fund. "Equality and Educational Excellence: Legal Challenges in the 1990s," reprinted by permission of the author and the *University of Minnesota Law Review*.

Vina Kay

Senior Researcher, Institute on Race and Poverty.